HO... ...PROPERTY
MAINTENANCE MANUAL

THE ULTIMATE HOME AND PROPERTY MAINTENANCE MANUAL

Joe Beck

McGraw-Hill

New York   Chicago   San Francisco   Lisbon   London
Madrid   Mexico City   Milan   New Delhi   San Juan
Seoul   Singapore   Sydney   Toronto

The McGraw·Hill Companies

Cataloging-in-Publication Data is on file with the Library of Congress.

1 2 3 4 5 6 7 8 9 0   DOC/DOC   0 1 0 9 8 7 6 5 4

ISBN 0-07-143930-7

The sponsoring editor for this book was Cary Sullivan, the editing supervisor was David E. Fogarty, and the production supervisor was Sherri Souffrance. It was set in Melior by Kim Sheran of McGraw-Hill Professional's Hightstown, N.J, composition unit. The art director for the cover was Anthony Landi.

Printed and bound by RR Donnelley.

 This book was printed on recycled, acid-free paper containing a minimum of 50% recycled, de-inked fiber.

McGraw-Hill books are available at special quantity discounts to use as premiums and sales promotions, or for use in corporate training programs. For more information, please write to the Director of Special Sales, McGraw-Hill Professional, Two Penn Plaza, New York, NY 10121-2298. Or contact your local bookstore.

CONTENTS

ACKNOWLEDGMENTS

A book of this kind is not possible without the help of many people. Accordingly, much thanks is hereby given to a variety of technical consultants, manufacturers' representatives, trades people, home improvement professionals, and public relations people to whom I turned in the course of writing it.

Thanks to my parents, Vic and Ella Beck, and my in-laws Herb and Susan Domroe, for their love and support. Particularly thanks to my dad, for his guidance and support and for showing me what a 9/16 inch wrench was all those years ago.

Thanks to Cary Sullivan, my editor, for receiving my work so graciously and providing invaluable advice and her expertise. Another thanks goes to Al Zuckerman, my agent at Writers House, for his belief and energy spent on the project.

To Tom Philbin, my friend and colleague, I owe special gratitude—he took me under his wing and then let me fly.

Thanks and love to my sons Andrew, for letting me use his computer and his list-making skills, and Ian, for reminding me to take breathers.

Above all, I am indebted to my wife Gail, whose inexhaustible love, support, and patience have made and always will make all the difference in my life.

INTRODUCTION

For most homeowners, house and yard maintenance is an ongoing activity—something always seems to be in need of maintenance and/or repair. It's no wonder—today's homes and properties are busy, sometimes complicated environments.

The everyday habits of adults, kids, and pets take their toll—windows and doors stick, roofs leak, faucets drip, screens rip, toilets back up, doorknobs loosen, and on and on.

Although you don't necessarily need a lot of maintenance skills to take care of your house, some skills and know-how help. *The Ultimate Home and Property Maintenance Manual* will help you develop those skills and know-how. The information included will help you avoid problems, identify them when they occur, and find solutions—even if the solution comes in the form of a contractor.

Lastly, I hope this book has a part in helping you enjoy your home and getting personal satisfaction from a job well done.

Joe Beck

JOB DIFFICULTY EXPLANATION

The home and property maintenance jobs described in this book range from easy to very difficult. To help you determine if this maintenance job is for you, I have rated the jobs for their complexity with regard to the level of skill required and the physical effort needed.

I have assumed the reader has a beginner handyman's (or handywoman's) knowledge, skills, strength, patience, and will to do a good job. I have rated the jobs as follows:

Easy: Would take a beginner with the proper tools roughly 1 to 2 hours to complete the job.

Fairly Easy: Would take a beginner with the proper tools roughly 2 to 5 hours to complete the job.

Difficult: Would take a beginner with the proper tools roughly 5 to 7 hours to complete the job.

Very Difficult: Would take a beginner with the proper tools roughly 7 to 10 hours or more to complete the job.

The House

Choosing and Using Tools

Hand Tools—Buy Quality

Hand tools rely on human power to make them work. Most are pretty small, portable, and come in sets. A lineup of good tools is essential to maintaining your house. Always compare and insist on quality. Following is a basic collection.

Hammers

Carpenter's hammers are designed for a specific purpose: to drive or draw (pull) nails. The hammer has either a curved or a straight claw. The face may be bell-faced, or plain-faced, and the handle may be made of wood, steel, or fiberglass.

The ball-peen hammer has a ball that is smaller in diameter than the face and is useful for striking areas that are too small for the face to enter. These are made in different weights, usually 4, 6, 8, and 12 ounces and 1, $1^1/2$, and 2 pounds. For most work a $1/2$-pound hammer or a 12-ounce hammer is good. However, a 4- or 6-ounce hammer is good for light work.

Using Hammers

Believe it or not, there is a right way and a wrong way to use a hammer. The most common fault is to hold the handle too close to the head, or choking; this reduces the force of the blow. It also makes it harder to hold the head in an upright position. Except for light blows, hold the handle close to the end, with four fingers underneath and the thumb along the side or on top of the handle. The thumb should rest on the handle and never overlap the fingers (see Fig. 1.1).

Try to hit the object with full force, holding the hammer at such an angle that the face and the surface being hit are parallel. This distributes the force of the blow over the full face and prevents damage to the surface, the hammer face, and your arm.

To drive a nail, hold it down near the point and set it on the surface, holding it straight. Give it a few light taps to get it started, then follow with full-force blows. If you do not want to risk damaging the surface of the work with a blow, you can drive the nail to within a fraction of the surface, then drive it the rest of the way with a *nail set*.

You can pull small nails by slipping the claw of the hammer over the head and prying backwards. For large nails, however, you can get extra leverage if you place a small block of wood under the hammer before pulling back.

Maintenance

Hammers should be cleaned and repaired, if necessary, before they are put away. Before using, ensure that the faces are free from oil or other material that would cause the tool to glance off nails, spikes, or stakes. The heads should be dressed to remove any battered edge.

The handle should always be tight in the head. If it is loose, the head may fly off and cause an injury. The eye or hole in the hammerhead is made with a slight taper in both directions from the center. Once the handle, which is tapered to fit the eye, is inserted in the head, a steel or wooden wedge is driven into the end of the handle that is inserted in

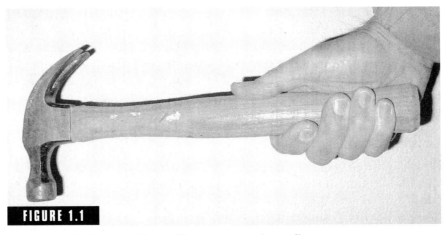

FIGURE 1.1

Correct use of a hammer will save time, energy, and your fingers.

the head. This wedge expands the handle and causes it to fill the oppo-site taper in the eye. Thus the handle is wedged in both directions. If the wedge starts to come out, drive it in again. If the wedge comes out, replace it before continuing to use the hammer. If you cannot get another wedge right away, you may file one out of a piece of flat steel, or cut one from a portion of the tang of a used, worn-out file. (The tang is the end of the file that fits into the handle.)

Safety

Hammers can be dangerous tools if used improperly. Here are some important things to remember. Do not use a hammer handle for hitting parts during any kind of assembly, and never use it as a pry bar. Such abuses may cause the handle to split; a split handle can produce bad cuts or pinches. When a handle splits or cracks, do not try to repair it by binding with string or wire; replace it. Always make sure that the handle fits tightly on the head.

Don't ever strike a hardened steel surface. Small pieces of steel may break off and injure someone in the eye or damage the work. It is all right to strike a punch or chisel directly with a ball-peen hammer, because the steel in the heads of punches and chisels is slightly softer than that in the hammerhead.

For around the house, the claw hammer, the type with a round striking end and turned-down nail-pulling section, is the most useful hammer to have. A 16-ounce weight is good, and you can expect to pay anywhere from $12 to $20 or more for one. Stanley and Plumb are two reliable brands; I like Plumb best.

Of course, if you plan to use the hammer only occasionally, you can get a real cheapo for around $7 to $8. These are likely to have the words "drop-forged" imprinted on them, as if this were an asset. It isn't: Drop forging creates a metal that is brittle—not a desirable feature in a hammer.

A framing hammer is another good tool to have. It has a striking surface and straight claw, good for slipping between framing members to pry them apart. One recommended brand is the Estwing, which has an all-steel form from head to handle. Plumb is a good brand, too. The average cost is about $30–$35.

Wrenches

A wrench is a basic tool that is used to exert a twisting force on bolts, nuts, studs, and pipes. No home should be without one.

The best wrenches are made of chrome vanadium steel. Wrenches made of this material are lightweight and almost unbreakable. Most common wrenches are made of forged carbon steel or molybdenum steel. These latter materials make good wrenches, but they are generally made a little heavier and bulkier in order to achieve the same degree of strength as chrome vanadium tools.

The size of any wrench used on bolt heads or nuts is determined by the size of the opening between the jaws of the wrench. The opening is manufactured slightly larger than the bolt head or nut that it is designed to fit. Hex nuts (six-sided nuts) and other types of nuts or bolt heads are measured across opposite flats (surfaces). A wrench that is designed to fit a nut or bolt usually has a clearance of from 0.005 to 0.008 inch. This clearance allows the wrench to slide on and off the nut or bolt with a minimum of "play." If the wrench is too large, the points of the nut or bolt head can be rounded and destroyed. This is called *stripping* the nut.

There are many kinds of wrenches. Each type is designed for a specific use. Following is a list of different kinds.

Open-End Wrenches

Open-end wrenches are solid, nonadjustable wrenches with openings in one or both ends (see Fig. 1.2). Usually they come in sets of from 6 to 10 wrenches with sizes ranging from ¼ to 1 inch. Wrenches with small openings are usually shorter than wrenches with large ones.

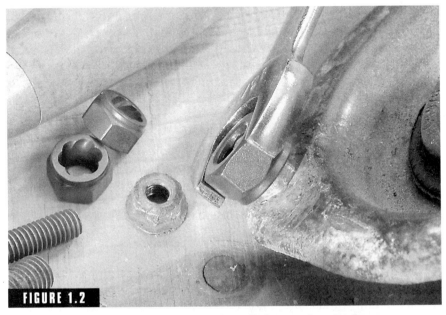

FIGURE 1.2

Open-end wrenches fit snugly on nuts and leave little room for mistakes.

This proportions the lever advantage of the wrench to the bolt, stud, or pipe and helps prevent wrench breakage or damage to the item.

Open-end wrenches may have their jaws parallel to the handle or at angles of up to 90 degrees. The average angle is 15 degrees. This variation permits selection of a wrench suited for places where there is room to make only part of a complete turn of a nut or bolt. If the wrench is turned over after the first swing, it will fit on the same flats and turn the nut farther. After two swings on the wrench, the nut is turned far enough so that a new set of flats is in position for the wrench.

Handles are usually straight, but they may be curved. Those with curved handles are called *S-wrenches*. Other open-end wrenches may have offset handles, which allow the head to reach nut or bolt heads that are sunk below the surface.

KEEP FAMILIES TOGETHER

When a hand tool is part of a set, it is important to return it to its carrying case right after using it. Misplacing or losing individual tools (particularly a common-sized one that is used often) makes the set incomplete, and sometimes useless. It's a good idea to keep them in the original packing case you bought them in. This way, you'll get years of use out of them and keep them together.

Box Wrenches

Box wrenches are safer than open-end wrenches, because there is less of a chance they will slip off the work. They completely surround or "box" a nut or bolt head.

The most frequently used box wrench has 12 points or notches arranged in a circle in the head and can be used with a minimum swing angle of 30 degrees. Generally, six- and eight-point wrenches are used for heavy-duty work, 12-point wrenches for medium work, and 16-point wrenches for light-duty work only.

One advantage of 12-point construction is the thin wall. It is better for turning nuts that are hard to get at with an open-end wrench. Another advantage is that the wrench will operate between obstructions, where the space for handle swing is limited. A very short swing of the handle will turn the nut far enough to allow the wrench to be lifted and the next set of points to be fitted to the corners of the nut.

A disadvantage of the box-end wrench is the loss of time that occurs whenever the user has to lift the wrench off and place it back on the nut.

Combination Wrenches

Combination wrenches are particularly useful because after a tight nut is broken loose, it can be unscrewed much more quickly with an

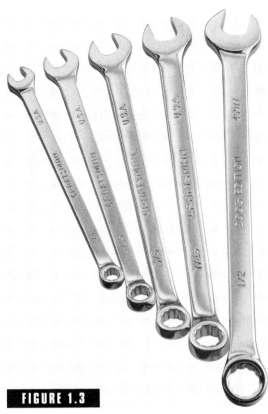

Combination wrenches are like having two tools in one—an open-end wrench and a closed-end wrench.

open-end wrench than with a box wrench. This is where a combination box-open-end wrench comes in handy (see Fig. 1.3). You can use the box end for breaking nuts loose or for snugging them down, and the open end for faster turning. The box-end portion of the wrench can be designed with an offset in the handle.

The correct use of open-end and box-end wrenches can be summed up in a few simple rules, most important of which is to be sure that the wrench properly fits the nut or bolt head. When you have to pull hard on the wrench, as in loosening a tight nut, make sure that the wrench is seated squarely on the flats.

Pull on the wrench—do not push. Pushing a wrench is a good way to skin your knuckles if the wrench slips or the nut breaks loose unexpectedly. If it is impossible to pull the wrench, and you must push, do it with the palm of your hand and hold your palm open. Practice will tell you if you are using the right amount of force on the wrench so that you can turn the nut to proper tightness without stripping the threads or twisting off the bolt.

Adjustable Wrenches

An all-around handy wrench that is a must for your toolbox is the adjustable wrench (see Fig. 1.4). These have jaws that can be opened or closed. Within the limitations of the individual wrench, they fit nuts, bolts, and pipes of various sizes. There are many different types of adjustable wrenches, several of which are used in plumbing.

ADJUSTABLE OPEN-END WRENCH

Use an adjustable open-end wrench on square or hexagonal nuts when you are working with the interior parts of faucets and valves. For most minor plumbing jobs, a 12-inch wrench is probably the best choice. (The size refers to the length of the tool; however, the jaws of larger wrenches do open more widely.) It is also handy to have an 8-inch or 6-inch wrench for smaller work.

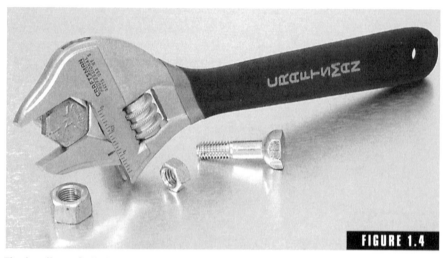

FIGURE 1.4

The handiest of all the wrenches—the adjustable wrench.

MONKEY WRENCH

A monkey wrench is used for the same purposes and in the same way as an adjustable open-end wrench. Turning force should be applied to the back of the handle (the side of the wrench opposite the jaw opening).

PIPE WRENCHES

For rotating or holding round work, an adjustable pipe wrench, sometimes called a basin wrench, may be used (see Fig. 1.5). The movable jaw on a pipe wrench is pivoted to permit a gripping action on the work (see Fig. 1.6). This tool must be used with discretion, as the jaws are serrated and always make marks on the work unless adequate precautions are observed. The jaws should be adjusted so that the bite on the work will be taken at about the center of the jaws.

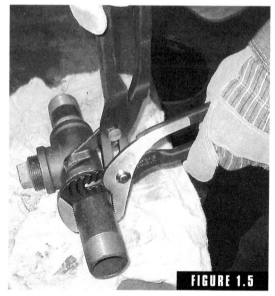

FIGURE 1.5

Chain Pipe Wrenches: A different type of pipe wrench, used mostly on large sizes of pipe, is the chain pipe wrench. This tool works in one direction only, but it can be backed partly around the work and a fresh hold can be taken without freeing the chain.

Two wrenches are used to twist pieces of pipe and/or couplings apart.

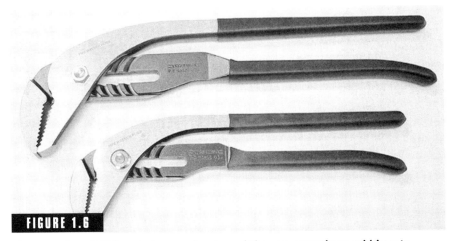

FIGURE 1.6

Pipe wrenches of different sizes are handy, and they are sometimes sold in sets.

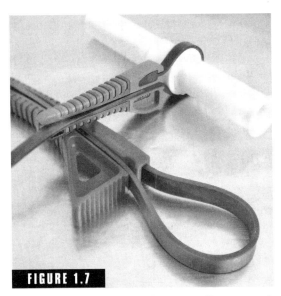

FIGURE 1.7

Strap wrenches are used when an ordinary wrench won't fit in a tight space.

To reverse the operation, the grip is taken on the opposite side of the head. The head is double-ended and can be reversed when the teeth on one end are worn out.

Strap Wrenches

The strap wrench is similar to the chain pipe wrench, but it uses a heavy web strap in place of the chain (see Fig. 1.7). This wrench is used for turning pipe when you do not want to damage the pipe (see Fig. 1.8).

Ratchet Wrenches

At first glance, ratchet wrenches appear just like box wrenches or combination wrenches, but when you take a closer look, you'll see that inside the round part are cogs (or what look like teeth). These are designed to grab the sides of a nut as the tool is slid over it, allowing the user to use the tool as you would a ratchet, and quickly tighten nuts or the heads of bolts without taking the tool of the nut (see Fig. 1.9).

Rules for Safety

It is important to use a wrench that fits the nut properly. Keep wrenches clean and free from oil. Otherwise they may slip, and serious injury to you or damage to the work may result. Do not increase the leverage of a

FIGURE 1.8

Strap wrenches are good for turning something you don't want to scratch or dent.

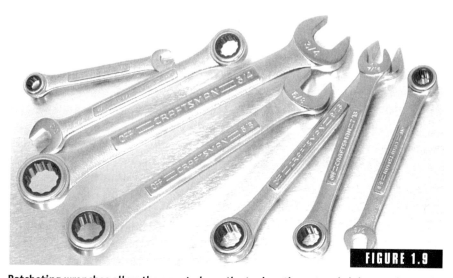

FIGURE 1.9

Ratcheting wrenches allow the user to keep the tool on the nut and tighten or loosen it.

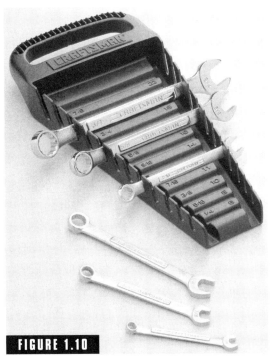

FIGURE 1.10

Wrench organizers keep all your wrenches where they are supposed to be.

SAFETY FIRST AND LAST

It's so simple: you want to get to a job and get it finished. In your haste you take a shortcut you didn't think about; next thing you know, you have a sliced finger or skinned knuckles. Whenever you work with hand or power tools, wear goggles or glasses to protect your eyes (you can't replace them), gloves, and loose, comfortable clothing (so you can easily bend, twist or crouch), and always stop and think before doing even a seemingly simple job. It's true—haste does make waste.

wrench by placing a pipe over the handle. Increased leverage may damage the wrench or the work.

Keep Wrenches Together

Provide some sort of kit or case for all wrenches (see Fig. 1.10). Return them to it at the completion of each job. Doing so saves time and trouble and facilitates selection of tools for the next job. Most important, it eliminates the possibility of leaving them where they can cause injury or damage to other equipment, you, or your house.

Determine the way in which a nut should be turned before trying to loosen it. Most nuts are turned counterclockwise for removal. This may seem obvious, but forgetting it could be unforgiving.

There are a number of different wrenches that it may be helpful to have around. One such is the pipe wrench. I recently saw a set of four in the Harbor Freight catalog for around $18, but although the price is right, I don't think the average homeowner will need that many. If you don't have any pipe wrenches, I would start by getting a 10-inch wrench and maybe a 14-inch one (the jaws go wider as the wrench gets longer). This should serve you well in almost any conceivable situation.

Ridgid is the top-of-the-line supplier of pipe wrenches, but I would stick with Fuller. The average cost of a 10-inch Fuller pipe wrench will be about $10, while a Ridgid will be almost twice that, or nearly $20. Like Ridgid, Fuller wrenches carry a lifetime guarantee. Another useful wrench is the adjustable open-end type, which has flat jaws and a chrome head and handle. This wrench has become synonymous with the brand name Crescent, which is top of the line; Fuller makes one for about half the price of a Crescent. I would suggest a Fuller, 10-inches long. Its cost should be under $12.

Metal-Cutting Tools

There are many types of metal-cutting tools, a few of which (snips and shears) are particularly good to have around the house. These are used for cutting sheet metal and steel of various thicknesses and shapes. Normally, heavier or thicker material is cut by using shears.

Snips

One of the handiest tools for cutting light (up to 1 inch thick) sheet metal is the *hand snip* or *tin snips.* Straight hand snips have blades that are straight and cutting edges that are sharpened to an 85-degree angle. Snips like these can be obtained in different sizes, ranging from small 6-inch to large 14-inch snips. Tin snips also work on slightly heavier gauges of soft metals, such as aluminum alloys.

Snips do not remove any metal when a cut is made. There is danger, however, of causing minute metal fractures along the edges of the metal during the cutting. For this reason, it is better to cut just outside the layout line. This procedure allows you to *dress* the cutting edge (keep it neat) while keeping the material within required dimensions. This makes cutting metal for things like roof flashing easier.

Cutting extremely heavy-gauge metal always presents the possibility of *springing* the blades. This means the rivet or bolt that holds the blades together comes out. Once the blades are sprung, hand snips are useless. If you use the rear portion of the blades for such cutting, you not only avoid the possibility of springing the blades but also get greater cutting leverage.

Many snips have small serrations on the blades. These serrations tend to prevent the snips from slipping backwards when a cut is being made. Although this feature does make the cutting easier, it mars the edges of the metal slightly. You can remove these small cutting marks if you allow proper clearance and dress the metal to size. Many other types of hand snips are used for special jobs, but the snips discussed can be used for almost any common type of maintenance work.

CUTTING SHEET METAL WITH SNIPS

It is hard to cut circles or small arcs with straight snips. There are snips especially designed for circular cutting. These have names such as circle snips, hawks' bill snips, trojan snips, and aviation snips.

To cut large holes in the lighter gauges of sheet metal, start the cut by punching or otherwise making a hole in the center of the area to be cut out. With aviation snips or some other narrow-bladed snips, make a spiral cut from the starting hole out toward the scribed circle and continue cutting until the scrap falls away.

To cut a disk in the lighter gauges of sheet metal, use combination snips or straight-blade snips. First, cut away any surplus material outside of the scribed circle, leaving only a narrow piece to be removed by the final cut. Make the final cut just outside the layout line. This will let you see the line while you are cutting and will cause the scrap to curl up below the blade during cutting.

To make straight cuts, place the metal on a bench with a marked guideline over the edge of a workbench. Hold the sheet down with one hand. With the other hand, hold the snips so that the flat sides of the blades are at right angles to the surface of the work, and cut. If the blades are not at right angles, the edges of the cut will be slightly bent and burred. The bench edge should act as a guide when you are cutting.

Generally, any of the hand snips may be used for straight cuts. When notches are too narrow to be cut out with a pair of snips, make the side cuts with the snips and cut the base of the notch with a cold chisel.

SAFETY AND CARE

Snips should always be oiled and adjusted to allow easy cutting and a cut that is free from burrs. If blades bind, or if they are too far apart, the snips should be adjusted by tightening the screw that holds them together.

Never use snips as screwdrivers, hammers, or pry bars. They break easily. Do not attempt to cut heavier materials than the snips are designed for. Never use tin snips, for example, to cut hardened steel wire or other similar objects.

Also, it is never a good idea to toss snips into a toolbox where the cutting edges can come into contact with other tools. Such contact dulls the cutting edges and may even break the blades. When snips are not in use, hang them on hooks or lay them on an uncluttered shelf or bench.

For some reason, there are a lot of junk tin snips on the market, so I think it is important to stay with what definitely works. Wiss makes very good snips. For intricate cutting, get what is known as *aviation snips* (models for cutting both left and right are made). These cost around $15. For straight cuts, get standard snips. These go for about $20–$22. The nice feature they offer is a slightly toothed blade that grips the metal being cut and tends to keep the cut straight.

Hacksaws

Hacksaws are used to cut metal that is too heavy for snips; for example, metal bar stock can be cut readily with a hacksaw. They are also fundamentally important in cutting many types of pipe.

There are two parts to a hacksaw: the frame and the blade. Common hacksaws have either an adjustable or a solid frame. Adjustable frames can be made to hold blades from 8 to 16 inches long, whereas those with solid frames take only the blade of the length for which they are designed. This length is the distance between the two pins that hold the blade in place.

Hacksaw blades are made of high-grade tool steel, hardened and tempered. There are two types, all-hard and flexible. All-hard blades are hardened throughout, whereas only the teeth of flexible blades are hardened. Hacksaw blades are about $1/2$ inch wide, have from 14 to 32 teeth per inch, and are from 8 to 16 inches long. The blades have a hole at each end that hooks to a pin in the frame. All hacksaw frames that hold the blades either parallel or at right angles to the frame are provided with a wing nut or screw to permit tightening or removing the blade.

The *set* in a hacksaw refers to how much the teeth are pushed out in opposite directions from the sides of the blade. The four different kinds of set are alternate set, double-alternate set, raker set, and wave set. The teeth in the alternate set are staggered, one to the left and to the right, throughout the length of the blade. On the double-alternate set blade, two adjoining teeth are staggered to the right, two to the left, and so on. On the raker set blade, every third tooth remains straight and the other two are set alternately. On the wave (undulated) set blade, short sections of teeth are bent in opposite directions.

USE CAREFULLY

Hacksaws are very often used incorrectly. Although they can be used with some success by almost any adult, a little thought and study given to proper use will result in faster and better work—and the added benefit of less dulling and breaking of blades.

Good work with a hacksaw depends not only on proper use of the saw but on proper blade selection. Coarse blades with fewer teeth per inch cut faster and are less liable to choke up with chips. However, finer blades with more teeth per inch are necessary when thin sections are to be cut.

To make the cut, first install the blade in the hacksaw frame so that the teeth point away from the handle. (Hand hacksaws cut on the push stroke.) Tighten the wing nut so that the blade is under tension; this helps make straight cuts.

Place the material to be cut in a vise. A minimum of overhang reduces vibration, gives a better cut, and lengthens the life of the blade. Have the layout line outside of the vise jaw so that the line is visible while you work.

When cutting, let your body sway ahead and back with each stroke. Apply pressure on the forward stroke, which is the cutting stroke, but not on the return stroke. From 40 to 50 strokes per minute is the usual speed. Long, slow, steady strokes are preferred.

For long cuts, rotate the blade in the frame so that the length of the cut is not limited by the depth of the frame. Hold the work with the layout line close to the vise jaws, raising the work in the vise as the sawing proceeds.

Metal that is too thin to be held can be placed between blocks of wood. The wood provides support for several teeth as they are cutting. Without the wood, teeth will be broken because of excessive vibration of the stock and because individual teeth must absorb the full power of the stroke. Pipe may also be placed in a miter box for cutting.

Cut thin metal with layout lines on the face and a piece of wood behind. Hold the wood and the metal in the jaws of the vise, using a C-clamp when necessary. The wood block helps support the blade and produces a smoother cut. Using the wood only in back of the metal permits the layout lines to be seen.

HACKSAW SAFETY

The primary danger in using hacksaws is injury to your hand if the blade breaks. The blade will break if too much pressure is applied, if the saw is twisted, if the cutting speed is too fast, or if the blade becomes loose in the frame. Additionally, if the work is not tight in the vise, it will sometimes slip, twisting the blade enough to break it.

Hacksaws come in various qualities, including a tubular framed type, which stores extra hacksaw blades, but you can get a perfectly serviceable one for $6 or $7. Great Neck is one manufacturer. If you want a hacksaw that will last forever, get a D-handle model. The cost will be about $16–$18. The D-handle's frame is made so that it protects the user's knuckles in case of a slip.

REMOVING FROZEN NUTS

To remove a frozen nut with a hacksaw, saw into the nut, starting the blade close to the threads on the bolt or stud and parallel to one face of the nut. Saw parallel to the bolt until the teeth of the blade almost reach the lock washer. Lock washers are hard and will ruin hacksaw blades, so do not try to saw them. Then, with a cold chisel and hammer, remove this side of the nut completely by opening the saw kerf. Put an adjustable wrench across this new flat and the one opposite, and again try to remove the frozen nut. Since very little original metal remains on this side of the nut, the nut will either give or break away entirely and permit its removal.

To saw a wide kerf in the head of a cap screw or machine bolt, fit the hand hacksaw frame with two blades side by side, and with teeth lined up in the same direction. With slow, steady strokes, saw the slot approximately one-third the thickness of the head of the cap screw. Such a slot will permit subsequent holding or turning with a screwdriver when it is impossible, due to close quarters, to use a wrench.

HACKSAW BLADES

For around-the-home use, four types of blades are all that are really needed, as described by the number of teeth per inch (tpi). The general idea is the more teeth, the smoother the cut. Hence, the following lineup: 18 tpi for molding, 24 tpi for general use, 32 tpi for very fine cuts, and 14 tpi for cutting wood.

Blades, of course, vary in quality. Blades labeled with the letters SS are the low end of the line and go for about 80 cents each. HSS, or high-speed steel, go for about $1.99 to $2.99 each. These are made of flexible molybdenum. They last indefinitely and do a good job cutting threaded rod, angle iron, and the like. They are a good buy, but they won't cut something like a heat-treated bolt.

The most expensive way to buy blades is a few in a package. Either buy them loose or in bulk—they come 10 to the package (but you might be old before you get to use them all). Lennox is one good brand.

Thin hacksaw blades are also available for use with a coping saw when special cuts are required. In terms of brand, I prefer Nicholson, followed by Stanley and Lennox.

Rod Saws

An improvement in industrial technology once again produces a tool where none existed before. The homeowner also benefits from this. A rod saw lets the user cut material that an ordinary hacksaw cannot even scratch. The rod saw acts like a diamond, cutting hard metals and materials such as stainless steel, glass, and stone. It cuts by means of hundreds of tungsten carbide particles permanently bonded to the rod.

A unique feature of this saw is its capability of cutting on both the forward and reverse strokes. It is designed to fit on a hacksaw handle and comes in varying lengths, usually from 8 to 16 inches long. A 10-inch rod saw typically sells for $2.75 or so, and larger ones can cost up to $4.00.

Pipe and Tubing Cutters and Flaring Tools

Pipe cutters are used to cut pipe made of steel, brass, copper, wrought iron, and lead. Tube cutters are used to cut tubing made of iron, steel, brass, copper, and aluminum. The essential difference between pipe and tubing is that tubing has considerably thinner walls. Flaring tools are also used to make single or double flares in the ends of tubing.

Hand-held pipe cutters are available from your local plumbing supply store or home center. They have models capable of cutting pipes from $1/4$ to $2^1/8$ inches wide. Brasscraft and Ridgid cutters are comparable in price, and the prices range from about $8 to $18. Flaring tools widen the ends of tubes from $1/4$ to $1/2$ inch and cost about $30. If you are unsure how to operate these, make sure you read the directions that come with them, or ask your supplier.

Chisels

Chisels are tools that can be used for chipping or cutting metal (or wood). They will cut any metal that is softer than the material that they are made of. Chisels are made from a good grade of tool steel and have a hardened cutting edge and beveled head. Cold chisels are classified according to the shape of their points; the width of the cutting edge indicates their size. The most common shapes of chisels are flat (cold chisel), cape, round nose, and diamond point.

The kind of chisel most widely used is the flat cold chisel, which serves to cut rivets, to split nuts, to chip castings, and to cut thin metal sheets and cast-iron pipe. The cape chisel is used for special jobs such as cutting keyways, narrow grooves, and square comers. Round-nose chisels make circular grooves and chip inside comers with a fillet. Finally, the diamond-point chisel is used for cutting V-grooves and sharp comers.

Using Chisels

As with other tools, there is a correct way of using a chisel. Select a chisel that is large enough for the job. Be sure to use a hammer that matches the chisel; that is, the larger the chisel, the heavier the hammer should be. A heavy chisel will absorb the blows of a light hammer and will do virtually no cutting.

As a general rule, hold the chisel in your left hand with your thumb and first finger about 1 inch from the top. It should be held steadily but not tightly. The finger muscles should be relaxed, so that if the hammer strikes your hand, it hand can slide down the tool, lessening the effect of the blow. Keep your eyes on the cutting edge of the chisel, not on the head, and swing the hammer in the same plane as the body of the chisel. If you have a lot of chiseling to do, slide a piece of rubber hose over the chisel. This will lessen the shock to your hand.

When using a chisel for chipping, always wear goggles to protect your eyes. If other people happen to be close by, see that they are protected from flying chips by erecting a screen or shield to block any airborne chips.

For wood, only a chisel 3 or 4 inches long with a metal cap is recommended. Since it takes a lot of punishment pounding with a hammer, better quality is recommended. Stanley makes a good one for around $13. A cold chisel for working on metal and masonry is also a good idea. A 1-inch-wide tool is good. Enders makes a good one that will hold its edge quite nicely. And this is important: Some cold chisels look good, but the edge gets dull after being used a couple of times. The Enders chisel costs around $13.

Files

There are a number of different types of files in common use, and each type may range in length from 3 to 18 inches. Files are graded according to the degree of fineness, and according to whether they have single- or double-cut teeth.

Single-cut files have rows of teeth cut parallel to each other. These teeth are set at an angle of about 65 degrees with the center line. Use single-cut files for sharpening tools, finish filing, and draw filing. They are also the best tools for smoothing the edges of sheet metal and burrs on pipe. Files with crisscrossed rows of teeth are double-cut files. The double cut forms teeth that are diamond-shaped and fast cutting. Use double-cut files for quick removal of metal, and for rough work.

Files are also classified according to the spacing and size of their teeth, or their coarseness and fineness. In addition to the grades shown, you may use some dead smooth files which have very fine teeth, and some rough files with very coarse teeth. The fineness or coarseness of file teeth is also influenced by the length of the file.

The length of a file is the distance from the tip to the heel, and does not include the tang. When you have a chance, in a home center or hardware store, compare the actual size of the teeth of a 6-inch, single-cut smooth file and a 12-inch, single-cut smooth file; you will notice that the 6-inch file has more teeth per inch than the 12-inch file.

File Shapes

Files come in different shapes. Therefore, in selecting a file for a job, the shape of the finished work must be considered, because that's what you're working toward.

Filing

When working with metal, your best ally is a file. You may be cross filing, draw filing, using a file card, or even polishing metal. Let's examine these operations. (When you have finished using a file, it may be necessary to use an abrasive cloth or paper to finish the product. Whether this is necessary depends on how fine a finish you want on the work.)

CROSS FILING

Cross filing means that the file is moved across the surface of the work in approximately a crosswise direction. For best results, keep your feet spread apart to steady yourself as you file with slow, full-length, steady strokes. The file cuts as you push it; ease up on the return stroke to keep from dulling the teeth. Keep the file clean.

When an exceptionally flat surface is required, file across the entire length of the stock. Then, using the other position, file across the entire length of the object again. Because the teeth of the file pass over the surface of the object from two directions, the high spots and low spots are readily visible after you have filed both ways. Continue filing first in one position or direction and then the other until the surface has been filed flat. Test the flatness with a straight edge.

DRAW FILING

Draw filing produces a finer surface finish and usually a flatter surface than cross filing. Small parts are best held in a vise. Notice that the cutting stroke is away from you when the handle of the file is held in the right hand. If the handle is held in the left hand, the cutting stroke is toward you. Lift the file away from the surface of the work on the return stroke.

USING A FILE CARD

As you file, the teeth of the file may clog with some of the metal filings and scratch your work. This condition is known as *pinning.* You can prevent it by keeping the file teeth clean. Rubbing chalk between the teeth will help prevent pinning, but the best method is to clean the file frequently with a file card or brush. A file card has fine wire bristles. Brush with a pulling motion, holding the card parallel to the rows of teeth.

Always keep the file clean, whether you are filing mild steel or other metals.

FILING ROUND METAL STOCK

As a file is passed over the surface of round work, its angle with the work automatically changes. A rocking motion of the file results, permitting all the teeth on the file to make contact and cut as they pass over the work's surface. Done properly, the motion tends to keep the file much cleaner and thereby produces better work.

POLISHING A FLAT METAL SURFACE

When polishing a flat metal surface, first draw file the surface. Then finish with abrasive cloth, often called emery cloth. Select a grade of cloth suited to the draw filing. If the draw filing was well done, only a fine cloth will be needed to do final polishing.

If your cloth is in a roll, and the job you are polishing is the size that would be held in a vise, tear off a 6- or 8-inch length of the 1- or 2-inch width. If you are using sheets of abrasive cloth, tear off a strip from the long edge of the 8- by 11-inch sheet.

Wrap the cloth around the file and hold the file as you would for draw filing. Hold the end of the cloth in place with your thumb. In polishing, apply a thin film of lubricating oil on the surface and use a double stroke, with pressure on both the forward and the backward strokes. Note that this is different from the draw filing stroke, in which you cut with the file in only one direction.

When further polishing does not appear to improve the surface, you are ready to use the next finer grade of cloth. Before changing to the finer grade, however, reverse the cloth so that its back is toward the surface being polished.

Work the reversed cloth back and forth in the abrasive-laden oil. Then clean the work thoroughly with solvent before proceeding with the next finer grade of cloth. Careful cleaning between grades helps to ensure freedom from scratches.

For the final polish use a strip of crocus cloth—first use the face and then the back—with plenty of oil. When polishing is complete, again carefully clean the job with a solvent and protect it from rusting with oil or other means.

Another way to polish is with the abrasive cloth wrapped around a block of wood.

POLISHING ROUND METAL STOCK

Round stock may be polished with a strip of abrasive cloth, which is seesawed back and forth over the surface.

Remember that the selection of grades of abrasive cloth, the application of oil, and the cleaning between grades applies to polishing regardless of how the cloth is held or used. Do not break in a new file by using it first on a narrow surface.

Protect file teeth by hanging your files in a rack when they are not in use, or by replacing them in drawers with wooden partitions. Files should not be allowed to rust—keep them away from moisture. Avoid getting the files oily. Oil causes a file to slide across the work and prevents fast, clean cutting. Files that you keep in your toolbox should be wrapped in paper or cloth to protect their teeth and prevent damage to other tools.

Also, never use a file for prying or pounding. The tang is soft and bends easily. The body is hard and extremely brittle. Even slightly bend or dropping it can cause a file to snap in two. Do not strike a file against the bench or vise to clean it—use a file card.

File Safety

Never use a file unless it is equipped with a tightly fitting handle. If you use a file without the handle and it bumps something or jams, the tang may be driven into your hand. To put a handle on a tang, drill a hole in the handle slightly smaller than the tang. Insert the tang end, and then tap the end of the handle to seat it firmly. Make sure you get the handle on straight.

Some people think files are used only for metal and rasps only for wood, but all you really need is one file of a specific size and style. I suggest an 8-inch half-round (half a circle in profile) with a so-called bastard (rough) cutting surface. It can be used on all kinds of metal and wood. A Nicholson is suggested. It costs about $10.

A close cousin of a file is Stanley's line of Surform tools, which are basically planes. They can be equipped with straight or round blades. They cost around $13 for the straight type and are also pretty useful around the house.

Rasps

Rasps (and files, their counterparts for metal) come in a bewildering number of types, shapes, and cutting surfaces. However, for occasional use around the home, such as slimming down a binding door, one type will serve you well: a 10-inch-long, half-round type (one side is curved, the other flat) with second-cut teeth. Second-cut refers to the coarseness of the teeth, which in this case is about the same as medium-grade sandpaper.

Twist Drills

Making a hole in a piece of metal is a pretty simple operation, and in most cases a precise job is required. A large number of different tools and machines have been designed so that holes may be made quickly and accurately in all kinds of material.

The most common tool for making holes in metal is the twist drill. It consists of a cylindrical piece of steel with spiral grooves, commonly called a bit. One end of the bit is pointed, and the other is shaped so that it may be attached to a drilling machine. The grooves, usually called flutes, may be cut into the steel cylinder, or may be formed by twisting a flat piece of steel into a cylindrical shape.

The principal parts of a twist drill are the body, the shank, and the point. The dead center of a drill is the sharp edge at the extreme tip end of the drill. It is formed by the intersection of the cone-shaped surfaces of the point and should always be in the exact center of the axis of the drill. The point of the drill should not be confused with the dead center. The point is the entire cone-shaped surface at the end of the drill. The shank is the part of the drill that fits into the socket, spindle, or chuck of the drill.

Twist drills are provided in various sizes. They are sized by letters, numerals, and fractions. Sets of drills are usually made available according to the way the sizes are stated; that is, "sets of letter drills" or "sets of number drills." Also, twist drills of any size (letter, number, or fraction) are available individually if desired.

PILOT HOLES

Always take the time to drill pilot holes in hard materials before driving. The hole should be slightly smaller in diameter than the screw and the same length as the screw, excluding the head. Pilot holes serve several purposes: they make it easier for the user to twist in a screw, they provide a precise location for the screw, and they are small enough to ensure a snug fit for the screw.

Drill Bits and Fittings

Many types of drill bits are sold for cutting different size holes in different materials. The most common sort are twist bits, used for drilling holes in metal and in wood up to the drill's capacity. Most of the time you will find these sold as sets. A set for your house is invaluable. Most sets have individual bits that range in size from about $7/32$ inch to about $1/2$ inch.

Larger holes in wood are drilled with spade-type or power bore bits. The spade bit has a flat tip with a center point and two cutting edges. The power bore bit has a round cutting tip for a somewhat smoother cut. A typical spade bit set consists of three individual pieces, including $1/2$-inch, $3/4$-inch, and 1-inch bits, and sells for about $6.

Forstner-type bits are used mostly in drill presses. They cut neat, flat-bottomed holes, but they have to be withdrawn and cleaned out during the drilling. Very large holes are drilled with spade bits up to 1 inch or hole saws up to 3 inches.

The hole saw has a revolving toothed ring attached to a central twist bit. The ring removes wood like a revolving pastry cutter. Different sizes of ring are available. Very long holes, such as those up the shaft of some lamps, are drilled with a power bit extension, This is a shaft held in the chuck with the bit held in a small set-screw chuck at the other end.

Other types of bits include countersink bits, for countersinking screw holes, and combination bits such as the Screw Mate, which are specially shaped to drill and countersink (or counter bore) a hole for a particular size of screw. A plug cutter is often used in conjunction with screw work to conceal screw heads in wood. This is the way it works: a bit the size of the screw head is used to counter-bore a screw hole (to recess the screw head some way into the wood) and then a plug, like a short cylindrical piece of wood, is cut from a matching piece of wood, glued into the recess over the screw head, and planed flat to give almost an invisible result. The grain of the plug runs across its diameter.

Drilling Masonry

For drilling hard masonry, special masonry bits are available. They look like twist bits, but have cutting tips made of a special hard alloy. If using a drill with rotary hammer action, then masonry percussion bits are required. This is most likely outside beyond the needs of the homeowner. These have specially hardened shoulders at the tip, to withstand vibration shock.

When using masonry bits, it is best not to drill fast. Doing so causes a lot of friction and heat, which will diminish the hole-making power of the bit. Slow and steady is the best way to use masonry bits.

Drilling Glass and Tile

Glass and tiles are drilled with a spear-point drill bit, which also has a hardened tip. This bit resembles an ice cream cone, in a way, because it is very sharp at the tip, but gets wider higher up, and has very sharp cutting edges on either side of the tip. When you shop for spear-point bits, be sure and ask the dealer if they are designed for glass and tile. You don't want to mistake a bit for something else: then you'll have a worthless piece of glass or tile on your hands.

Homemade Depth Gauges

Some drill bits have a thickness of plastic wrapped around the shank of the drill to provide depth indication. This can be moved up and down, according to what you are drilling. You can make a homemade depth stop by sticking adhesive tape around the bit. Bright fluorescent tape is best because it is easily seen. Drill to the lower edge of the tape and you should be fine.

The Bit Sharpener

Sharp and accurate drill bits will produce better-quality work, without undue time losses or frustration—and bits lose their sharpness with continued use. You can restore the edge on a grinder or use a special drill-bit sharpener. You can change the position of the bit inside the sharpener with an adjusting knob. In this way you can control the cutting of the first two angles.

When using a sharpener, set the adjusting knob on the front in the vertical position and insert the drill into the smallest hole of the top plate into which it will fit. If you insert it into a larger hole the bit will be misshaped. The point of the bit should be in the center, otherwise the bit will drill oversized holes, which will result in badly finished work and possibly the waste of a valuable piece of lumber. You can control the point position by the pressure you apply to the bit during sharpening. Turn the knob in a clockwise direction to increase the angle of cutting and in a counterclockwise direction to decrease the cutting relief.

Drill bits should be sharpened only when they are dry. When sharpening, do not use water or any other liquid as a coolant. Sharpening makes the bit hot, so do not touch it with your fingertips immediately after you have extracted it from the machine. Only high-speed steel or carbon steel bits can be sharpened in the machine. Masonry and other bits with specially hard tips, or of a different tip shape, should not be put into the machine, or they will be ruined. Make sure you ask your dealer which bits can be safely sharpened in the machine.

Metal-Cutting Jobs

Many hand and power tools have been designed for the specific purpose of cutting metals quickly and accurately. This section describes some metal-cutting operations that can be performed with chisels and drills.

Holding the Work

Most work is held for drilling by some mechanical means such as a vise or clamp. If it is not well secured, the work may rotate at high speed or fly loose, and become a high-speed projectile. When one is drilling in small pieces with a hand-held drill, it is best to hold the work in a vise. Also, always wear goggle or eye-protecting glasses.

Metal Cutting with Chisels

When struck with a heavy hammer, a cold chisel is capable of cutting metal. With a chisel and a hammer, you can cut wires, bars, rods, and other shapes of metal and also cut off the heads of rivets and bolts.

Cutting Wire

Mark off a guideline on the stock and place the work on the top face of an anvil or other suitable working surface. Place the cutting edge of the chisel on the mark in a vertical position and lightly strike the chisel with a hammer. Check the chisel mark for accuracy. Continue to strike the chisel until the cut is made. The last few blows of the hammer should be made lightly to avoid damage to the anvil, the supporting surface, or the chisel. Heavier wire stock is cut in the same manner, except that the cut is made halfway through the stock; then the work is turned over, and the cut is finished from the opposite side.

Cutting Off a Rivet or Bolt Head

Hold the work in a heavy vise, or secure it some other way so that the work will not move. Hold the chisel with one face of the bevel flat on the surface of the job. Strike the head of the chisel with the hammer as you loosely hold and guide the chisel.

To cut off a rivet head, select a chisel of about the same size as the diameter of the rivet. Cut through the center of the rivet head, holding one face of the bevel flat on the surface of the job, and then sever the center of the head from the shank or body.

To remove a rivet head when there is not room enough to swing a hammer with sufficient force to cut the rivet, first drill a hole about the size of the body of the rivet in and almost to the bottom of the rivet head. Then cut off the head with a cold chisel.

To cut off a bolt head, make sure the object is held securely in a vise. Line a cold chisel up with the bolt and strike the chisel until you have cut part way through the bolt. Open the vice and move the bolt to the opposite direction. Strike the chisel again, on the other side, until the head comes off. Be careful not to hit the chisel too hard; the cutting surface is tough—usually tougher than bolt heads.

Cutting Holes in Metal

In drilling any metal, there are several general steps to be followed. First, mark the exact location of the hole. Second, secure the work properly and then use the correct cutting speed. You can judge this by the effectiveness of the drill on the metal as you start to drill. It is assumed that you have selected the correct drill size.

The exact location of the hole must be marked with a center punch. The punch mark forms a seat for the drill point, ensuring accuracy. Without the mark, the drill may have a tendency to "walk off" before it begins to cut into the metal.

Wood-Cutting Hand Saws

Wood-cutting hand saws come in a variety of types. Two useful ones for the homeowner are the crosscut saw and the ripsaw. The crosscut saw is for cutting boards across or at an angle to the grain of the wood; the ripsaw is for cutting with the grain, or lengthwise.

Saws are made with varying numbers of teeth per inch. The more teeth the saw has, the smoother the cut will be. To tell quality, look for a springy, well-finished blade.

What kinds of saws will serve you well? For crosscutting—cutting across the grain—a 20-inch-long saw with 10 tpi (teeth per inch) will work well. For ripping—cutting with the grain of the wood—a 26-incher with 8 tpi is good. Stanley makes good saws in the $14–$22 range, but of course shopping around may get you an even better price. Saws, by the way, are one of the items that can be kept going for years by resharpening them and taking care of them.

Saw Precautions

A saw that is not being used should be hung up or stored in a toolbox. A toolbox designed to hold saws has notches that hold them on edge, teeth up. Storing saws loose in a toolbox may allow the saw teeth to become dulled or bent by coming into contact with other tools.

Before using a saw, be sure that there are no nails or other edge-destroying objects in the line of the cut. When sawing out a strip of waste, do not break out the strip by twisting the saw blade. Although this is a common practice, it dulls the saw and may spring or break the blade.

Be sure that the saw will go through the full stroke without striking the floor or some object. If the work cannot be raised high enough to obtain full clearance for the saw, you should carefully limit the length of each stroke to avoid accidents.

Using a Hand Saw

To saw across the grain of wood, use the crosscut saw; to saw with the grain, use a ripsaw. Look at the teeth in both kinds of saws so that you can readily identify the saw that you need. If you still have questions about what saw to use, find a professional carpenter; if you can't find one, ask your hardware or home center salesperson.

Place the board on a sawhorse or some other suitable object. Hold the saw in your right hand (or your left hand, if you are left-handed) and extend the first finger along the handle. Grasp the board and take a position so that an imaginary line passing lengthwise along your right forearm will be at an angle of approximately 45 degrees with the face of the board. Be sure that the side of the saw is plumb (or at right angles) with the board face. Place the heel of the saw on the mark. Keep the saw in line with your forearm and pull it toward you to start the cut.

To begin, take short, light strokes, gradually increasing the strokes to the full length of the saw. Do not force or jerk the saw; that only makes sawing more difficult. The arm that does the sawing should swing clear of your body so that the handle of the saw operates at your side rather than in front of you.

Use one hand to operate the saw. You may be tempted to use both hands at times, but if your saw is sharp, one hand will serve you better. The weight of the saw is sufficient to make it cut. Should the saw stick or bind, it may be because the saw is dull and is poorly set, or because the wood has too much moisture in it, or because you have forced the saw and thus have caused it to leave the straight line.

Keep your eye on the line rather than on the saw while sawing. Watching the line lets you see instantly any tendency to leave it. A slight twist of the handle, and taking short strokes while sawing will bring the saw back. Blow away the sawdust frequently so that you can see the line.

Final strokes of the cut should be taken slowly. Hold the waste piece in your other hand so that the stock will not split when you take the last stroke.

Short boards may be placed on one sawhorse to be sawed. Place long boards on two sawhorses, but do not saw so that your weight falls between them, or your saw will bind. Place long boards so that your weight is directly on one end of the board over one sawhorse, while the other end of the board rests on the other sawhorse.

Short pieces of stock are more easily cut when they are held in a vise. When you rip short stock, it is important that you keep the saw from sticking, so it may be necessary to take a squatting position. The saw can then take an upward direction and thus work more easily. When you rip long boards, it will probably be necessary to use a wedge in the saw to prevent binding.

ON-LINE SHOPPING FOR TOOLS

The Internet is a good tool shopping source for homeowners. You can get some good bargains on brand-name tools for your home and property. This is because some tool suppliers that sell over the Internet don't have the standard overhead costs that other retailers might have. This translates to savings for them and you. Try the following sites:

www.Brookstone.com	www.ToolKing.com
www.NorthernTool.com	www.Toolpost.com
www.SnapOn.com	www.ToolSeeker.com

To find more Internet tool suppliers, go to www.google.com and type in the name of the tool you are looking for.

Screwdrivers

A screwdriver is one of the most basic hand tools used (see Fig. 1.11). It is also the most frequently abused of all hand tools. It is designed for one function only—to drive and remove screws. A screwdriver should not be used as a pry bar, a scraper, a chisel, or a punch. Use screwdrivers only on screws—not as pry bars. Whenever possible, use only a screwdriver whose tip fits screw slots snugly. This avoids slippage and stripped screws.

Standard Screwdrivers

There are three main parts to a standard screwdriver. The portion you grip is called the *handle,* the steel portion extending from the handle is the *shank,* and the end that fits into the screw is called the *blade.* The steel shank is designed to withstand considerable twisting force in proportion to its size, and the tip of the blade is hardened to keep it from wearing.

Standard screwdrivers are classified by size, according to the combined length of the shank and blade. The most common sizes range in length from 2$\frac{1}{2}$ to 12 inches. There are many smaller and some larger

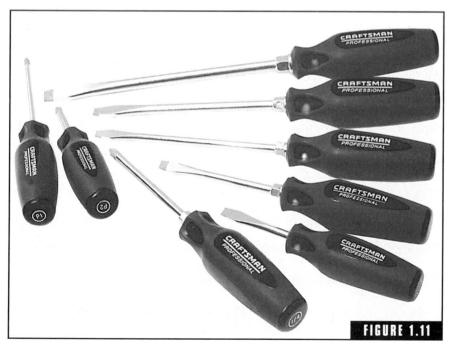

FIGURE 1.11

Most screwdrivers are sold in sets. This way they stay together, as a family.

for special purposes. The diameter of the shank, and the width and thickness of the blade, are generally proportionate to the length, but again there are special screwdrivers with long thin shanks, short thick shanks, and extra wide or extra narrow blades for specific uses.

Screwdriver handles may be wood, plastic, or metal. When metal handles are used, there is usually a wooden hand grip on each side of the handle. In some types of wood- or plastic-handled screwdrivers the shank extends through the handle, whereas in others the shank enters the handle only a short way and is pinned to the handle. For heavy work, special types of screwdrivers are made with a square shank. They are designed in this way so that they may be gripped with a wrench, but these types are the only kind on which a wrench should be used.

When you use a screwdriver, it is important to select the proper size so that the blade fits the screw slot properly. Proper fit prevents burring the slot and reduces the force required to hold the driver in the slot. Keep the shank perpendicular to the screw head.

Phillips Screwdrivers

Another type of screwdriver that is essential for your toolbox is the Phillips. The head of a Phillips-type screw has a four-way slot into which the screwdriver fits. Three standard-sized Phillips screwdrivers handle a wide range of screw sizes. Their ability to hold helps to prevent damaging the slots or the work surrounding the screw.

It is a poor practice to try to use a standard screwdriver on a Phillips screw, because both the tool and screw slot will be damaged. Use the same technique for driving and removing screws as for standard screwdrivers.

Screwdrivers come in a variety of sizes and tips—Phillips, standard, etc.—so if you buy a manual screwdriver for specific screws to be turned, this can get expensive. It is better to buy a combination screwdriver, one that consists of a handle and interchangeable tips. Stanley makes one that will accept two sizes of Phillips heads and two sizes of standard heads. With this one tool you will be able to do 90 percent of the jobs around the house. The cost should be about $8–$10.

Another option is to buy a set of screwdrivers. Lots of these are sold with popular sizes in both Phillips and standard points and are fairly inexpensive. You can get a set of six for under $10. These should also handle most of the projects you have around the house.

Another screwdriver to have is the magnetic type, which holds the screws to the tip magnetically. This is a really valuable feature if you have ever tried to drive a screw that is recessed in a wall somewhere. Not only do you never get it screwed in straight because it falls off the tip of the screwdriver, you risk losing the screw altogether behind a wall or some place you can't easily reach.

Finally, a screwdriver with a rubber grip is good for electrical work. If the screwdriver slips during the work and contacts live wires, you will be fully protected. This is very important, for obvious reasons.

Pliers

Pliers allow the user to firmly hold a variety of objects still for cutting, twisting, or to move one part while the other remains still (see Fig. 1.12).

Wrench (Vise-Grip) Pliers

Vise-Grip is the brand name of a locking-grip pliers, a wonderful tool. It can be used as a straight pliers, but its big advantage is that it can be clamped tightly on an object and then turned. This allows the user to put a great deal more pressure on the item.

Vise-Grip pliers can be used for holding objects regardless of their shape. A screw adjustment in one of the handles makes them suitable for several different sizes. The jaws of Vise-Grips may have serrations or may be clamp-type. The clamp-type jaws are generally wide and smooth and are used to work with a variety of materials.

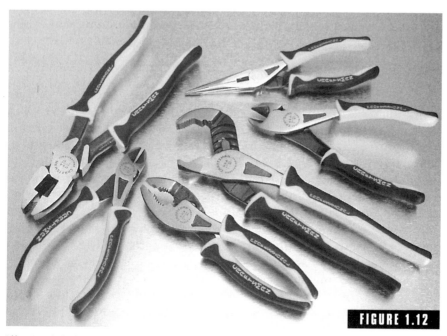

FIGURE 1.12

Pliers and their users are happiest when all the sizes stay together.

Vise-Grips have an advantage over other types of pliers in that you can clamp them on an object and they will stay, leaving your hands free for other work. A homeowner can use this tool in a number of ways. It may be used as a clamp, a speed wrench, and a portable vise, as well as in many other applications where a locking, plier-type jaw is useful. These pliers can be adjusted to various jaw openings by turning the round adjusting screw at the end of the handle. Vise-Grips can be clamped and locked in position by pulling the lever toward the handle.

Vise-Grip pliers should be used with care, since the teeth in the jaws tend to damage the object on which they are clamped. Do not use them on nuts, bolts, tube fittings, or other objects that must be reused.

Locking pliers come in various sizes and in different brands, including the original Vise-Grips. In my view, the original brand is still the best, and you should shop around for them. As stated before, they come with smooth as well as serrated jaws and in various sizes. I suggest the 7-inch-long model, which goes for around $12 or $13.

Water-Pump Pliers

Water-pump pliers were originally designed for tightening or removing water-pump packing nuts. They were excellent for this job, because they have a jaw adjustable to seven different positions. Water-pump pliers are easily identified by their size, jaw teeth, and adjustable slip joint. The inner surface of the jaws consists of a series of coarse teeth formed by deep grooves, a surface cleverly adapted to grasping cylindrical objects.

Channel-Lock Pliers

Channel-lock pliers are another version of water-pump pliers and are easily identified by the extra-long handles, which make them a very powerful gripping tool (see Fig. 1.13). Their shape is approximately the same as that of the pliers just described, but the jaw-opening adjustment is different. Channel-lock pliers have grooves on one jaw and lands on the other. The adjustment is effected by changing the position of the grooves and lands. Consequently, these pliers are less likely to slip from the adjustment setting when gripping an object. They should be used only where it is impossible to use a more adapted wrench or holding device. Many nuts and bolts and surrounding parts have been damaged by improper use of channel-lock pliers. Ask other homeowners.

A couple of kinds will serve well. One is the 6-inch or 8-inch slip joint pliers. Crescent makes a good one for around $12, but Fuller has a perfectly adequate one for only $8.50. Another recommended type is a 10-inch or 12-inch water-pump pliers. This has a lot of power and can give you extra torque when needed.

FIGURE 1.13

Channel-lock pliers are good for exerting pressure and a turning motion on nuts and bolt heads.

Vises and Clamps

Vises

Vises are used for holding work when it is being sawed, drilled, shaped, sharpened, riveted, or glued. Clamps are used for holding work that cannot be satisfactorily held in a vise because of its shape and size, or in the absence of a vise. Clamps are generally used for light work.

A machinist's bench vise is usually a large steel vise with rough jaws that prevent work from slipping. Most of these vises have a swivel base with jaws that can be rotated. A similar light-duty model is equipped with a cutoff. These vises are usually bolt-mounted onto a bench and are fine for the homeowner who wants such a tool.

The bench and pipe vise has jaws for holding pipe from 1 to 3 inches in diameter. The maximum main jaw opening is usually 5 inches, with a jaw width of 4–5 inches. The base can be swiveled to any position and locked. These vises are equipped with an anvil. To be sure you are getting what you need, ask your dealer when you shop.

The pipe vise is specifically designed to hold round stock or pipe and has a capacity of 1–3 inches. One jaw is hinged so that the work can be positioned and then the jaw brought down and locked. This vise can also be used on a bench.

CARE

Keep vises clean at all times. They should be cleaned and wiped with light oil after using. Never strike a vise with a heavy object and never hold large work in a small vise, since these practices will cause the jaws to become sprung or otherwise damage the vise. Keep jaws in good condition, and oil the screws and the slide frequently. Never oil the swivel base or swivel jaw joint; its holding power will be lessened.

When the vise is not in use, bring the jaws lightly together or leave a very small gap. (Heat may cause the movable jaw of a tightly closed vise to break because of expansion of the metal.) Also, it is best to leave the handle in a vertical position to prevent any injury to the vise or people.

You can pay a lot of money for an excellent vise, such as the ones Columbia makes, but I think a low-cost vise can be used with perfectly good results. For instance, I bought a 4-inch utility vise from the Harbor Freight catalog for about $22, and it works very well. Fuller also makes good, low-cost vises. I also got a very solid vise for virtually nothing at a garage sale.

Clamps

Clamps are valuable tools for the homeowner. They are used to hold something still, which frees working hands, while working on something else or the object being clamped, as it were.

A C-clamp is shaped like the letter C. It consists of a steel frame threaded to receive an operating screw with a swivel head. It is made for light, medium, and heavy service in a variety of sizes.

Threads of C-clamps must be kept clean and free from rust. The swivel head must also be clean, smooth, and grit free. If the swivel head becomes damaged, replace it as follows: pry open the crimped portion of the head and remove the head from the ball end of the screw. Then replace it with a new head and crimp.

Safety Precautions

When closing the jaw of a vise or clamp, avoid getting your hands or body between the jaws or between one jaw and the work. When holding heavy work in a vise, place a block of wood under the work as a prop to prevent it from sliding down and falling on your foot. Do not open the jaws of a vise beyond their capacity, as the movable jaw will drop off, perhaps hurting you.

Rules and Tapes

There are many different types of measuring tools. If very accurate measurements are required, a caliper is used. On the other hand, if accuracy is not extremely critical, the common rule or tape suffices for most measurements around the house.

A steel rule will serve you well. This rule is usually 6 or 12 inches in length, although other lengths are available. Steel rules may be flexible, but the thinner the rule, the easier it is to measure accurately, because the divisions of marks are closer to the work.

Generally a rule has four sets of graduations, one on each edge of each side. The longest lines represent the inch marks. On one edge, each inch is divided into eight equal spaces, so each space represents 1/8 inch. The other edge of this side is divided into sixteenths. The opposite side is similarly divided into 32 and 64 spaces per inch, and it is common to number every fourth division for easier reading.

There are many variations of the common rule. Sometimes graduations are on one side only; sometimes a set of graduations is added across one end for measuring in narrow spaces; sometimes only the first inch is divided into sixty-fourths, with the remaining inches divided into thirty-seconds and sixteenths.

A metal or wood folding rule may be used for measuring purposes. Folding rules are usually 2 to 6 feet long. Folding rules cannot be relied on for extremely accurate measurements, because a certain amount of play develops at the joints after the ruler has been used for a while.

Steel tapes are made in lengths of 6 feet and longer. The shorter lengths are frequently made with a curved cross section so that they are flexible enough to roll up, but remain rigid when extended. Long, flat tapes require support over their full length when you are measuring, or the natural sag will cause an error in reading.

The flexible-rigid tapes are usually contained in metal cases into which they wind themselves when a button is pressed, or into which they can be easily pushed. A hook is provided at one end to hook over the object being measured so that one person can handle it without assistance. On some models, the outside of the case can be used as one end of the tape when inside dimensions are being measured.

The newest measuring devices resemble something straight out of *Star Wars.* Straightline and Black and Decker make laser measuring devices that let the user point it to an opposite wall in a room, click a button, and a digital readout indicates how far away the wall is. They are able to measure 50 feet and cost about $39. Another valuable product (that is used less for measuring but for finding, then measuring) is an electronic stud finder. When passed along a wall, lights on the handle blink when it passes over a stud and two horizontal laser beams shoot out of each side. These lights indicate a level, horizontal line for use in hanging pictures and anything else that requires a straight line. This also sells for about $39 and is worth the price for the homeowner. Black and Decker makes a similar device that emits horizontal and vertical beams simultaneously. This sells for about $68 and is worth the expense.

Measuring Procedures

To take a measurement with a common rule, hold the rule with its edge on the surface of the object being measured. Doing so will eliminate errors that may result because of the thickness of the rule. Read the measurement at the graduation that coincides with the distance to be measured, and state it as being so many inches and fractions of an inch.

OUTSIDE PIPE DIAMETERS

To measure the outside diameter of a pipe, it is best to use some kind of rigid rule. A folding wooden or steel rule is good enough. Line up the end of the rule with one side of the pipe, using your thumb as a stop. Then, with the one end held in place with your thumb, swing the rule through an arc and take the maximum reading at the other side of the pipe. For most practical purposes, the measurement obtained by using this method is satisfactory. It is necessary that you know how to take this measurement, as the outside diameter of pipe is sometimes the only dimension given on pipe specifications.

PIPE CIRCUMFERENCES

To measure the circumference of a pipe, a flexible rule that will conform to the cylindrical shape of the pipe must be used. A tape rule or a steel tape is good. When measuring, make sure that the tape has been wrapped squarely around the axis of the pipe to ensure that the reading will not be more than the actual circumference. This is extremely important when large-diameter pipe is measured.

Hold the rule or tape against the pipe. Take the reading, using the 2-inch graduation, for example, as the reference point. In this case the correct reading is found by subtracting 2 inches from the actual reading. In this way the first 2 inches of the tape, serving as a handle, will enable you to hold the tape securely.

INSIDE DIMENSIONS

To take an inside measurement, such as the inside of a box (or studs), a folding rule that incorporates a 6- or 7-inch sliding extension is one of the best measuring tools to use. To take an inside measurement, first unfold the folding rule to the approximate dimension. Then extend the end of the rule and read the length that it extends, adding the length of the extension to the length on the main body of the rule.

To measure an inside dimension using a tape rule, extend the rule between the surfaces, take a reading at the point on the scale where the rule enters the case, and add 2 inches. The 2 inches is usually the width of the case. The total is the inside dimension being taken. To measure the thickness of stock through a hole with a hook rule, insert the rule through the hole, hold the hook against one face of the stock, and read the thickness at the other face.

OUTSIDE DIMENSIONS

To measure an outside dimension using a tape rule, hook the rule over the edge of the stock. Pull the tape out until it projects far enough from the case to permit measuring the required distance. The hook at the end of the rule is designed so that it will locate the end of the rule at the surface from which the measurement is being taken. When a length measurement is taken, the tape is held parallel to the edge. For measuring widths, the tape should be at right angles to the lengthwise edge. Read the dimension of the rule exactly at the edge of the piece that is being measured.

It may not always be possible to hook the end of the tape over the edge of stock being measured. If so, it may be necessary to butt the end of the tape against another surface or to hold the rule at a starting point from which a measurement is to be taken.

DISTANCE MEASUREMENTS

Tapes are generally used for making long measurements. Secure the hook end of the tape. Hold the tape reel in your hand and allow it to unwind while you walk in the direction in which the measurement is to be taken. Stretch the tape with sufficient tension to overcome sagging; at the same time, make sure that the tape is parallel to an edge or to the surface being measured. Read the distance.

Care

Rules and tapes should be handled carefully and kept lightly oiled to prevent rust. Never allow the edges of measuring devices to become nicked by striking them with hard objects. It is preferable to keep them in a wooden box when not in use.

To avoid kinking tapes, pull them straight out from their cases. Do not bend them backward. With the wind-up type, always turn the crank clockwise; turning it backward will kink or break the tape. With the spring-wind type, guide the tape by hand. If it is allowed to snap back, it may be kinked, twisted, or otherwise damaged. Do not use the hook as a stop. Slow down as you reach the end.

There are a number of measuring tools the active do-it-yourselfer should have in his or her arsenal. One is a 25-foot-long tape with a 1-inch-wide blade. Blades also come $1/2$ in wide, but when you extend a $1/2$-inch blade it does not maintain stiffness as a 1-inch-wide blade does, so fewer one-hand operations are possible. Two good brands are Stanley and Lufkin.

Be alert to sales on these tapes. Stanley has regular sales, and Lufkin often will offer a free tape if you buy a quantity of another product. Shopping around can yield quite dramatic results.

A 6-foot folding ruler is also recommended. These are available in wood and in fiberglass; fiberglass costs more. Some people don't like the feel of fiberglass, and I agree. Two lengths are suggested for the homeowner: a 6-footer and an 8-footer. The 6-footer is good for plumbing applications, while the 8-footer is good for carpentry, because most carpentry materials such as paneling, studs, and Sheetrock are usually available in lengths of 8 feet.

An 8-foot folding rule from Lufkin sells for around $20. A 6-footer goes for about $14. You want extra good quality in rules. Also, remember, pay homage to the old adage: "Measure twice and cut once."

Squares, Plumb Bobs, and Levels

Squares are used primarily for testing and checking the trueness of an angle or for laying out lines on materials. Most squares have a rule marked on their edge, so they may also be used for measuring. For the plumber and the homeowner alike, a carpenter's square is most useful.

CATALOG SHOPPING

Catalog shopping is a good way to get name-brand tools at great discounts. Most of these tool suppliers ship them all over the country, sometimes within days of your order. They often offer significant discounts over retail stores for the same items. Here are a few that I like:

Harbor Freight: 1-800-444-3353

Trendlines: 1-800-328-0457

Tool Crib: 1-800-232-9366

Carpenter's Square

The size of a carpenter's steel square is usually 12 × 8 inches, 24 × 16 inches, or 24 × 18 inches. The flat sides of the blade and the tongue are graduated in inches and fractions of an inch. (The square also contains information that helps to simplify or eliminate the need for computations in many woodworking tasks.) The most common uses for the square are laying out and squaring up large patterns, and for testing the flatness and squareness of large surfaces. Squaring is accomplished by placing the square at right angles to adjacent surfaces and observing whether light shows between the work and the square.

Squares may be made of either aluminum or steel; aluminum is more expensive. My choice is steel. Though heavier than aluminum (a factor which may count when holding it above one's head), it doesn't get scratched as aluminum does, making the markings difficult to read. Two manufacturers of good, medium-priced squares are Stanley and Handyman. The average cost is between $12 and $14.

If you want a better square—which really isn't necessary for occasional use—you can expect to pay around $22. At the high end, Stanley makes a black level with numbers and markings in white.

Another good square to have is a speed square, which is an offbeat tool that acts as a guide for cutting wood at an angle; it also has markings to help one calculate and cut rafters. It's faster to use than a regular square, hence its name. Cost for a 7-inch speed square in metal is $12; in plastic, $6. Hint: Get the plastic and save $6.

Plumb Bobs

A plumb bob is a pointed, tapered, brass or bronze weight that is suspended from a cord for determining the vertical or plumb line to or from a point on the ground. Common weights for plumb bobs are 6, 8, 10, 12, 14, 16, 18, and 24 oz.

A plumb bob is a precision instrument and must be cared for as such. If the tip becomes bent, the cord from which the bob is suspended will not occupy the true plumb line over the point indicated by the tip. A plumb bob usually has a detachable tip; if the tip should become damaged, it can be replaced without replacing the entire instrument.

The plumb bob is used to determine true verticality when vertical uprights and corner posts of framework are erected. Surveyors use it for transferring and lining up points. Homeowners can use it for the same purpose.

To locate a point that is exactly below a particular point in space, secure the plumb bob string to the upper point. When the plumb stops swinging, the point is exactly below the upper point.

Levels

Levels are tools designed to prove whether a plane or surface is a true horizontal or true vertical. The level is a simple instrument consisting of a liquid, such as alcohol or chloroform, partially filling a glass vial(s) or tube(s) so that a bubble remains. The tube is mounted in a frame, which may be made of aluminum, wood, or iron. Levels are equipped with one, two, or more tubes. One tube is built in the frame at right angles to another. On the outside of the tube are two sets of graduation lines separated by a space. Leveling is accomplished when the air bubble is centered between the graduation lines.

Levels must be checked for accuracy. Place the level on a true horizontal surface and note where the bubble is. Reverse the level end for end. The bubble should also be centered.

Do not drop or handle a level roughly. To prevent damage, store it in a rack or other suitable place when not in use.

A level is a most important tool to have, and you want to make sure you have one that works. M & D makes good levels, and they have the advantage of being the only manufacturer (that I know of) that offers replacement bubble vials. You just screw the new bubble vial in place if you break it, and therefore you don't have to discard the tool. (Incidentally, if a bubble is off, most levels can be reset if they're sent back to the factory.)

M & D makes aluminum levels and, although they are expensive, you might want to opt for one. Perhaps the best buy of all, though, is the American-brand level. These normally sell for around $65, but they go on sale a few times a year for about $55.

Ratchets and Sockets

Ratchets

A ratchet is a long-handled metal tool with a square, metal nub at the top that fits into the female end (of the same size square opening) of metal sockets. The ratchet has an adjustment switch that locks the turning direction of the nub, and also the socket that is attached to it. It can be set to turn clockwise or counterclockwise. For the homeowner, ratchets are available in $3/8$-inch up to $1/2$-inch sizes, and some tool makers have gone to a slimmer design (the head) to fit in tight places (see Fig. 1.14).

FIGURE 1.14

Ratchets are now made with thin profiles to fit into narrow spaces where ordinary ones won't.

Craftsman makes ratchets individually and as part of ratchet-and-socket sets. You can spend anywhere from $8 or $9 for individual ratchets up to $60 or $70 for top-quality ratchet sets that include several popular sizes. It is probably best to shop for these at your local home center or from catalogs.

Sockets

These are round, hollow tubes of metal with a square hole at one end to receive the nub of a ratchet. The other end of a socket is designed to slide over a nut and break it free with leverage from the long handle of a ratchet (sometimes known as a socket wrench). Some are extra long (known as deep sockets) and serve as plumber's sockets. They are available in a wide range of sizes and are usually sold as sets (see Fig. 1.15).

Other Hand Tools

Described here are some other common hand tools that the human (see the sidebar) homeowner should have handy for maintaining his or her home.

Rivet Guns

A rivet gun is a manually operated tool designed to install "blind" rivets. It acts on the same principle as a paper stapler, except that the

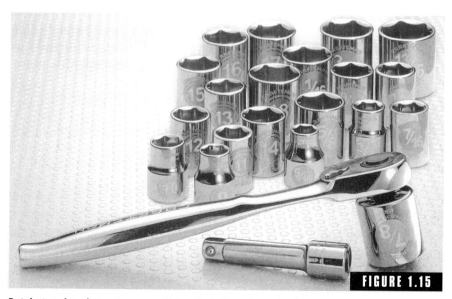

FIGURE 1.15

Ratchet and socket sets are available in U.S. and metric sizes.

staples are heavy. This tool lets you fasten pieces of material together when the other side is not accessible.

Caulking Guns

Several kinds of caulking guns are available, but for me the best is the half-barrel type with the ratchet plunger. As you squeeze the trigger, the plunger presses against the bottom of the caulking cartridge and forces the material out. I like the gun because it is easy to get the cartridge in and out, and it is easy to stop the caulk flow: just flip the end of the plunger. It's a good idea to get a decent caulking gun; for a good-quality one, expect to pay around $4.

Cement-Finishing Tools

Many types of cement-finishing tools are available, but for most do-it-yourselfers I think only two types are needed: a small pointing trowel which can be used to apply mortar to block or brick, and a brick trowel for applying mortar when building. A good brand is Marshalltown. A brick trowel goes for $16–$19 and a pointing trowel for around $7. If you don't get a Marshalltown pointing trowel, make sure that the blade flexes; if it doesn't flex, the quality is probably not great.

Chalk Boxes

For chalk boxes, staying with high-line quality is best. Straight-line is a good one. The cord they use is strong, it holds chalk well, and it is easy to get chalk refills. See your home center salesperson for more information on these. They cost about $4 for a 50-footer.

Coping Saws

Coping saws with square, rigid frames are better than ones with round frames that can bind and break. Stanley and Great Neck make good ones. These are useful around the house for cutting that odd-something that always seems to need cutting. These go for about $10.

Glue Guns

A while back, the glue gun burst on the scene, then more or less expired because it had technical problems. It worked by melting and extruding hot-melt glue sticks, but sometimes the process was chaotic.

Today the method is reliable, and the tool is excellent for any quick gluing job—the extruded glue dries in 30 seconds—and it can also be used for caulking. I like the Stanley-Parker line of glue guns. The GR 70 is good, and so is the GR 60. The cheapest place, by far, to buy the guns is in KMart. Last time I looked, the GR 60 was on sale for around $15. I've seen it elsewhere for nearly double that.

Also, if you use a lot of glue sticks, buy them in bulk. KMart sells packages of several. A quick note: Stay away from glue sticks sold in crafts stores, which are typically of poor quality.

Miter Boxes

The miter box is used to guide a saw to the cutline so that the user can make angled cuts. They are great for cutting molding. A wide variety is available, but for home use I recommend one made of maple wood; these sell for around $8 and will work very well. (Recently I saw a plastic Stanley miter box for around $19 in a local Caldor store; you can pay $23–$24 for a metal one. That's a lot of extra money to pay for something that's not needed. Wood miter boxes are just as good as others and costs much less—maybe $10 less.)

Paintbrushes

Many grades of paintbrushes are available, but to some degree what you buy relates to how well you take care of tools. If you take good care of them, then by all means pay the money and get a high-quality brush. If they usually end up looking like a rock with a handle, then don't. Whatever you do, don't buy a cheap brush for painting (or applying any finish) where smoothness counts. A low-quality brush just won't do the job. These brushes are fine for applying tar or epoxy or the like, when the brush is going to be discarded after use, but that's about it.

FOAM BRUSHES

For one-shot use, foam brushes are an excellent buy. They can be used on exterior and interior trim of all kinds (including windows) and on small walls and ceilings, such as in a bathroom. They don't work well, however, on exterior oil-based paint. You've probably seen them in hardware stores: small blocks of foam with chisel-cut edges and a short wood handle.

If you wish, you can clean them and use them again. Believe it or not, I know a guy who has foam brushes that are over 10 years old.

Foam brushes come in a range of sizes, such as 1, 2, 3 inches and wider; choose the size the same way as you'd choose a bristle brush size. Foam brushes are not going to make you poor, ranging in price from around 99 cents to about $3. Foam brushes are really quite a bargain: they work beautifully and cost peanuts. If you are the kind of person who takes care of tools well, then by all means read on.

BRISTLE BRUSHES

Brushes in general are lumped under the heading bristle brushes, but technically this isn't an accurate description. Pure bristle brushes are those made with animal hair, such as that of a pig, and in fact they are very expensive and work well only with oil-based paints. Try using a pure bristle brush with water-based (latex) paint and the bristles will become soggy and limp, just as a pig's hair does when wet.

What manufacturers call bristle may be a blend of animal and synthetic hair, or pure synthetic, such as nylon. What you should buy depends on what type of paint you will be using. If you are using oil-based paint, varnish, or other non-water-thinned material, I recommend pure bristle brushes.

You should go for quality. There are various ways to check for this, including observing the amount of bristles, flagged ends (split), and general bulk; thick brushes are better than thin. In this regard, if you examine various cheap and more expensive brushes you will start to notice differences.

Still, perhaps the safest way to choose a quality brush is by price. I suggest that you buy one 3-inch brush (this can handle all trim and small walls and ceilings) costing anywhere from $14 to $20.

Once you have spotted what you like, ask the dealer for a discount. When I was in a Sherwin-Williams paint store I asked the dealer what kind of discount he could give me, and he offered 20 percent. Or you can write down the brand name and call other stores to see if they have the same brush, and at what price. If you plan to use the brush for latex as well as oil-based coatings, then you should get a synthetic bristle brush. The same quality criteria apply (flagged ends and bulk), and so does price: between about $14 and $20 for a 3-inch brush is about right.

Paint Rollers

Paint rollers actually consist of two components: the handle, which is the handle and the cage for the roller, and the roller itself. You can get rollers in various sizes, but the standard size is 9 inches long. In terms of a handle, get the birdcage kind. The roller is simply easier to slip on and off. There are various kinds of rollers, but I think the following kinds are useful.

Mohair is a short-nap roller used for applying varnish, polyurethane, and enamel over broad areas, such as walls and ceilings in kitchens and baths. One complaint against it is that it leaves an "orange peel" texture, but this can be gotten around by first using the mohair, then following immediately with a brush to smooth it out. For walls and ceilings you can use a 9-inch roller with a nap of Dynel or some other synthetic fabric. Since this can get complicated, I would suggest using price as a criterion. A good roller costs around $6, but if you clean it properly you can use it for years and the difference in ease of working and the finished job will be quite dramatic.

Say you want to paint a chain-link fence? A cage-type roller handle is easiest to operate. You should expect to pay around $5 for a quality roller, but it will last a long time and work well. For a rough surface, such as stucco or cement, a roller with a nap 1 inch long is suggested. Again, buy quality. Average price here will be around $7.

One special alert: avoid those combo deals that offer pan, roller, and handle for $5 or so. They are invariably of poor quality. One tip on using a roller: use a stick, which is a wood handle with a threaded end that can screw into the handle on the roller. Reason: you will be using two hands, which gives you better control and more strength.

Roller pans are available in either plastic or metal. You should get a good one with a deep well. My advice is to go for the plastic; you'll save money. For example, I recently saw a metal pan at a local hardware store for $3 and a plastic pan for only $2.50. Also, plastic pans are easier to clean than metal ones if you use latex paint.

Planes

A 3½-inch block plane is all most do-it-yourselfers will require. It doesn't come cheap, costing around $35. Stanley and Handyman are two good brands. It can pay to shop around. This could be a particularly good situation in which to ask if there are any discounts available.

Incidentally, if you expect to be doing a lot of planing, you might think about an electric plane. Makita makes a nice model for around $100, and, of course, this greatly simplifies the planing task. A block plane from Stanley normally sells for around $45, but you can get it for $10 less if you shop around.

Scrapers

A scraper consists of a 3-inch-wide thin blade mounted in a handle. It is essential for interior paint jobs, not only for general wall and ceiling prep but for patching cracks and small holes.

Scrapers are available in a variety of grades, including ones with mirror-polished blades and riveted wood handles, but the key is flexibility: you can get a scraper for about $4 that will work well as long as the blade is flexible. Only this type of blade works well in applying patching material.

Shop Aprons

If you want to save your clothes while you work around the house, shop aprons are money savers because they do just that. I like the denim kind that covers the front of the body. They go for around $20, and with proper care and cleaning they should be around for years to come.

Soldering Guns

A number of soldering guns are available, but the pencil-tip, 140-watt gun from Weller is a good unit. I have seen it ranging in price from $14 to $28, so it emphatically pays to shop around. Ask your hardware dealer or home center sales rep about these. Education pays.

Staple Guns

Staple guns are very handy for installing acoustical ceiling tile, insulation, and performing a myriad of other jobs. Staples are loaded into the gun and the handle is squeezed to fire it. The way to save money on a staple gun is to buy one that uses standard-size staples, because hardware and other stores will sometimes run sales on standard staples and you can pick them up for a good price. This is not true for offbeat sizes.

Staple guns are also sometimes on sale. Three brands of staple gun are common: Stanley, Parker, and Bostich. I like the Stanley and Parker models, which go for around $23. The Bostich stapler is kind of expensive, around $34. Staples normally run $3 plus, but during sales they are priced around $2. This may sound like a small amount to save, but staples can be gobbled up at a very rapid rate and the pennies can add up, so you want to be able to buy staples that are competitively priced.

Propane Torches

For a propane torch, I would stick with the Turner or Bernzomatic brand names. The reason is that when you need replacement parts such as a tip, replacement orifice, or gas, they'll be easier to find than an off-brand. The torch comes with a needle tip, which is useful in soldering and many other tasks. You can save a bit by buying the Turner brand. The cost is around $14.

Utility Knives

Utility knives are good for cutting everything from carpeting to Sheetrock. They come in a couple of different models. One type has a push-pull blade, while the other is permanently fixed. I don't like the push-pull type; it's inconvenient. Better, I think, is to invest in a small holster and sheathe the knife in it. When it is needed, it can easily be pulled out. Utility knives come with regular and heavy-duty blades. Regular is fine. Stanley makes a good utility knife. Figure around $3 for the knife and $3 for the holster.

Power Tools

Power tools help the user with the aid of an electric or sometimes gasoline-driven engine to increase the strength or the endurance of the tool and get the job done more quickly. For our purposes, though, it's probably best to consider power tools as ones with electric motors for the homeowner. Like hand tools, power tools come in gradations of quality, and there are quite a few types available. For the active do-it-yourselfer, though, I think only a few are truly useful enough to have in your home.

Power Drills

Power drills can be used for far more than just boring holes. A large number of accessories can be fitted to the basic drill unit, enabling it to do many types of work that would otherwise require a specialized power tool. Basically, a power drill is a compact electric motor fitted with a projecting shaft at one end on which is mounted a chuck, a revolving clamp that grips and drives drill bits or other attachments. The motor unit is held in the hand by a pistol grip and the motor is started by pressing a trigger at the top of the grip. For safety reasons, the motor stops if pressure on the trigger is released. However, most drills have a locking pin that can be engaged to hold the trigger in the "on" position.

Electric power is supplied to the drill by a cord that enters the machine through the bottom of the handle. On many modern drills, a

POWER TOOL SAFETY

A helpful hint: whenever you are using power tools, always unplug them immediately after using them. Even if it means unplugging a saw while you take a measurement, it's better to do that—and have to plug it back in—than to have an accident by hitting the switch inadvertently. Also, if you have a safety device on the trigger of the power tool, use it. And it's a good idea to take all attachments out of power tools immediately after you are done with them. Think about a power drill, plugged in, with a large bit in it—you walk away for a second, that's all it takes—and kids' inquisitive hands are near it. You also don't want to make the mistake of accidentally hitting the trigger if you have a cluttered work space. You've heard it before: power tools are dangerous if they are not used properly. Lastly, don't use power equipment if you're not feeling 100 percent or you're taking medication. The risk of accidents is simply not worth it.

complex system of insulation, known as double insulation, is built in to keep the user from getting an electric shock. In addition to extra user safety, it is usually not necessary to ground such tools.

The motor is cooled by a built-in fan that draws air through slots in the sides of the drill. These slots must be kept uncovered and free of sawdust or the motor may overheat and burn out. Should any power tool become hot, through heavy or prolonged use, the quickest way to cool the motor is to hold it safely away from yourself and the work, and run it at full speed in free air. This allows the fan to provide maximum ventilation.

Many drills can be adjusted to run at different speeds. The normal type is a drill with a two-speed geared reduction, to run at up to 1000 rpm and at 2500 and 3000 rpm. These speeds are suitable for most household jobs, and a machine with a two-speed gearbox is the best buy for the ambitious amateur. Some drills have been made with two speeds achieved electronically, through a diode switch. This is certainly a low-cost method, but the speed range is narrower, typically 1700 rpm and 2500 to 3000 rpm, and there is some power loss at the lower speed.

Variable-speed drills, in which the speed can be infinitely varied by an electronic device, are also available. This control can either be built into the trigger, working by finger pressure, or through a feedback system, an electronic chip which enables a speed to be "dialed" and then maintains it constantly, whatever the applied load.

When choosing a drill, you may want to consider a drill that provides rotary hammer action. This will be of no practical use for carpentry, but it will be very useful if you have to drill into brick, concrete, or masonry. At the flick of a selector switch, the rotary hammer action can be engaged for easy drilling into such materials. As the drill bit rotates, it also hammers up and down, to break up hard aggregate in its path. Disengage the hammer selector for normal rotary drilling and attachment driving. This feature adds to the cost of the drill, but is well worth it for the additional scope it offers around the home.

Power drills come in various sizes, which are graded by the capacity of their chucks, that is, by the largest drill bit that can be fitted into the chuck.

Common drill sizes are $1/4$, $3/8$, and $1/2$ inch. In most cases, using a narrow-shanked bit, they will drill holes at least double these diameters in wood, and sometimes even more, using that bit.

The larger machines have more powerful motors. A medium-sized machine should be adequate for all ordinary jobs. The $1/4$- and $3/8$-inch sizes fall into this category and are the most suitable for the household carpenter. An indispensable accessory that every drill user will need is an extension cord. This will enable you to use the tool at a distance from a power source. Cords are available in standard lengths from 25 to 100 feet or more, or you can make your own. The longer the cable, the thicker the wires must be to prevent power loss.

A wide variety of accessories are available for drills, from drill bits of varying kinds to sanding wheels and screwdriver bits. I think that a screwdriver bit, reamer bit, and some speed bores will handle just about any job you have.

Sanding Tools for Use with Power Drills

Several types of sanders can be fitted to a power drill. The most commonly used is the disk sander. It is used for rough sanding of wood. A flexible rubber disk is mounted in the chuck of the machine and an abrasive paper disk is fastened to it with a recessed central screw. The sander is used at an angle so that only one side of the disk touches the surface being sanded. If the disk is laid flat against the surface or pressed too hard against the surface, it produces circular marks called swirl marks, which may be deep and difficult to remove. Even with the disk used at the correct angle, slight swirl marks are often unavoidable.

A special type of disk called the Swirlaway reduces these marks to a minimum. The disk is made of metal and is flat and completely rigid. To give it flexibility in use, the shaft on which it is mounted can be tilted (by means of a ball joint) at a slight angle while it is turning. This allows for normal power drill operation.

Another type of sander is the drum sander, which consists of a wide revolving drum made of rubber, with an abrasive belt fastened around its perimeter. It makes no swirl marks, but should be used only for sanding curved edges of small objects or narrow strips of wood.

Drum sanders are available in a wide range of widths and sizes. They can be used on convex and small flat surfaces, across or with the grain of wood. The arbor of the drum is fitted into the chuck of the drill. A tubular cover of abrasive material makes a band that fits around the cylinder. When the cylinder spins, it is moved against the surface of the lumber. The abrasive is held on the drum by tightening a nut on the shaft, which expands the rubber.

Power Saws

Saber Saws (Jigsaws)

The saber saw, also known as a jigsaw, is a powered saw with a thin blade which makes a vertical stroke (see Fig. 1.16). It will let you make curved and straight cuts in wood and light metal. Most are light-duty machines and are not designed for extremely fast cutting.

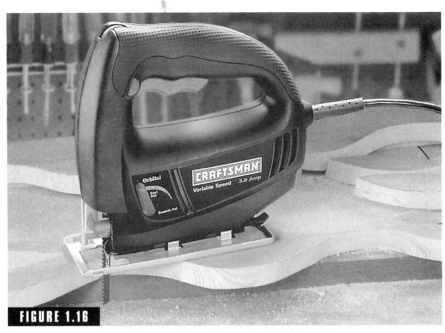

FIGURE 1.16

Jigsaws are great for making curved cuts in wood and light metal.

There are several different blades designed to operate in a saber saw, and they are easily interchangeable. For faster cutting of wood, a blade with coarse teeth may be used. A blade with fine teeth, on the other hand, is designed for cutting metal.

The best way to learn how to handle this type of tool is to use it. Before trying to do a job, clamp down a piece of scrap plywood, draw some curved as well as straight lines to follow, and practice cutting.

You will develop your own way of gripping the tool, and this will be affected to some degree by the particular tool you are using. On some tools, for example, you will find guiding easier if you apply some downward pressure on the tool as you move it forward. If your grip is not firm, the tool will tend to vibrate excessively, roughening the cut. Do not force the cutting faster than the design of the blade allows, or you will break it.

To make intricate cuts in wood, such as curves and sharp angles, the saber saw is a must. Its thin, vertically moving blade makes this possible.

GENERAL OPERATION

In using a saber saw, always hold the saw firmly on the work, which should be solidly supported. Be sure that the blade can cut along the required course without striking the work support. (If the work is resting on sawhorses, you don't want to cut the sawhorse.) If you're cutting into the work from the edge, keep the saw blade a short distance from the edge (with the saw resting on the work) when you start the saw. Allow a few seconds for the saw to reach full speed before you move the blade into the work, and move it gently.

Don't force the saw along the cut; move it at a rate that results in a steady cutting speed without noticeable slowing of the motor. Low-powered saws will, of course, cut at a slower rate than high-powered ones. Suit the rate of cut to the saw. If you have never used a saber saw before, practice on scrap material before you tackle an actual job. Usually, it takes only a few minutes to get the feel of the saw and the knack of using it.

In making curved cuts, keep the saw moving forward and steer it along the line to be cut. Don't try to make right-angle turns. If you must cut out an opening with sharply squared corners—perhaps in plywood—first cut it out with rounded corners inside the square cornered outline. Then use the saw to square the corners by cutting inward to the sharp corner from both adjoining sides.

In all saber saw work, keep your hands out of the saw's path, and do not try to turn the work to you. Let the saw do the work.

GENERAL CUTS

A rounded cut can be performed in one careful operation, but several passes are needed for oblongs and squares. The first side should be cut to its fullest extent before bringing the blade back down the cut and curving it gently away from the cut to carve out the second side. The piece left in the corner can be cut out later. Keep the motor running throughout this procedure.

Cut the remaining sides in the same way. A keyhole-size opening can be cut by moving the blade backward and forward and making slight stabs at the wood. The saw can also be used to cut straight lines, although a circular saw is preferable for this. Keep long lines accurate by using a clamped batten as a guide.

POCKET CUTTING

To start a cut in the middle of the lumber, tilt the saw forward and allow it to make its own starting hole, as described earlier. This works less well on thicker wood, and it may be necessary to drill a hole first before inserting the blade.

Circular Saws

Three basic types of circular saws are generally available, two of which are stationary shop tools. The most familiar form is the *bench table saw*. It consists of a metal table with a circular saw blade protruding upward through a slot near the table center. The blade can be raised or lowered by means of a saw projection hand wheel. This makes it possible to set the blade height to the depth of cut desired. For example, you can set the blade to cut only $1/2$ inch into a thicker piece of wood, if you merely want to cut a slot in it, rather than cut all the way through it.

The blade can also be tilted to an angle to cut a bevel rather than a square edge. The angle of tilt is controlled by a saw tilt hand wheel. This angle of tilt in some saws, chiefly older ones, is controlled by tilting the table rather than the blade. Saws that control the angle of cut by tilting the blade are called *tilt arbor saws,* and those that control the angle by tilting the table are called *tilt table saws.*

THE FENCE

Both types of bench, or table, saws mentioned are usually equipped with a *fence.* This is an adjustable metal guide running parallel to the saw blade. It can be moved and locked to provide the desired space between itself and the blade, thus automatically setting the width of the piece cut, as when ripping a wide board lengthwise to make two narrower boards. In most cases the space between the blade and the fence should be measured with a ruler for accuracy, even if the saw has its own measuring scale. In all cutting of this type, however, allow for the thickness of the blade's cut (*kerf*), as it must be subtracted from the total width of the remaining wood.

THE MITER GAUGE

In addition to the fence, most table saws are equipped with a *miter gauge.* This is a guide that slides in slots parallel to the saw blade, and can be adjusted to any required angle. Thus, it is possible to set the edge of a piece of wood against the adjusted miter gauge, and push the piece through the saw so as to cut off the end of the piece at the preset angle.

You can, for example, set the miter gauge at 45 degrees to cut a miter, or at any other angle that happens to be required. Most miter gauges are also provided with removable *rod stops* that make it possible to cut any desired number of duplicate parts. As designs vary with the brand, follow the manufacturer's instructions in adjusting and operating the saw and its accessories.

BENCH SAW SAWING TECHNIQUES

It is dangerous to feed small pieces of wood into the blade with your hands, because your fingers get uncomfortably close to the blade and the slightest slip may cause a serious accident. Wood is very likely to slip on a bench saw because of possible flaws in the wood and the tremendous torque of the blade. This is a problem, especially when using the miter gauge at an angle.

Small pieces of lumber should be pushed toward the blade with a push stick, a piece of lumber with a V-shape cut out of the end so that it can hold the piece of wood firmly. It does not matter if the pushed stick gets cut, because you can make another one in seconds. Fingers are not so easily replaced.

MITERING

Mitering, or cutting wood at a 45-degree angle to make a mitered joint, can be done quickly and accurately. To cut a miter across the face of a piece of wood, as in making a picture frame, set the protractor on the miter gauge accurately to 45 degrees. Then lay the wood against the guide and slide the guide and wood together down the table into the saw blade.

As a general rule, when crosscutting, the lumber should be held with both hands on one side of the blade and the off cut allowed to fall away freely. If you push from both sides, the pressure tends to close up the cut around the blade, causing it to jam and buck dangerously. If you must hold both sides, apply pressure in such a way as to hold the cut open.

To cut a bevel or miter along the edge of a piece of lumber, set the tilt protractor to a 45-degree angle. On some bench saws the table tilts instead of the blade. Slide the wood along the fence toward the blade in the normal way, but be sure the cut is of the correct width you require.

Taper ripping is cutting a very shallow taper on a long length of wood so that it is narrower at one end than the other. It is used, for example, when cutting legs for tables, so that the finished result is smooth and graceful.

Taper work is best done by making an adjustable jig out of two moderately long battens. Set them face to face and fasten them together by a hinge at one end and a slotted metal strip fastened with wing nuts on the other. By moving the free ends a distance apart and locking them at this distance with the strip and wing nuts, the jig can be set at any shallow angle.

In use, the jig is slid along the fence together with the wood to be cut. This method is particularly convenient when there are a large number of identical designs or shapes that must be cut, to make sure they match exactly.

As with any kind of bench saw operations, make sure you are completely familiar with the saw's operation. If you have any questions whatsoever, be sure and ask them of a professional. Never attempt a technique you haven't tried before without consulting a carpenter or expert craftsman first.

FIGURE 1.17

The circular saw is a portable powerhouse with many uses.

PORTABLE CIRCULAR SAWS

The portable circular saw (Fig. 1.17) is probably the most popular portable power saw. This is the tool used for cutting and ripping boards and manufactured wood products of all kinds. Various kinds are available, ranging from high-powered types to ones that are very ordinary.

With a portable circular saw you can do many of the jobs possible with table saws. But instead of moving the work through the saw, you move the saw along the work. The saw can be adjusted to tilt the blade to various angles to cut bevels. Another adjustment raises or lowers the blade to cut to various depths, as in grooving work.

On most portable saws there is also an adjustable rip guide that can be set and locked at varied distances from the blade to act like the fence of a stationary saw in ripping boards to specified widths. Angle cuts, as in mitering, may be made by guiding the saw along a marked line. Various types of miter and angle guides are also available. Before buying one, however, make certain that it can be used with the brand of saw you own.

Blade Sizes

Power saw sizes are commonly designated according to the diameter of their blades, and the diameter varies over a considerable range, depending on the type of use. Typically, table saws likely to be used in a home shop take blade diameters from $7\frac{1}{4}$ inches to as large as 12 inches. Radial saws are also likely to be in the $7\frac{1}{4}$–12-inch blade diameter range.

The portable circular saw ranges in blade size from as small as $6\frac{1}{4}$ inches to 8 inches. The smallest size blades are used for such things as trim, plastic laminates, and composition boards. A very popular size, the 7-inch blade, is readily available at most tool and hardware suppliers.

The important point in selecting any circular saw by blade size is its ability to cut the thickest material you are likely to use. A typical 7-inch saw, for example, can cut through a piece of lumber 2 inches thick at 90 degrees. This is adequate to handle most house framing work and, of course, work on thinner materials.

Blade Types

You buy blades for your power saws according to the type of work to be done. One of the most popular blades for general use in rough cutting is the combination or all-purpose wood-cutting blade. This cuts both across the grain and with the grain. For plywood, you will do best with a blade made for the purpose, with fine teeth that don't fray the surface. If you are cutting into wood that may contain nails, use a flooring blade, which has specially hardened teeth that can retain their sharpness even if the blade shears through occasional nails. Use this type of blade also if you are cutting used lumber that may contain nails. For light-gauge metal there are metal-cutting blades, and for heavier metals there are abrasive disks that replace the blade. Similar disks are available for cutting masonry block and other, similar materials. If you need a blade for any special job or material, tell your hardware dealer what the blade must do. He can then recommend the right blade for the job.

About Saw Guards

When using any power saw equipped with a blade guard, use the guard on all work where its use is possible. On a typical bench or table saw, the guard (which covers the exposed portion of the blade above the table) can be used on practically all work in which the blade cuts all the way through the wood, as in ripping and end cutting. In most cases when the cut is not a through-cut, as in grooving, however, the guard must be removed.

The guard on a portable circular saw consists of two sections, an upper one fixed in position and a lower one that is retractable. As you push the saw into the work, as in cutting the end off a board, the retractable (spring-loaded) section of the guard springs upward as it comes in contact with the wood being cut, and snaps back in position as it passes over the far side of the wood.

The guard can be used for practically all work except when the saw moves into the wood at a very fine angle. If this results in jamming the guard against the wood during entry, the lower guard may be retracted manually by means of a retracting lever on the guard.

Follow the manufacturer's instructions on this, as in all phases of operation. And in all types of power saw operation, keep your hands well clear of the blade at all times, and never attempt repairs or adjustments with the saw plugged into the power outlet.

Wet Saws

Wet saws are smaller units that usually sit in a rectangular plastic tub with water in it. The deck, blade, and motor sit above the water line, and a small tube (attached to a submersible pump that recycles the water) feeds water to the spinning blade—hence the name.

Water is needed to keep the blade—and the object being cut—cool, because friction quickly heats it up. The water is also used to reduce dust and debris that may flake off the material being cut.

The blades look like pressed cement chips molded together and often have diamond chips in them. The blade needs to be tough—wet saws can cut up to 1-inch-thick ceramic tile, quarry stone, marble, slate, or terra cotta.

Good wet saws have decks that can tilt 45 degrees and can work all day long. As remarkable as they are, the homeowner usually won't need one, unless you have a large tile job, such as installing a kitchen floor or tiling a bathroom. For the few times you may need one, it is probably a better idea to rent one from a rental center. Check your Yellow Pages for the nearest rental center. Follow all directions and safety advice when operating this kind of saw.

Reciprocating Saws

Users often refer to all reciprocating saws by the very descriptive brand name Sawzall. This saw lives up to its name. Users have told me over the years that they have used them to cut through metal railings, fences, doors, molding, tree branches, metal pipes—you name it (see Fig. 1.18).

This saw weighs about 8 pounds and has a distinctive shape, kind of like the space shuttle *Challenger*—when it's landing, of course. The back part has a large part with a built-in handle for the user and the front tapers to a tough-looking blade that shoots out and back inside a housing at a rapid speed.

The good part about these saws is that precision cuts aren't usually needed, or expected. They are commonly used for demolition work: cutting through wall framing, doors, stubborn window sills, and the like. They are tough, have a long reciprocating stroke (horizontal blade

FIGURE 1.18

Reciprocating saws are very powerful and can handle most house framing.

coming in and out at high speeds), and high powered. They can accept a variety of different blades for a variety of uses.

They can cut just about anything, and they last. The only problem is that for the homeowner, they may be impractical. However, I would-n't necessarily say go rent one. If you have a large demolition job to do, you may want to buy one. It will probably be worth the investment. DeWalt sells a good model with its own carrying case and some blades for $85. Milwaukee Sawzall also has one for $100. On the other hand, if you need one only once, you may want to ask your neighbor or a friend to borrow his.

Sanders

Electric sanders do the job of hand sanding, but they do it faster, more thoroughly, and can sand larger areas of wood. Believe me, hand sand-ing can be brutal on your hands, arms, and elbows. Some popular types of sanders for the homeowners are belt sanders and orbital sanders.

Orbital Sanders

An orbital sander can be used to give a fine finish to any flat surface. It is an integral tool with its own motor and a large, flat sanding pad covered by an abrasive sheet. This moves backward and forward in a small circle and leaves no visible swirl marks. Many can also be adjusted for recipro-cal (back and forth) motion. Abrasive disks, belts, and sheets are avail-able in many coarse, medium, and fine grades, as well as special types, such as "wet-or-dry" and "preparation" for rubbing down paintwork.

The sandpaper used on these machines is important to consider. The finish on sandpaper depends on the number of particles or granules. The grains are widely spaced on "open-coat" paper, to allow the dust to fall from the sander when it is removed from the lumber. This minimizes clogging when sanding painted wood. The backing paper is tough and specially made to withstand the harsh action of the power sander. Note: ordinary sandpaper is not suitable for use with a power sander. You need special sandpaper. Check with your local dealer or the hardware section of your local home center.

Belt Sanders

It is of great advantage to use an integral belt sander (see Fig. 1.19). The belt sander is powered by a motor housed in the sander body. There is an on/off switch and a second handle so that you can control it with two hands. The sanding belt travels over two rollers, one at the front of the sander and the other at the rear, driven by the motor-operated roller, usually the rear one. To remove material fast, the sander can be

Belt sanders are serious tools for doing heavy sanding work.

used at about 45 degrees to the grain of the wood, first pointed to one side, then the other.

Keep the sander moving over the area to be sanded, so as not to make hollows in the surface. On rough work, start with a fairly coarse sanding belt and progress through medium to fine. Belt changing with most types takes less than a minute.

Wet/Dry Vacuums

Wet/dry vacuums are the industrial equivalent of your mother's old Hoover. These units are powerful, dependable, and can handle nearly

THE IMPORTANCE OF BUYING QUALITY TOOLS

Buying quality tools that last cannot be overstated. Take this example: My father bought a hand-held Craftsman 7-inch circular saw from Sears in the late 1960s. He bought it to make a fence around our house. All I knew as a kid was that it weighed a ton when I helped him and it was all metal. It also came in its own metal case. It was a serious tool, and he did serious work with it over the years—nearly every weekend. I never remember it being broken or missing. Guess what? He still uses it, nearly 40 years later! Think it was worth buying top of the line?

RENTING VERSUS BUYING

Sometimes, as mentioned before, it can pay to rent a tool rather than buy it, particularly if you have a specialized need. Why buy a tool you are going to use only once or twice, say, in 10 years? Rental tools are also good when you need a lot of muscle. These tools are industrial-strength and can do things their non-industrial-strength brothers can't do. What types of tools are available, and for what jobs? Let's put it this way: just about everything you can imagine is available. Look under "Tool Rental" in your local Yellow Pages.

It is very important to shop around, since rental prices on tools can vary hugely, up to 50 percent. Rental dealers expect you to ask the price and will be happy to furnish it. So use your phone book and your Yellow Pages.

Also, if you plan to use something for a long time, perhaps you can work out cheaper rates than you'd normally pay. It is also important to have your job set up before you rent the tool. You want to make sure you use the tool for every minute you pay for. If it's an outdoor job, make sure you can use the tool when you rent it—right when you get home with it. If you figure on purchasing a tool, it sometimes pays to try out a rental unit first. It can quickly tell you if the tool's for you.

Incidentally, make sure you know what you are renting. Many times there are extra charges, such as for drill bits, saw teeth wear, and for the drill bits themselves. Be sure and ask before you sign on the dotted line for the rental.

any mess—wet or dry. They are simple in design: hollow tubs on castors-style wheels with latched lids (that house the motor) and a series of hoses and attachments (see Fig. 1.20).

Most models feature two holes on either side of the motor, one for the vacuum feature and another that works as a blower. Simply pull the hose off one and attach it to the other. Other differences between models are in motor horsepower, tub size, hose size, and the length of power cords. Most units have cartridge filters that can be taken out and rinsed with water.

Homeowners have a lot of choices. Craftsman makes a 16-gallon unit with a 6.25-horsepower motor for about $130. Ridgid offers a 12-gallon unit with a 4.25-horsepower motor for about $75. Ridgid also has a smaller, 6-gallon model for about $40.

I suggest the 12-gallon unit for homeowners. It has the tub capacity you need, the engine power required, and enough attachments to clean up different messes in different rooms of your house and in the garage (see Fig. 1.21).

FIGURE 1.20

These vacuums are durable, powerful, and a good investment.

Buying Hints

As with other tools, stick with good names. For example, helpful features on a saber saw include variable speeds (so you can slow down the blade to cut various materials), and double insulation as protection against electrical shock. This is true of many power tools, and you should ask your dealer if the power tool you want to buy is double-insulated.

Also, ask about warranties and rebates. Some tools also have rebates attached to them. A final, general rule when buying hand and/or power tools: buy quality, name-brand tools. The idea here is that you truly get what you pay for. Most reputable tool manufacturers have been around a long time because they have consistently produced quality tools—and it's safe to say they will continue to do so.

However, there are exceptions. In some cases, tools that are of decent but not top-notch quality can be bought at less than half the price of their more costly counterparts. For example, you can get perfectly fine pipe wrenches from the Fuller Company at far less than half of what you'd pay for them from Ridgid. The main difference is that Ridgid is more suitable for a full-time plumber. Fuller guarantees their tools 100 percent under normal use, so if you break one, the manufacturer has instructed retailers to exchange it for a new one with no questions asked.

Still, for the most part, I suggest only top-notch quality for the active do-it-yourselfer. Generally, hardware stores and lumberyards/building supply dealers charge the highest prices for tools, and home centers charge less. On the other hand, you may not want to trek over to a home center to save $2, say, and so will get the tool at your local hardware store.

One cheap outlet that I've found is in the Trendlines tool catalog. They carry brand-name as well as good quality off-brand tools. Harbor Freight Tools also carries brand-name tools as well as offbeat brands at very low cost. Their phone numbers are printed in this chapter.

With catalog shopping you may also save on sales tax if your state has it and if you shop interstate, and, possibly, shipping charges. For example, if your order from Harbor Freight is over $50, the shipping is free. As an example, I recently saw a Stanley 25-foot power tape on sale for $9.99 in the Harbor Freight catalog, which is a good price, but shipping would add about $4.00 to the cost, which was still a lot less than at two local hardware stores, one of which had

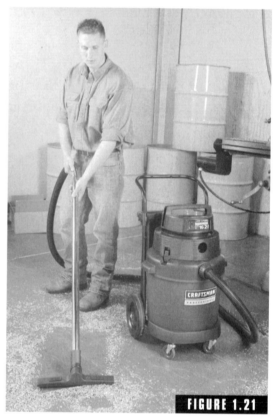

FIGURE 1.21

Wet/dry vacuums are easy to operate and are built for many uses.

TOOL REVIEWS

Homeowners are faced with dilemmas about what tools to buy. How do you decide what to buy when you see two different brands of the same tool? Do you shop for quality? Price? Ease of use? Following are some Internet sites that contain valuable information; professionals have done some of the work for you and have rated some of the most common tools.

www.OnlineToolReviews.com

www.Epinions.com

www.ToolSeeker.com

www.WoodZone.com

the tool for almost $21, another for $17. (The Home Depot had it for about $8.00.)

The bottom line: shopping around pays—and may save you money.

Buying versus Renting

Many times a do-it-yourself job can be made much easier with the right tool, but it might cost plenty to buy. Consider renting the tool. Special rental stores (see your Yellow Pages) will rent you everything imaginable—portable power tools, spray units for cabinets, concrete hammers, plumber's tools, generators, power saws, floor nailers, and power augers for digging post holes, to name a few. These tools are usually in good repair and industrial size—they can do a quicker, better job than standard consumer models. Make sure you think the job through. If it looks like you can do the job more quickly with an industrial-sized tool, and you have enough confidence that you can work it, proceed with a rental.

Roof, Chimney, and Gutters

Roof Repair

Most of us don't spend much time thinking of our roofs. When I began to, I realized something that should have been pretty obvious: the roof takes more abuse than any other part of the house. The sun beats down on it, rain lashes it, snow settles on it, and wind whips it. Roofs are built to last, but any damage they sustain should be promptly corrected.

In general, repairing most types of roofing is fairly easy, but it is not something to attempt if height makes you queasy. There's no need to have to get yourself repaired. In any case, you should wear sneakers or shoes with soles that provide traction on the surface of the roof and work only on a nice, relatively wind-free day.

Safety Ladders

Many outdoor repairs—on gutters, roofs, or high windows, for example—will require the use of a ladder. Today, the range of ladder designs, types, sizes, and materials is broad enough to fit your particular needs.

In laying roofing or in making repairs, a long wooden ladder or a so-called chicken ladder may be used for safety. This is not to be confused with the ladder you use to get on the roof. The chicken ladder is made by nailing 1- × 2-inch wooden cleats about a foot apart on a 1- × 10-inch plank or similar long board. Either type of ladder may be hooked over the ridge of the roof. Hooks are made by nailing a strong piece of wood to each leg near the upper end of the ladder at an angle with the legs. This angle should conform as nearly as possible to the slope of the roof, and the pieces which form the hooks should be braced or stiffened by nailing short boards between them and the legs of the ladder.

Asphalt Shingles

The most common kind of residential roofing is asphalt shingles—the kind with the granular surface (see Fig. 2.1). One of the more common problems is that over time, the shingles crack. You can use roofing cement and a trowel and fill the crack with the material. This material expands and contracts with weather—it won't crack like roofing tar. If you get the roofing cement on shingles, wipe it away with a kerosene-soaked rag.

It's a good idea to clean up any stray roofing cement. The material is black, so it will show up against a light-colored roofing. Roofing cement is available at home centers and hardware stores. A 5-gallon can of wet/dry roofing cement is about $20 and should be more than enough for most routine repairs.

Popped Nails

A common problem with asphalt shingles is popped nails. These are usually caused by strong winds: They lift the shingle, taking the nail right with it. Incidentally, if you are installing a new roof, consider installing shingles with adhesive tabs—they can withstand hurricane-force winds.

FIGURE 2.1

Shingles work hard to keep your house dry, so you don't have to.

The solution to popped nails is simple. Use new galvanized or aluminum nails and hammer them in place. Nails should be flush with the shingle surface, not below it. Or, you can adhere the shingle with a couple of globs of roofing cement. Cover the heads of new nails and old holes with roofing cement to prevent water penetration. Use a small putty knife for this.

Replacing Asphalt Shingles   *EASY* **1–2 hours**

Shingles may also require replacement. For example, the granular material may have worn away—look for dark gray or black patches which signal this. You may also find the granular material washed into gutters. Or, pieces of shingles may have been lifted off by wind, or they may be cupped (curled at edges) or very badly split. Heavy rains or wind can finish these shingles off. A hot day when shingles are pliable is the best time to do any shingle repair work.

Check the placing of original nails on the shingle to be replaced. This way, you'll be able to match the pattern with the new shingle that replaces it. Just lift the shingle and pry the nails loose with a pry bar, and slip the shingle out. Secure the new shingle with $1^1/_2$-inch roofing nails, placing the nails in the same pattern used when removing the bad shingle.

STUBBORN SHINGLE?

You may find that the shingle is secured by additional nails at the top edge, securing the overlapping shingle. In this case, remove your first set of nails from the middle of the shingle. If you can lift the shingle above to get at the top nails, fine. If not, pull the shingle straight out, ripping it free from the nails. Use the damaged shingle as a pattern and cut small cutouts in the top edge of the replacement shingle where the old nails were. Then simply slide the new strip in place.

The cutouts will let you do this without the top nails interfering. Then, secure it with nails as high up as you can place them, and use roofing cement under the flaps as extra security. If the shingles are damaged down at the edge of the house, you may have to put in a so-called starter course before nailing on a new shingle. A starter course refers to the first row of shingles on the edge of the roof. It sets the pattern that an installer follows. Ask your shingle supplier about this process. It is important to start the job correctly so it comes out the way you want.

Replacing Asphalt Ridge or Hip Shingles   *FAIRLY EASY* **2–5 hours**

Shingles that are located along the ridge, or spine, of the house or the hip may also need replacement (see Fig. 2.2). Here, you may be able to use the damaged shingle as a pattern for cutting the new one. Or, remove

FIGURE 2.2

Ridge shingles are the highest shingles on your roof—keep them securely fastened.

a good shingle and use that. Nail in place following the nail placement pattern used on the other shingles. Remember, water and wind are the enemies. Pay particular attention to this when replacing these, the highest shingles on the roof.

Wood Shingles

Wood shingles are another fairly common kind of roofing material. One problem these shingles develop is splitting. This type of shingle is rigid and you can't easily lift it to remove the nails securing it. So demolish it in place—break it up into pieces—with a hammer or small ax, being careful not to damage other shingles or the paper and sheathing underneath it. Then, slip a hacksaw blade under the shingle where it is nailed and saw the nails flush with the surface, or as close to the surface as you can get.

Cut a shingle to the width needed. Slide it in place, until its edges are aligned with adjacent shingles. Drive a nail in the middle of the shingle, then cover the head with a dot of roofing cement. Whether you use one or more shingles, they should be placed so that the joints between them or adjacent shingles do not coincide with shingle joints above or below.

Replacing Shingles in More Than One Course

FAIRLY EASY **1–2 hours**

If you find that shingles in a number of courses need replacement, follow this procedure. Split up and pull out damaged shingles in the uppermost row and hacksaw off nails. This will make it easy to remove damaged shingles in rows below. When the area is clear, start securing new shingles, following the nailing pattern observed when you removed the damaged ones, except for the top row: Face nail these in place, covering nail heads with dabs of roofing cement.

Any patch will stand out on the roof, but trying to stain them to match existing roofing isn't easy. It's usually better to let them weather naturally. Eventually their appearance will catch up with the rest of the roof.

Slate and Tile Roofs

Tile and slate roofs are very durable indeed, but they can develop cracks. To repair these, you can use roof cement, wiping up any mess with kerosene. Replacing either type is really a job for a professional. This involves calling a reliable contractor and getting some estimates.

Built-up Roofing

EASY **1–2 hours**

Built-up roofing is one of the easiest kinds of roofing to repair, because it is laid relatively flat: You can walk around on it without having to be careful of your balance.

One problem is that the roofing curls up at the edges. This is because material gets underneath it. Use a brush to clean out accumulated debris under the edge. Then spread some roofing cement under the curled-up edge and nail it down securely with large head nails. Apply roofing cement over the edge and on nail heads.

Splits

If the roofing is split, use a utility knife to cut away all ragged edges. Spread roof cement over the spot and 2 inches out from all sides. Put a piece of felt (available at home centers and roofing supply stores) and press it tightly into the cement, then nail it in place. Apply more cement along the edges, and over nails. Sprinkle a little gravel over the patch for protection against weathering.

Flashing

Metal Flashing

Metal flashing is a bright, aluminum, flexible sheet. It comes in various gauges (most common is 26 gauge) and 6-, 8-, 12-, 14-, and 18-inch widths, and in 50- and 100-foot rolls. It can be bought a few feet at a time as well as by the roll.

It is best to purchase flashing that is as close to the gap (you need to cover) in width as possible. This makes it easier to work with. For example, if the gap is 8 inches, get 10-inch-wide material. It cuts easily with tin snips.

Copper Flashing

Copper flashing comes in rolls of different gauges, but is usually only 12 inches wide. Copper is much more expensive than aluminum but might be the way to go if you want to match existing décor. Copper flashing is sometimes used on older houses, and although it is fully functional, it can also add charm to a roof and the house. For most homes, however, aluminum flashing will suffice.

Flashing is most often used on roofs to seal gaps between the roofing material and other materials, such as between roofing and a chimney, between roofing sections such as in the valleys of a roof, between siding and roofing, or around windows and doors.

Flashing Repair

EASY **1–2 hours**

One problem with flashing is rust. This can form and eventually eat through the metal. Water then has free passage to the interior of the house. If you see rust, use a wire brush to remove it and apply good metal paint. If there is a small hole, patch it with roofing cement. If the hole is large, obtain a piece of flashing, cut out a patch, and secure it with roofing cement. Make sure that water can't get in under the edges.

Use Extreme Caution on Roofs

Always wear heavy gloves when working with flashing. The edges are sharp and slice open skin easily. Also, whenever you are up on the roof, always wear shoes with a sole that provides traction. Knee pads and arm pads are also a plus. Also, wait until the roof is dry to do any kind of repair. Finally, don't work on a windy day—your body could act like a kite—you don't need to be blown off the roof. Better safe than sorry.

Skylight Flashing

It is important that flashing around skylights be secure and rust-free, especially on the higher part of the skylight if the roof has a pitch to it. If nails pop out or caulking around the outside becomes brittle, be sure and apply a fresh coat of caulk or roofing cement.

Gaps

Also, check for gaps at flashing. One vulnerable spot is where flashing overlaps. If there are gaps, plug them up with butyl rubber caulking compound. Another vulnerable spot is where the flashing meets the chimney. This commonly has a cap flashing which is bent over and stuck into the mortar. When this mortar crumbles, the flashing can get loose and water running down the chimney can get behind it.

You can replace the mortar with fresh mortar, resecuring the edge of the flashing, but a better method is to plug it up with caulk. This has a much better chance of sticking. Before doing this, force the metal as firmly as possible into its slots in the mortar.

Vent Pipes

One other particularly vulnerable spot for leaks in a roof is around and above plumbing vent pipes. The point where they disappear into the roof is commonly covered with a metal or plastic collar with lips, or flanges, that extend under the shingles. The top of this preformed piece is usually caulked where it meets the pipe, and this caulk may work loose or dry out. The answer is to apply fresh caulk (remove all crumbly or dried out material first). Roofing cement is equally good if you have it on hand (see Fig. 2.3).

Finding a Roof Leak

DIFFICULT **5–7 hours**

Sometimes, one can make all obvious repairs on a roof in an attempt to stop a leak, and the leak persists. Where do you go from there? To find the part of the roof that is leaking can be quite sneaky, because water flows, and the source of the leak can be far from where you notice the water. For example, water can enter at the top of a house, run along sheathing, then down onto roof rafters, run a little farther there, then run along the backside of plasterboard and be 10 or 15 feet from where it entered.

To find the leak, you need a hose and a helper. Stand on the roof directly above where the water is showing up inside. Someone should be stationed inside, directly below the spot. Turn on the hose and start running the water over that spot. Keep the water trained on the spot for a few minutes. If water appears inside, the helper should yell. If not, keep moving up the roof, repeating the procedure until you find the leak.

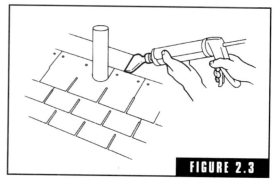

FIGURE 2.3

Flashing above vent pipes should be sealed with roofing cement.

Examine Area

Examine the area closely. If you see the source of the leak, plug it up. If not, remove shingles, including the felt beneath them, over a large enough area so that you are sure to uncover the source. Then install new felt and shingles.

Is It Worth Repairing?

While roof repair is vitally important if you want to stay dry, some roofs may not really be worth the trouble—they're so far gone that only a new roof will do. If asphalt shingles are in generally bad shape, replacement is likely called for. However, there are treatments available that may give your roof a few more years of life.

Professionals apply preservatives to wood and solvents or paint to asphalt. Usually, the pros will guarantee their work (if they don't, forget them), so they'll be inclined to tell you truthfully if the treatment is worthwhile, or if it is time for a new roof. If you want to confirm this, or you have questions about your roof, call a few roofing contractors and pick their brains.

A New Roof   VERY DIFFICULT 7–10 hours

If you have to have a new roof, you can do the job yourself, but you have to be fairly handy. Manufacturers supply instructions with bundles of shingles. The roofing can go right over the existing roof, as long as it's the original roof. However, more than two layers of roofing weighs too much.

Consider getting a heavyweight shingle if asphalt is your choice. These weigh from 265 to 385 pounds per square (10 × 10 square feet of roofing), come in various colors and textures, and are guaranteed to last 25 years. The average roof lasts 15 to 20 years (see Fig. 2.4).

Replacing Ridge Vents   FAIRLY EASY 2–5 hours

Circulating air is an important part of effective insulation in your house. This is achieved through the proper amount of and strategic location of air vents in your roof. Without this, warm, moist air escapes through insulation and condenses in your attic when it hits colder air. The resulting moisture accumulation dampens wood and causes mildew, and eventually rot.

One of the best ways to ensure that there is enough air circulating is to install continuous ridge vents. These are just what the name says: They are vents that straddle the ridge (the peak) of the roof and run the

FIGURE 2.4

A new roof is a beautiful thing to behold, and it keeps the moisture out.

length of the roof. After they are covered with shingles, ridge vents are much less noticeable than traditional roof vents. They also provide the most air possible because they are so long. Although they are often installed during new roof construction or repair, they can and often are retrofitted onto existing roofs. If you are simply replacing old ones, pry the old ones off and install the new ones.

Continuous ridge vents simply straddle a gap along the top part of the roof and are nailed down and covered with shingles. If you are installing them for the first time, it is best to have a contractor handle this type of job. As always, if you are unsure of yourself or being on the top of your roof isn't your idea of a good time, it might be wise to call a contractor. Installing vents usually is a job that can be done fairly quickly with the right equipment and energy.

Installing Exhaust Fans   *DIFFICULT* **5–7 hours**

A common problem for homeowners is having too much heat collect in the attic in the summer when it is hot and when the sun is strong. This is particularly true of dark-colored shingles on roofs. The darker the color, the more they absorb the heat from the sun's rays. Too much heat in your attic and house makes the air conditioning system work harder than it has to.

This means more energy and money is being spent to keep the house comfortable. A solution to this problem is to install a powered vent—an exhaust fan—in the roof (see Fig. 2.5). This kind of unit has a thermostat-controlled fan that will increase air circulation and pull warm air out of the attic and vent it to the outside.

Since the fan is electrically powered, it is probably best to let an electrician install it. However, if you'd like, you can install the fan and call an electrician to hook up the wiring. Here's what to do: Start by driving a nail through the roof from inside to mark the position of the vent hole. Make sure you are going to place the unit between roof rafters so you don't have to do more cutting than is necessary.

Next, remove the shingles and the tar paper from the area on the roof. Measure the outside dimensions of the unit (without the flanges). Transfer this measurement to the sheathing (the plywood part of the roof). Drill four pilot holes in the roof on each corner of your measured space. Next, using a reciprocating saw (see the power tool section of Chap. 1), connect the dots.

Remove the sheathing and slide the top edge of the flange (the outside lip of the unit) under the shingles immediately above the hole you cut. Center the unit over the hole and set it into place. Nail the unit in

FIGURE 2.5

Attic exhaust fans pull warm air out of the house, making your air conditioner work less and your house more comfortable.

place with galvanized roofing nails. Install new flashing over the space between the top of the unit and the rest of the shingles. Seal all the gaps with roofing cement and make sure there are no gaps.

Cover the nail holes and the seam between the base and the roof with roofing cement. Secure shingles to the bottom edge and make sure they are properly placed. You don't want any gaps where rainwater can get in. Now you're ready to call the electrician.

Gutters

Gutters are common enough on our houses, but we don't seem to pay much attention to them until there is a problem. Most gutter problems could be avoided with regular maintenance. Gutters are worth maintaining. They serve an important function: channeling water away from our houses.

Clogged Gutters

Probably the most common problem with gutters is simply that they get clogged with waste material—twigs, leaves, seeds, and other debris. Left alone, this material can build up to the point where water can't run freely down the gutter. In warm weather, it overflows onto the ground, saturating it; after a while the water can seep through the foundation wall, or perhaps find its way in by cracks. Indeed, excess ground water is a common cause of damp basements. Also, trapped water can become stagnant in warm weather, providing a nice breeding ground for mosquitoes.

In winter, trapped water turns to ice. Now the water may also overflow, but it can also back up under roof shingles and get into the house. This can wreak havoc on walls and ceilings. Or, if water turns to ice, the weight can rip the gutters right off the house.

Cleaning Out Gutters   *EASY* **1–2 hours**

Gutters should be periodically checked for debris, especially in the fall and spring when waste can accumulate quickly. You can use a small trowel to scoop most of the waste out, then flush the gutter with a hose. If you don't have a trowel, you can get a device called a Gutter Getter, which is simply a plastic scoop that bends and conforms to the general shape of the gutter, allowing you to scoop as much as possible in one pass.

Installing Barriers

To prevent having to clean out your gutters every spring and fall, you can install a mesh grid, strainer, or plastic cover over the top of the gutter. These allow water to flow into them and keeps everything else out. There are a variety of kinds available at your local home center, and they usually are pretty simple to install. Most just snap or clip into place.

Branches over the Roof?

Finally, if your leaf and debris problem becomes chronic, you may want to have some tree limbs trimmed back if they hang over your roof. This is a last resort, though, because trees and their limbs are just—well, lovely. Unless they are jeopardizing my roof or any other part of my house, trees always have a home on my property.

Equipment

All that's really required to work on gutters is the wherewithal to get up on a ladder, and somebody to help you maneuver the ladder. If you feel queasy about the whole thing, don't do it. Nervousness could cause an accident.

If you do go up, make sure you use a good ladder. If you're getting a new one, get aluminum—it's light, yet strong. A 16-foot extension ladder can handle the jobs on most homes. Also, while you're up there, have someone hold the ladder at the bottom while you're at the top; or put something heavy against the bottom of the ladder on the outside. Then there's no real chance the bottom can slide out. (Caution: Be careful using an aluminum ladder near power lines.)

Lean the ladder against the house, or against the gutter if that's necessary for proper ladder placement. Sight down the gutter. Wherever you see debris, move the ladder into position and scoop it out with a garden trowel or other implement. You can drop the material in a plas-

Do Your Part, Recycle!

My father-in-law, Herb Domroe, came up with a clever idea for recycling the swampy material he took from his gutters. It saved him from having to bag it and dispose of it. Instead, he built a simple screening device that trapped large branches and debris, while letting the smaller parts slip through, into a bucket. He later used it as fertilizer (most organic material will do) for plants around his house. He was doing his part to recycle, and it saved him from having to bag the material or take it off his property.

tic bucket hooked to the top rung (with a piece of hanger wire) or simply drop it on the ground and clean it up later.

Proceed around the house. When all the blockages are cleared, lug a garden hose up the ladder and run water into each gutter to clear it completely. If the water does not run quickly out the downspout, it means the downspout is clogged. Try to clear it with a steady stream of water from the hose. If this doesn't do the job, you can use a "snake," the same thing you use to clear a clogged sink drain. Simply feed the pointed end of the snake down into the downspout. When you hit a blockage, move the snake up and down to shake it loose. Follow it by shooting a stream of water down the spout.

As a final treatment, direct a jet stream of water by holding your finger halfway over the hose nozzle down the downspouts to make sure they're cleared.

Leaking Gutters

FAIRLY EASY **2–5 hours**

Gutters made from aluminum, galvanized metal, and wood may eventually develop leaks. At any rate, experience might or might not tell you where the leaks are. This is because small pinholes might develop from rust and the leak might be so small you don't notice it at first. On the other hand, a broken joint (particularly common over time, by downspouts) may have water pouring through it during strong rains. How do you check them?

If you don't know, wait until the first rainy day, then grab your umbrella and go outside and look. Note where the leaks are. On the first sunny day, repair them. To repair small holes in a galvanized or aluminum gutter, you should use roofing cement. Hardware stores and home centers sell roofing cement for around $6 a gallon, all you'll need for this particular job.

Start by cleaning the inside of the gutter and rinsing it. When it is dry, use a scouring pad and/or a wire brush to scrape it down to bare metal. You can also use emery cloth, a special sandpaper used for metal. This is available at hardware stores. Use a clean cloth to wipe off any metal shavings or dust. Then simply use a thin putty knife and apply roofing cement over the hole. If you have a few small holes, you might want to use a caulking gun to apply it (roofing cement is also available in tubes). Be sure and feather it down on the sides so when the new patch dries, water can flow over it easily.

For larger holes, a patch made from burlap or glass fabric (available at home centers and hardware stores) is used. Prepare the inside of the gutter the same way. Start by cutting a piece of fabric or burlap that is slightly larger than the hole. Use the putty knife to smear roofing cement over the hole and around its edges. Make it about 1/4 inch thick.

Lay the patch in the cement (spread it out to make it smooth), and spread a coating of cement over the patch. Again, remember to try and smooth it out: Water needs to flow over it.

If the leak is at a joint—where gutter sections join—use the same procedure as for a hole.

Gutter Care and Repair

Keeping gutters shipshape is more important than most people realize. Gutters that are not functioning properly can lead to other problems that you can easily live without.

INCORRECT PITCH   *EASY* **1–2 hours**

Gutters should be pitched, or slanted, so they slope a minimum of 1 inch for every 30 feet of length, or a maximum of 1 inch every 10 feet. If pitched incorrectly, water can overflow or be trapped in the gutter. It is very difficult to tell if pitch is correct by eye alone. To check, climb up on a ladder after a rainfall and see if water is standing in the gutter. If so, it's incorrectly pitched. Or, you can simply pour a bucket of water in and see how well it flows to the downspout.

To correct pitch, the first thing to do is establish a perfectly level line on the fascia—the trim board along the top of the house that the gutter is mounted against. This line can then serve as a reference guide to correct pitch. Most roofers or handymen who pitch gutters incorrectly do so because they assume the house is perfectly level. Houses settle, though, and are hardly ever level. In essence, you establish your level line as if the house weren't there.

ESTABLISHING LEVEL   *EASY* **1–2 hours**

First, make a mark about an inch below the gutter at the high end, and an inch below it at the downspout end. Drive a nail into the ends of the fascia at these points and draw a line of string tightly between them. With a helper, and using a level, raise or lower the line until it is perfectly level. When doing this, it is best to hold the level parallel to but not actually touching the line. Touching it can throw it out of level. When level, mark the fascia at the ends—where the line is.

ESTABLISHING PITCH   *EASY* **1–2 hours**

Next, check to see if the top of the gutter at the high end is touching the shingles. It should be. If so, simply raise your line and refasten so it is parallel with the bottom of the gutter. Then move the line down at the other end so it runs at the proper pitch, and fasten in place.

For example, if the bottom of the gutter on the high end is 1/2 inch above the level mark, and the gutter is 30 feet long, the downspout end should be ¹/₂ inch lower than the other mark—that will give you a 1-inch pitch in 30 feet. If the high end of the gutter happens to be 1 inch above the level mark, the other end guideline could be right at the level mark. When you are finished, the pitch will be correct, but it will appear level to the naked eye. (See Fig. 2.6.)

RESETTING THE GUTTER   *EASY* **1–2 hours**

Next, you remove the gutter and reset. For this job you'll need a number of aluminum 2-inch no. 6 or no. 7 sheet-metal screws; one on each side and the bottom should do it, but use more if it looks like the gutter needs it. Before fastening, apply a good coat of sealer between sections. Hardware stores sell an aluminum type that is good. Be sure to remove excess sealer that squeezes out. A buildup of this can trap debris and cause water blockage.

If you have seamless gutters (made from one piece of aluminum), make sure you have the right hardware (save the hardware you take out—the long aluminum spikes and collars they slip through—that hold the gutters to the fascia). If these are broken or bent, home center stores and hardware stores carry them.

DOWNSPOUT LEAKS   *EASY* **1–2 hours**

Leaks at the downspout are usually caused by improper installation of the outlet piece—the lipped fitting on top that connects the downspout

FIGURE 2.6

Correctly installed gutters should appear level to the naked eye.

Keep downspouts free of leaks. They serve an important purpose: channeling water.

to the gutter proper (see Fig. 2.7). Instead of locating it so the lip is on the outside of the gutter, it is installed so it is inside, which seems more logical. The cure here is to remove the piece (or buy a new one) and reinstall it properly with sheet metal screws and a healthy bead of sealer. The end pieces of the gutter can also leak, and these should be secured with screws and sealer.

To minimize the chance of a downspout developing leaks at the joints, make sure it is securely anchored to the house. This prevents movement. Strapping iron and lag screws should be used for anchoring.

The lowest end of the downspout should be a few inches above ground level unless it enters an underground drain. A splash block (a formed piece of concrete or plastic) under the end will prevent damage to the grass and surrounding shrubbery.

Splash Blocks   *EASY* **1–2 hours**

Splash blocks are underrated, simple devices that serve an important purpose: They direct water away from the foundation of your house. Believe me when I tell you this: water is your home's worst enemy. If it is not drained away, standing water can damage the foundation or cause damp basement walls. In addition to house damage, standing water can help mosquitoes breed, draw other animals to drink, and make your yard a mud slick.

Start by making sure there is a slash block under each of the downspouts on your house. Make sure the block (it can be cement or plastic, in a rectangular, fan-shaped block) extends at least 3 feet from the house and that the grade slopes at least 6 inches every 10 feet. This way, water will flow down the slope, ensuring even after it flows off the splash block it stays away from your house.

Over time, splash blocks often settle (sink) into the ground and you have to build up the ground underneath them until they are properly supported again. This involves moving the block temporarily, reflattening the ground and packing it down with new dirt, and then simply replacing the splash block where it once stood.

You may want to check the splash block by spraying a hose onto the roof and watching the water come down through the downspout and off the splash block. This way, you'll know that during the next rainstorm you'll have nothing to worry about.

Pest Control

Preventing Unwelcome Visitors

EASY **1–2 hours**

Did you ever have invited dinner guests that simply wouldn't leave? Vermin are easier to keep out of your house. There are many things you can do to prevent pests from getting into your house. Following are some suggestions.

Start by making sure your chimney has a chimney cap that is in good working order and is securely fastened. Next, make sure screens on all windows are not torn or ripped and are securely in place. After that, make sure all outside doors are completely sealed. A quick check of this involves inspection to see if light can be seen under the door when it is closed. If it can, insects can get into your home. Also, check for plumbing leaks and seal off any gaps between pipes behind cabinets or furniture. Still another tip is to check the grout and caulk seals around bathtubs, toilets, or pipes that come out of the walls.

Some common-sense tips also include making sure all your food is in tightly sealed containers, avoid any unnecessary clutter, not leaving pet food or water out overnight, and finally, believe it or not, checking your grocery bags and packages you bring into your house. Pests and pest eggs can hitch a ride into your home inside these.

Some outdoor tips include sealing soffits and gable and roof vents, checking gutter drains so that water is channeled away from the house, and making sure leaf and debris litter doesn't accumulate in gutters.

How Do You Handle the Invaders if They Make It Inside?

There are some pretty clear telltale signs that pests have made their way inside your house. The obvious ones are just that you walk into your kitchen for your morning coffee and there's a cockroach waiting for you on the floor. Others might include mice, silverfish (they like to climb walls), ants, and flies. They make their appearance and you head for the telephone to call the exterminator.

Other, less noticeable signs are what looks like wood or pencil shavings. Chances are, this is the work of termites boring into the wood of the framework of your home. Of all the critters that can invade your home, these guys can do the most damage and, over time, cause irreversible damage. All exterminators offer termite inspection services.

It's best to have an inspection done if you are unsure whether you have termite damage.

Another sign is what looks like tunnels. These are signs of wasps and hornets. They may stay outside, but they have been known to invade garages, crawl spaces, and tool sheds. Also, at the risk of being ghoulish, check for droppings (pellets) and/or discarded wings or other body parts. Lastly, be on the lookout for food packages and containers that look chewed or as though they have been nibbled on.

As with most pest invasions, contact a reputable extermination company for advice and/or an inspection of the problem.

Hire a Pro to Solve the Problem

Forget the Raid and other spray cans of insecticide. They will solve your problem temporarily. My suggestion is to hire a pro to keep vermin out of your house permanently. Although most homeowners have the option of controlling pests, most people lack the expertise that professionals have to solve the problem effectively, safely, and permanently.

For instance, professionals are trained to safely handle and apply materials used to control pests. When looking for a company, make sure their technicians are certified, ask for references from other customers, look for memberships in industry associations, and finally, make sure the company is licensed, insured, and has the correct application certificates.

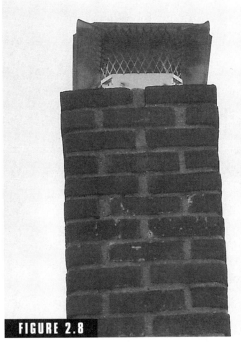

Chimney caps are an often unseen, but important part of house maintenance.

Chimneys

The Importance of Chimney Caps

Chimney caps (see Fig. 2.8) serve a very simple but important purpose. First, they prevent rain, snow, and any other debris from entering your chimney. Second, and just as important, they keep animals, especially birds, squirrels, and raccoons, from entering your chimney and making it their home. They also keep ice and rain off the chimney crown, a vital area that includes the cement over the top of the chimney. This will prolong the life of the crown and prevent flue tile damage. Finally, chimney caps increase the draft of chimneys, particularly in windy areas.

Chimney caps are usually made of stainless steel, copper, or aluminum. A solid top and screened side keeps rain and small critters out while allowing exhaust smoke to escape.

Installing or Replacing a Chimney Cap   *EASY* **1–2 hours**

Replacing or installing a chimney cap begins in the same way. But before you climb the ladder for the roof, make sure you have older, loose-fitting, comfortable clothes on. Also, be sure you wear sneakers or some other shoes that will allow you to walk safely on the roof and not slip.

You'll want to have a partner on the ground who can either hand you the new chimney cap or help you pull it up in a bucket on a rope. This will let you obey a golden rule: never climb a ladder with anything in your hand.

If you are replacing a chimney cap, simply use a screwdriver or wrench to loosen the screws or bolts that secure it to the chimney and lift it off. If the bolts or screws are rusted or corroded, spray some WD40 or silicone spray on the bolts. Let it sit for a little bit and try to loosen them. If the unit doesn't want to come up, take it with both hands and wiggle it up off the chimney.

Before installing the new cap, check the flue, the surrounding cement, and the bricks surrounding them to be sure they are in good repair. If they need repairing, now is the time to do it (see the next section). If the chimney is in good working order, reverse the steps and install the new one according to the manufacturer's instructions. The hardware should be included with the unit. Make sure the unit is securely in place, and remember to take the tools down off the roof!

Repairing Flue Damage   *DIFFICULT* **5–7 hours**

The flue is the inner part of the chimney. This is the part that contains and vents the exhaust (the products of combustion). On most masonry chimneys the flue is made out of clay; on some prefabricated chimneys it is made of metal. The purpose of the flue is to safely vent the toxic gases that result from fires in a fireplace that burns wood or a boiler that heats a house.

It is critically important to maintain your flue, because if part of it collapses from age and wear, or debris such as leaves and animals fall into it, the results can be harmful—and potentially fatal. This is because carbon monoxide, one of the deadliest gases that is produced in working chimneys, can seep into your house through cracks or holes in flues that need repair. The first part of maintenance begins with yearly, or more frequent, inspections by a trained professional.

Maintaining your flue also involves tackling another equally important problem that is best left to professionals: creosote buildup. Creosote is a natural by-product of burning wood, and over time it builds up on the inside of the flue and is itself highly flammable. To prevent potential fires within the chimney structure itself, have the flue inspected, and cleaned if necessary, by a qualified chimney professional.

A proper inspection includes an examination of the structure for signs of deterioration or weakness, exterior staining due to gases seeping through the outside walls, broken or dislodged bricks, and atrophy of mortar joints. In some extreme cases, chimney professionals have been known to bring in video inspection equipment to check the inside of the flue for possible damage.

In any case, for the best results, ask the technician if he is going to clean the flue before he does the rest of the inspection. Doing so will yield the best results. Special rods, chimney brushes, and vacuums are used to minimize the potential for a mess. You'll rest easy knowing the job was done properly.

What Can You Do between Inspections? *EASY* **2–5 hours**

The smartest thing you can do is have working carbon monoxide detectors in your house and check them regularly. It is best to have them placed on each floor and near sleeping areas so they can be heard at night.

Another is to make sure you burn properly seasoned firewood. This includes not only staying away from green and/or moist wood, but letting your firewood age before you burn it. Store it in a dry place and keep it off the ground. Letting firewood age for a whole season is not unheard of. Lastly, whenever it is possible, burn your fires as hot as possible. This will keep the flue clearer for longer. Doing these simple things should help stave off problems that could lead to expensive repair bills, and will keep you and your family safe.

Grout and Brick Repair *FAIRLY EASY* **2–5 hours**

Bricks and mortar that are exposed to the elements (wind, rain, and sun) eventually start to show signs of wear (see Fig. 2.9). Depending on how deteriorated they are, different kinds of repairs are occasionally needed as regular maintenance. Over time the face of bricks may shale or fall off. Given enough time, whole bricks may fall out of the chimney.

There is something you can do to prolong the life of your chimney before a problem develops. As long as the chimney and mortar are in good repair, you can apply a water-repellent product to seal out the elements. One brand is called Chimney Saver, and it's pretty simple to

FIGURE 2.9

Chimneys suffer when the grout between the bricks begins to decay.

apply. It is available at home centers and fireplace stores. Read the label and follow the manufacturer's directions.

If you do have a chimney that needs repair, the job of fixing crumbling mortar is not a hard one. First, you'll need a few tools. These include a grout rake (a tool used to scrape out loose mortar between bricks), a water spray bottle, a wire brush, a tuck-pointing tool (available at home centers or a mason supply store), a hammer, acrylic concrete and grout fortifier, grout or masonry mix, a trowel, a bucket, a tarp, and a wet/dry shop vacuum.

Start by spreading out the tarp below where you will be working. Next, using the grout rake, scrape out all the loose mortar between the bricks and remove any parts of the bricks that come loose. Vacuum out the remaining pieces and dust. Next, scrape the remaining grout seams with the wire brush to remove more dust. Vacuum this dust again.

Using the water spray bottle, dampen the joints so that the new mortar adheres well. Using the bucket, mix the mortar and fortifier according to directions. Make sure the mixture is thick but still workable. Give it some time to sit and soak up water. Use the tuck-pointing tool to pack the joints full of mortar. Next, use the tip of the tool to pack even more mortar tightly into the joint, until it is flush with the bricks.

FIGURE 2.10

Metal bands that secure antennas to chimneys are best left alone unless you remove the antenna (and the bands that hold it on) completely.

After letting the mortar dry for at least an hour or two, use the trowel to scrape off any excess mortar. Spray water on the mortar again so it won't dry too quickly. This will prevent the mortar from cracking prematurely. Finally, a few days later, go back and brush the chimney for the last time with a brush. This will help get rid of any remaining sand or dust.

Antennas

An important part of antenna maintenance is making sure it is securely fastened to the roof or chimney. More often than not, it is attached to the chimney by metal straps that lash the antenna to the chimney.

Visually inspect the antenna and make sure the straps are not rusted, bent, or ripped in any way. With both hands, grab the shaft of the antenna and gently shake it to make sure it is securely in place. If you have to do any grout and brick work on the chimney, there's really no need to take down the antenna. Doing so will probably make more work for yourself, and you will risk not being able to secure it again. This is because even galvanized, waterproof hardware used to secure the antenna to the chimney can become locked in position and will break if you take a wrench or screwdriver to it. If this happens, you'll be forced to get new hardware if you rely on an antenna for television.

Sometimes the best maintenance is no maintenance. Until you are ready to go to satellite TV or cable and take it down permanently, if it is securely in place, don't mess with it. In this case, take the advice of the old adage: "If it ain't broke, don't try and fix it." (See Fig. 2.10.)

Plumbing Systems

Basic Plumbing

Chances are, your house is hooked up to a municipal water system that also supplies fresh water to many other houses. Knowing how the system works is important because this will help you maintain it. Residential plumbing usually consists of two systems: fresh water coming into the house, which feeds all the fixtures and appliances: and the drainage system that drains the same fixtures and appliances.

Water travels through the system's pipes until it reaches the meter outside your home. It travels through the meter, where usage is measured, continues through a large gate valve, and then through one or more pipes into your house. This pipe is called the *main service line* (usually it is 3/4 inch in diameter). From there it branches out into a pair of narrow pipes (usually 1/2-inch-diameter copper pipes) that travel side by side throughout the house and end at the appliance or fixture that uses the water.

One of the lines is for cold water and the other is for hot. Water becomes hot because it is first routed through the hot water heater or the coil in a furnace or boiler before it is sent through the house. Names are given to pipes according to the direction they travel in your house. Those that travel horizontally to fixtures and appliances are called *branch lines* and ones that travel vertically (at least one floor) are called *risers.*

The second part of the system is the drainage system. It consists of waste pipes, a soil stack, traps, and vents. This is also known in the plumbing trade as the DWV system. Its name describes what it does: it *drains wastes* at the same time it *vents* them.

The easiest way to explain how this system works is to use the operation of a sink as an example. Waste drains out of a sink through a series of pipes that leads to the waste pipes (usually $1\frac{1}{2}$–2 inches wide), which are sloped to empty into the soil stack. The soil stack is an even larger pipe (3–4 inches in diameter) that runs from the lowest point in the house to the highest and sticks up about 6 inches above the roof.

From the soil stack, the waste travels to the building drain. This is a horizontal pipe that travels across the house and leads to the sewer line and to the disposal system. Depending on the location of your house, your disposal system consists of a sewer, septic tank, or cesspool.

Locating the Water Main
EASY

A golden rule for maintaining your plumbing system is to make sure every family member knows the precise location of the main water shutoff valve and how to turn it off (see Fig. 3.1). In the event of an emergency such as a burst or leaking pipe, this valve can be quickly turned off, stopping any more water from coming into the house and causing further damage. This is because water is pumped from a cen-

FIGURE 3.1

The valve on the water main should be turned clockwise in an emergency.

tral station and enters your house under pressure, about 50 pounds per square inch (psi), and the shutoff valve, in an emergency, could be the only thing between your house and a swimming pool.

This is why, when you turn on a faucet, the water is always ready and flows freely. The bad part is because of this pressure, if a pipe or fitting springs a leak, the water usually sprays out with a lot of force. When this happens, shut off the main house valve and call a plumber immediately. If you don't have an emergency, there are a lot of things you can do without the help of a plumber. Some of them are described here.

Outside Taps (Sillcocks)

Most houses have one or more sillcocks for outside water use. These are not immune to leakage and should occasionally be inspected and maintained. A practical problem that can be taken care of is a summertime one. Leakage can and does occur when sillcocks are left on with garden hoses attached to them. This leaves the spray nozzle at the end of the hose as the only valve stopping the water from leaking.

This is a problem, because most hoses are not designed for constant pressure and the valves inside spray nozzles are not as durable as the ones in sillcocks. As a result, over time, leaks happen. Sometimes, leaks are not detected until an ocean of water is lost. (See Fig. 3.2.)

FIGURE 3.2

Make sure to keep these turned off when not in use. To be sure, disconnect hoses from them.

Another problem is that leaving sillcocks on during the winter or freezing weather can cause pipes or hoses to rupture and create pretty bad leaks. How do you maintain them so they work properly? Inspect them a few times a year, regulate their use with some of the techniques mentioned above, and have them replaced by a certified plumber if they leak.

Dripping Faucets   EASY **1–2 hours**

Dripping faucets are a common problem around the home, but this is definitely not something you need to call a plumber about. Repair will likely take all of 5 minutes and cost a grand total of 75 cents or so.

Of course, the time you're most likely to notice a dripping faucet is in the middle of the night, when the house is quiet. And that's no time to repair anything. You needn't. You can silence the drip temporarily and make the repair in the morning.

To do this, find a long piece of string, or a shoelace. Wet the string thoroughly, then tie one end of it to the faucet nozzle, letting the rest hang down into the drain. Fiddle with the tied-on end until the dripping water runs down the string. This will carry it silently to the drain. That's it. If you don't have a piece of string, use a rag or a sock or a towel. First, of course, wet it thoroughly.

To make the repair, you should know how a faucet works. A faucet is a simple device for controlling water flow. Water comes up through the hole in the faucet. When the handle is turned off, the washer presses against the hole and won't let the water out. When the handle is turned on, the washer lifts off the hole and the water flows.

The handle of the faucet is attached to a shaft, called a spindle, with a threaded part that screws down against and covers a hole inside the faucet body—the part that's attached to the sink. Water is constantly being fed through pipes to the faucet, but when the faucet is off, the bottom of the spindle acts like a cork—water pushes against it but can't get out. When you turn the faucet on, the spindle screws up out of the hole and water flows.

The thing that really seals off the hole is the washer on the bottom of the spindle. This is a rubber or fiber device shaped like a little black doughnut. It's soft, and makes a good seal to prevent the water from slipping out past the edges of the spindle. With time, however, this washer wears out or loses its shape. Then it doesn't seal off the water completely. Just a little gets by, and you get a drip.

Your first inclination is to turn the faucet tighter. And this will stop the drip temporarily, because the washer will press more tightly in the hole. Ultimately, however—in a day or two or a week—the washer will become so worn that you will have a drip no matter how tightly you turn off the faucet.

To make the repair, simply replace the washer. To do this, you need to take apart the faucet. First, though, turn off the water supply going to the dripping faucet. How do you do this? You turn off the pipe valve.

Pipe Valves

A pipe valve looks like a little spoked wheel or an oval-shaped piece of metal. In most homes, the valve is located under the sink. There will be two, one for the hot water and one for the cold. Feel the pipes. The one that is warm will be the hot water pipe; the cold one will be for the cold water. When you locate the right valve, turn it off by turning it to the right as tightly as you can.

Of course this can be confusing; there may be a number of valves under there. If this is the case, and you are not sure which one to turn, just turn off all the valves you can see. No harm will be done. But first turn on both faucets. When you turn the right valve off, the water will stop.

In some homes you won't see any valves under the sink at all. If that's the case, look on the walls—any valves there? If all else fails, you can turn off the main valve. This will be located right next to the water meter on the main pipe—the one that brings all the water into your house. The valve will be on the left side of the pipe. Turn it to the right. If you aren't sure where the main valve is, call your water company. They'll know—or have someone come over and show you.

Taking the faucet apart will depend on what kind you have, but the process is basically the same for all faucets. You unscrew or turn the things that look like they can be unscrewed or turned and the faucet comes apart. There's no great mystery involved. One common type has the faucet shaft, or spindle, held on the faucet body by a big chrome nut. Obtain an adjustable wrench (one for $8 or $9 at Sears will be good enough), with jaws that open at least 1 inch wide—or a type of wrench with jaws that open that wide.

Pliers can also be used. Wrap some cloth or tape around the chrome nut to protect its shiny finish, then place the jaws of the wrench on the nut, tighten them up, and turn counterclockwise—to the left. After a few turns, you should be able to turn the nut by hand. Loosen it all the way, then turn the faucet handle in the "on" direction until the whole shaft comes up and out of the faucet body.

At the bottom of the shaft, as mentioned, is the washer, held on by a tiny screw. Take the little screw off with a screwdriver and remove the washer. On some shafts, you can lift it right off. Others will have to be pried a little with the point of a knife.

Take the old washer and screw down to your dealer and ask for ones just like them—the same size and shape. Brace yourself; they will cost you about 50 cents. Make sure you get a brass screw—not one that's colored to look like brass. Pure brass won't corrode; steel ones will. To make absolutely sure it's brass, if your dealer is not, try a test: Use a magnet to pick up the screw. If you can't pick it up, that's good—brass can't be picked up with a magnet. Steel, however, can.

Place the new washer on, insert the little screw, and tighten. Then just screw the shaft down into the faucet body and tighten the big fat nut. Do it slowly, don't force it, and keep the shaft and nut straight as you do. That's it.

Stopped-up Sink   *EASY* **1–2 hours**

When a kitchen, bathroom, or other sink becomes stopped up or the water drains slowly, you can try a number of things to get the water flowing again. First, carefully reach down through the water (a knife or other sharp object may be lying in wait) and feel around the drain strainer. Sometimes lint, soap scum, food, or the like can collect quickly and clog things up. Pick out whatever you can with your fingers. After the water drains, remove anything else you can see. For this, a pair of tweezers may come in handy.

The Plunger

If that doesn't get the water flowing, try the next thing: the plunger. You've probably seen one of these. It consists of a handle that looks like a sawed-in-half broomstick on one end of which is a rubber cup.

You may be able to borrow a plunger, but buying one is a good investment. I recommend one that is good for clearing both sink and toilet blockages. The cup has a little bulb on it that fits snugly into the hole in the toilet (when you're using it for that purpose). To use it on a sink, you snap the bulb inside the cup. At any rate, get a hefty one—six inches in diameter. You can pick one up at your local home center or hardware store for under $10.

The plunger works by getting the water lying in the pipe to move back and forth, alternately pushing against the blockage and sucking it upward, and thus working it free.

To use the plunger, first make sure the sink has at least 6 inches of water in it. If the blocked water is not 6 inches deep, run some more in. This is to ensure that the plunger cup is under water at all times while you're plunging.

Place the cup over the drain and push down hard, compressing the plunger, then jerk up so the cup lifts off the drain about a half-inch. Push down again, lift off, and continue like this, trying to keep a nice, steady rhythm. Keep the bottom of the plunger under water at all times.

Every 30 seconds or so, jerk up extra hard and check to see if the water is going down. If it is, continue plunging until it is all gone.

Then turn on the faucet full blast to see if the water goes down freely. If it does, the blockage has been knocked loose and is heading for the sewer line. As a final treatment, turn on the hot water for a few minutes.

Not so incidentally, if the sink has a little overflow outlet (this will be above the drain on the back side of the sink), this must be plugged with a sopping wet rag while you plunge. Or if you're plunging one of a pair of sinks, you must plug the other sink's drain. Of course, you'll need a helper. If you don't plug that other opening, the suction you're creating by plunging will escape and you won't get much result.

If the plunger doesn't do the job after 5 minutes or so, call it quits. You'll be ready to, because plunging is hard work.

The Trap

The next step, in that case, is to clean out the *trap.* This is a V-shaped section of pipe directly under the sink. Its purpose is to "trap" a little water, which in turn serves as a seal to prevent sewer gas from backing up the drain pipe and out the drain. But the trap is also a perfect place for things like knives, forks, toothbrushes, spoons, rings—you name it—to collect and eventually block the water.

Some traps have a plug at the very bottom. Place a pan or pail under this plug and use a wrench or pliers to turn the plug counterclockwise to loosen it, then unscrew it with your fingers. When you do, it's likely that whatever was causing the blockage—plus the water in the sink— will plop down into the pan or pail.

Some traps don't have plugs in them. If this is the case, take a wrench and loosen each of the big nuts that are at the top ends of the "D." Slip these nuts up and off the D and, gently, rock it back and forth until you can take it out. If something is wedged inside the trap, poke inside it with a piece of hanger wire or something else you don't mind getting dirty. Then put back the pipe and tighten the nuts. Make sure you get them on straight.

Whenever you clean out a trap—one with or without a plug—always finish the job by letting the hot water run for 5 minutes. This will clear away any grease deposits that might have collected where the blockage was.

The Snake

Your final try to clear a blockage is to use a snake. A snake is a flexible wire cable with

TRAPS

Traps are safety devices that get their name from what they do. They are pipes that are shaped to trap water so that harmful gases and vermin can't get back into the house through sink or tub drain holes. Even toilets have traps built into the bottom of them. There is also a trap and fresh-air inlet where the soil pipe leaves your house.

a point on one end and a tubelike handle on the other. Snakes come in various lengths. One about 8 feet long is good enough. To get quality, pay $10 or so for it. As with a plunger, it doesn't pay to buy a small tool.

First, take off the trap plug, or the trap itself. With your hands, feed the snake into the pipe that goes into the wall. When it is firmly implanted, slide the tubelike handle down along the cable until it is a couple of feet from the pipe opening and lock it in place by turning the little screw on it. Then push the snake in, at the same time turning the tube handle, which will turn the snake.

If the snake becomes stuck, it may just mean that it's ensnarled in a bend in the pipe. On the other hand, you may have located the blockage. Push and pull and twist. If it feels like it's really stuck, pull it all the way out. The little hooked end may have caught on the blockage and you may be able to drag it out. If not, start all over again.

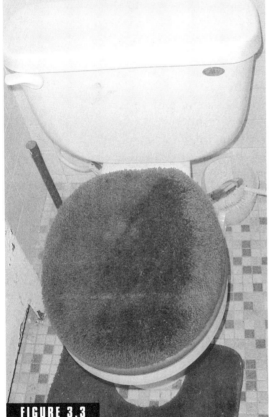

FIGURE 3.3

This toilet's tank has too much clutter around it. The top and the back of it (below where the water supply lines are) should be kept clear so you have easy access to it for inspection and repairs.

As you feed the snake into the pipe, keep sliding the handle down and setting it in position. If the blockage still is not cleared when you have fed all of the snake in that you can, it's time to call the plumber. The blockage is either wedged in too hard and requires bigger equipment to clear it, or it is located beyond the reach of your snake

Repairing Toilets   *DIFFICULT* **5–7 hours**

Toilets vary in general design and in the design of the flushing mechanism. They are, however, enough alike that general repair instructions can be given for all designs.

Checking the Tank

Problems with a toilet usually occur because something goes wrong in the flush tank—the squarish box above the toilet which holds the flush water. It's a good idea to get thoroughly familiar with how a toilet works before doing any repairs. (See Fig. 3.3.)

First, lift off the top of the tank. Do this carefully. If you drop it, it could chip or break. Set it aside and look down into the tank (see Fig. 3.4). Looks like a hopeless

FIGURE 3.4

It's really not as complicated as it looks. Repairs usually consist of replacing the float, the arm of the handle, and the ball at the bottom of the tank.

jungle of piping, doesn't it? It's really not complicated. Turn the tank handle just a little. When you do, you'll see that it moves a vertical rod (or chain) upward a little. Next, turn the handle fully to flush the tank. See what happens?

The rod (or chain) lifts a rubber ball that's resting in a hole in the bottom of the tank. When the ball is lifted out of the hole, the water in the tank runs out into the bowl, flushing it. Then the tank fills up again, automatically.

Flush the tank again and watch what happens to the float. Depending on what kind of hardware you have inside the tank, the float will look like either a round plastic ball attached to a small rod or a plastic device that slides up and down on a vertical shaft.

As the water runs out, the float, which of course is floating, goes down with the water level. This float does two jobs. First, when it gets near the bottom of the tank, the end of the rod it's on opens up a water inlet valve, and new water starts to rush into the tank. At the same time, the ball at the bottom of the tank, which has been held up by water rushing past it through the hole, drops down and closes the hole because there's no more water to keep it open. Second, as the water level rises, the float rises, and the end of the rod it's on gradually closes off the water inlet valve. So the float turns the water on and off.

While the tank is filling, a little tube shoots water into the overflow tube and fills up the bowl itself. If for some reason the incoming water flow is not shut off, the water will flow out the overflow tube into the bowl. There is no way that a toilet tank can overflow. There are other parts to a toilet tank mechanism, but knowing those mentioned will enable you to make the majority of the repairs required. Now, let's cover some common problems.

Common Problems

First, if you have a problem, take off the tank top so you can see what is going on. If, after flushing, water keeps on running into the bowl and yet the tank doesn't fill up all the way, it usually means that the little rubber ball at the bottom of the tank is defective. What's happening is that it is not plugging up the hole completely.

The cure is to replace the ball. First, shut off the water to the tank. This is done by turning off the water supply to the tank. You can do this by turning off the valve (little wheel) either below the tank or somewhere on the bathroom wall. An easier way, however, is simply to lift the rod that the float is on as high as you can, then tie it in that position to something above the tank (such as a cabinet door knob). As you may remember, this closes off the inlet water valve.

Flush the tank, emptying it. When it's empty, hold the rod (or chain) that the ball is on and unscrew the ball with the other hand. Place it aside and gently wipe off the edges of the hole the ball rests in with a clump of fine-grade steel wool (available at hardware stores).

Take the ball down to your local hardware store and ask for one just like it. If, when you took the ball off, you noticed that the rod it was attached to was bent, get a new one of those, too. A bent rod can keep the ball from going in straight and plugging the hole completely.

With the rod in place, screw the new ball onto it. Untie the float rod or turn the water supply valve back on. Flush the toilet. If the water still runs out of the tank, and the tank doesn't fill all the way, the ball is not fitting into the hole properly. This may be because the little guide arm that the rod fits through is not positioned properly. Just turn off the water supply again, then loosen the little screw holding the arm to the overflow tube and jiggle the arm back and forth until the ball drops into the hole perfectly. Then, tighten the screw to hold the rod permanently in that position.

Another problem is that the tank fills up all the way but the water continues to run until it goes out the overflow tube. If this is happening, you'll not only see the water running out the overflow pipe, you will also hear a hissing noise. Something is wrong with either the water inlet valve or the float or its particular rod.

Lift up the float. If the hissing noise stops and the water stops flowing, the problem is in the float or the rod. Flush the toilet, emptying the tank. Tie the rod as before to shut off the water. Keep it off by turning off the water supply valve.

Unscrew the float and shake it. If there is water inside, the float must be replaced. Simply trot down to your local hardware store and get one just like it (about $10). Screw the new float in place, untie the rod (or turn the water supply valve on), and flush the tank. The tank should fill up but not overflow.

If you find when you take off the float that it doesn't have water in it, the problem is in the rod that it is on. To correct this, screw the rod in tightly and then simply bend the rod downwards with your hands, so the float is another half-inch or so down into the tank. Flush the toilet. The float should be positioned so the water stops about an inch from the top of the overflow pipe. If it doesn't, bend the rod a little more to achieve this.

If your first test of lifting the rod up does not shut off the water flow, something is wrong with the water inlet valve. Fixing this is probably a job for a plumber.

Tank "Sweating" *EASY* **1–2 hours**

When cold water enters a toilet tank, it may chill the tank enough to cause "sweating" (condensation moisture in the air on the outer surface of the tank). This makes the tank "drip" with water beads on it. This can be prevented by insulation. Insulating jackets or liners that fit inside toilet tanks keep the outer surface of the tank warm, so the outside of the tank stays dry. These liners or jackets are available from plumbing supply dealers. They are pretty easy to install; check the instructions.

Stopped-up Toilet *DIFFICULT* **5–7 hours**

Every homeowner has encountered a stopped-up toilet at one time or another. Solving this problem is similar to handling a stopped-up drain. However, when water starts to rise in the bowl, the first thing you need to know is how to turn off the water going into it. The quickest way is to lift up the rod that the float is on (as explained in the previous section). Just take off the top of the flush tank, grab the rod, and pull up. This will stop the water. Then tie the rod to the nearest cabinet knob or something else to hold it in position.

The first thing to use to clear the blockage is a plunger. The best kind to get is the two-way force cup, mentioned in the stopped-up sink section. This has a bulb on the end of the rubber cup, which fits snugly into the hole at the bottom of the bowl. When you plunge you get better suction. A 6-inch-diameter one will be good.

Plunge the bowl as you would a sink. Place the plunger bulb into the hole at the bottom and press forcefully down on the plunger, compressing it. Pull up about an inch, then press down again. Go up and down in a steady rhythm, every now and then pulling up hard. If you see the water starting to go down, continue to plunge until it is all gone. As a final test to see if the blockage is cleared, flush the toilet. Be ready to grab the rod to stop the water flow if the blockage isn't gone.

If, before you start to plunge, the bowl is filled to the brim with water, take an old pot or pail and ladle out some of it, say 6 inches. Otherwise, when you start to plunge, the water will spill on the floor.

If 5 minutes of plunging doesn't do the trick, you have to take sterner measures. The name of the game here is the *closet auger,* a "snake" that is especially designed for clearing toilet blockages. It gets its name from "water closet."

A closet auger is like the snake described in the stopped-up sink section, being a wire with a pointy end, but it is thicker and less flexible and it has a crank handle. Closet augers are sold in various sizes. One 6 feet long will be good. Sears and Home Depot both sell good-quality ones.

To use the auger, feed the end in with your hands. When it's inside the hole, push it upward. The end has to get over a humplike part just beyond the hole in order for it to get to the drain pipe.

Keep pushing it in with your hands. When enough of it is in so you can push it with the handle, do so, at the same time cranking it. This will turn the end of the auger.

If the auger becomes stuck, it may mean that you've contacted the blockage. Push extra hard, also turning. If it feels as though the point on the end of the auger has caught on something, pull out hard. You could drag the thing out. Of course, it could also mean that the auger is wedged into a pipe bend. Anyway, just keep pushing and turning until all of the auger has disappeared. If the toilet still isn't clear, it's time to take off the gloves, as they say. There is something else you can do—it's drastic, but it is effective.

Removing the Toilet Bowl

DIFFICULT **5–7 hours**

An obstruction in the bowl itself (the bottom part of the toilet) or leakage around the bottom of the bowl may require removing the bowl, though obstructions can usually be cleared with a plunger. If using the plunger doesn't work, follow these steps to remove the bowl:

1. Shut off the water.

2. Empty the tank and bowl by siphoning or sponging out the water.

3. Disconnect the water pipes to the tank.

4. Disconnect the tank from the bowl if the water closet is a two-piece unit. Set the tank where it cannot be damaged. Handle the tank and bowl carefully; they are made of vitreous china or porcelain and are easily chipped or broken.

5. Remove the seat and cover from the bowl.

6. Carefully pry loose the bolt covers and remove the bolts holding the bowl to the floor flange. Jar the bowl enough to break the seal at the bottom. Set the bowl upside down on something that will not chip or break it.

7. Remove the obstruction from the discharge opening.

8. Place a new wax seal around the bowl horn and press it into place.

9. Set the bowl in place and press it down firmly. Install the bolts.

Other Bathroom Problems

Clogged Faucet Strainer

EASY

Many faucets are equipped with a little strainer-like device that screws onto the end of the faucet. Its purpose is to aerate the water so it doesn't splash when it hits the sink. When one of these gets clogged with soil, the water starts to jet—and splash—rather than flowing in a soft stream.

To cure the problem, first remove the device from the faucet. Sometimes you can do this by simply turning it to the left or right—whichever way the thing goes with your fingers. If necessary, use a pair of pliers, first wrapping a little tape around the device to protect its shiny finish from the jaws of the pliers.

Remove the little screens (or screen) from the device. You can poke them out with your finger or pick them out with the point of a knife. Note where each goes, so you can reassemble them properly later. (Some screens may not come out, so just brush the exposed screen vigorously. That usually does the trick.)

Using an old toothbrush and a little hand soap, brush the screens thoroughly, even if dirt isn't visible (see Fig. 3.5). Rinse them thoroughly, replace them, and then screw the device back onto the faucet and tighten carefully.

Erratic Shower Spray

If a shower head ejects water in a hard stream, it probably means that inside is a buildup of scale and soil. Some of the little holes where the water comes out are clogged, so the water is virtually fired out of the other ones.

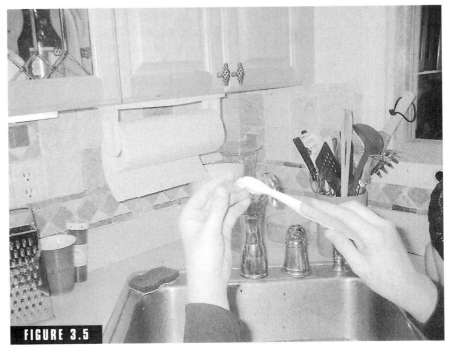

FIGURE 3.5

Removing debris from a clogged strainer helps the water flow freely.

First, grip the shower head in your hand and turn it counterclockwise. It should come right off. If you need help, use a wrench or pliers. Using a flashlight, look down into the hole in the back of the head. You'll likely see some foreign matter. If you hold the head to the light, you'll see that some of the holes are blocked.

Soap up a Q-Tip, or a toothpick with cotton on the end, and work it down inside the shower head, clearing the holes and wiping the entire inside of the head. After a few minutes, discard the Q-Tip and run hot water through the hole in the head so it emerges from the little holes. Repeat the procedure four or five times until a Q-Tip emerges as clean as it went in. This is a good sign that you have removed the material.

Screw the head back on the shower and turn on the water. If water doesn't come out properly, repeat the Q-Tip procedure as needed.

Leaky Pipes

FAIRLY EASY **2–5 hours**

You may be surprised to know that you can probably repair a leaky pipe. Not one that's spewing water—that's a job for a plumber—but the pinhole or small-hole leaks that drip or even spray a fairly steady stream of water.

The first thing to do is to turn off the water. As with a faucet, there are valves controlling water flow through particular pipes. Ideally, you'd simply turn off the valve that would stop water flowing through the damaged pipe. If you're not sure which valve controls what, you can turn off the main water valve, as described under "Dripping Faucets." As you know, however, this will turn off both hot and cold water everywhere in the house.

The repair can be made in a variety of ways. One way is with an epoxy putty. The Oakly brand is good. You can buy this at a plumbing supply store or at a home supply center. It comes in a large tube and looks like clay when it comes out. It will cost you about $7. It's worth the cost.

To use it, first wipe the damaged area of the pipe absolutely dry. Clean it by rubbing it briskly with steel wool. Then, following label directions, mix the two-part adhesive/filler together and swab it onto and around the hole. That's it, but the material does take 10 hours or more to dry. This is obviously impractical if you have to turn off the main water valve.

Better, if you are going to turn off the main valve, is a clamp-type patch obtainable at hardware stores. It comes with a rubber patch that looks like a bicycle tube patch. This will only cost you about $4, and they come in different sizes. Place this patch over the hole, then slip the clamp device over the patch; tighten the clamp with the bolts provided. This presses the rubber hard against the hole, and water can't get out. You can turn the water on right away; it's a 5-minute repair which will last awhile.

Both of these repairs—the epoxy and the clamp—will last indefinitely.

For a hole in a drain pipe under the sink, you can make a quick repair with rubber tape. Tight Seal is a good brand name to get. It is rubber tape with adhesive on one side of it. You can get a 10-foot roll for about $5. First wipe the pipe dry. Peel off the paper backing on the tape and wrap the pipe tightly. If the leak is near a joint, you can form the tape with your fingers so it fits snugly.

Plan before Replacing Fixtures in a Bathroom

An important part of plumbing work is installing fixtures, particularly the sink, tub, and toilet. Before you install new fixtures in an existing bath, it is a good idea to think carefully about what you will do.

A new bath job may range from just taking out the fixtures and installing new ones to ripping out everything to the studs and starting from scratch. If the bathroom is very old, probably the best thing is to go down to the studs. If there is only one bath in the house, you will have to go slowly. Plan your work so that you do not inconvenience anyone. Take the fixtures out only when you are ready to put the new ones in. Of course, if the work is new, you need not worry about any of the above.

Removing Fixtures

DIFFICULT **5–7 hours**

There are certain things that you must do when removing fixtures. The first is to turn off the water supply. Usually, as explained earlier, there are valves for turning off the basin and toilet. Basin valves (there are two) are under the sink; the toilet valve is under the toilet itself. Tub valves (two) are in your cellar beneath the tub, or they may be in a panel in a wall behind the tub.

If you don't have a basement and your house rests on a slab, the valves may be in the utility room. If you cannot find the appropriate valves, you can turn off the main valve in the basement, turning off all water, hot and cold, in the entire house.

When you disconnect any fixture, pay careful attention to how it is connected. It will make the job of putting the new one in easier.

Removing Kitchen Sinks

To remove a kitchen sink, you will have to loosen the clips that hold the sink to the countertop. The faucet has two thin supply pipes leading from it that hook up with water pipes coming out of the wall; a basin wrench is handy for removing nuts that are up close to the back of the sink.

The basin also is tied into the waste line. Here, there is a slip nut (you pull it up with your fingers) that holds the drain pipe in place in the trap. When all nuts are loose, you can just lift the sink up and out of the way.

Removing Toilets

If you are removing a toilet, first flush the bowl. Use a pot to remove all water from the bowl (or as much as you can); sponge out the rest. One type of bowl has a flush elbow, which is connected to the tank. Unscrew with a wrench and take the bowl and tank out separately. New types of toilets have the tank and bowl in one piece. In either case, toilets are connected to the floor flange with two or four bolts that must be removed before you can lift the toilet out of the way.

Removing Tubs

If the tub is the old-fashioned type with decorative "feet," the piping is exposed, and it is a simple matter to disconnect the tub. Just use a wrench on the exposed nuts.

Another type of tub is built into the wall. To remove it, you have to open up the walls first to reach the connection of the tub to the water and waste lines. If the wall is plasterboard, just rip it off with a pry bar, first removing the escutcheons (the decorative pieces below the faucet handles). If the wall is plaster, use a sledgehammer. A hammer is useful in either case.

For removing any tub from the waste line, check downstairs in the cellar (if you can) to see if the waste line from the tub can be unscrewed from the waste line proper. If you can, just loosen the nut and lift straight up on the tub; the attached waste line will come up and out. It may be that the waste line on the tub is connected to the main line by a slip nut instead of a normal nut. If this is the case, just push the slip nut up out of the way with your fingers.

If you cannot disconnect the tub waste line from the waste line proper, the only recourse is to disconnect it at the drain flange from inside the tub. Doing so may be difficult, because it is usually corroded. At any rate, fit the handles of a large wrench into holes in the drain, then slip a screwdriver between the handles for leverage and turn.

Incidentally, if the piping is ancient (lead water pipes), or very old (galvanized iron pipe), or just old (brass pipes), it ought to be replaced with copper pipe.

Bathtubs are made from a number of different materials. Some are cast iron with a porcelain enamel coating, some are made of steel with porcelain over, and others are made of molded glass fiber reinforced with an acrylic resin. These last tubs are commonly known as fiberglass tubs.

Sizes and shapes vary. Commonly, bathtubs are rectangular, usually 4–6 feet long (commonly 5 feet), with heights ranging from 12 to 16 inches from floor to rim top. The actual water depth of the tub is, of course, from the bottom of the tub to the overflow drain.

Cast iron is the heaviest (up to 500 pounds) type of tub and is more durable and less susceptible to damage than other types. Formed steel tubs are light (about 100 pounds) and less expensive than cast iron. Many plumbers use them for upper-story installations because of their manageability and because they do not usually require that the floor be reinforced. This may be your best choice if your bathroom is on the second floor of your house. Incidentally, some steel tubs are made of two sections welded together, but a seam shows and many people do not like this. This may be something to consider when you shop.

Steel tubs are more apt to make noise than cast-iron tubs. Some companies therefore offer them with an undercoating that helps deaden sound.

The fiberglass tub is a relative newcomer to the plumbing scene. The surface is especially smooth and easy to keep clean, but it does scratch relatively easily. Some companies make kits that you can use to remove scratches. Coming into more popular use lately is the one-piece fiberglass tub-shower unit. An advantage of this type of unit is that it eliminates the need for making a joint where the tub meets the wall; this joint often breaks open, allowing water to penetrate into walls behind the tub.

Fiberglass tub-shower combination units come in many different sizes and are molded in various shapes, but the most common is the 5-foot-long rectangular one.

In position, the tub stands on the floor, but the back rim also rests on a ledger strip nailed to the studs. You can make this ledger strip out of any wood available, from a 1 $\times$ 3 to a 2 $\times$ 6.

Installing Fixtures

VERY DIFFICULT **7–10 hours**

Installing new fixtures in your bathroom is exciting. However, after the stylistic choices are made, the real work begins. That is, coordinating not only what fixtures fit comfortably in your bathroom, but how easily they can be connected to water service and drainage lines. Following is information and tips on installing fixtures in your bathroom.

Installing a Tub

VERY DIFFICULT **7–10 hours**

First, measure the tub from the underside of the lip to the floor to determine the exact height. It should not be too low, so add an extra $1/2$ inch and be certain that it is level. If the floor is very far out of level, you will have to take this condition into account.

Use your level to check floor levelness. If the floor is more than $1/4$ inch out of level from the back wall to the face of the tub, put the tub in place and then shim it up temporarily with under-course shingles or pieces of wood.

Use a straightedge board cut to length to level the tub end to end at the back wall and then front to back on each end. If one end happens to be out of level, it should pitch toward the front, the way the water runs.

After you are satisfied that the tub is level, mark the studs where the top of the tub is. Slide the tub away from the wall. Measure the thickness of the back edge of the tub. Allow this amount from the lines on the studs to the top of the ledger and nail the ledger solidly to the studs. Now move the tub back into place and shim the front edge. It should now be level and rest solidly on the ledger and the floor and shims.

If you have easy access to the tub connections from the outside (i.e., if they are open to an unfinished area), a tub is easy to connect. Indeed, always try to trim the tub (put on drain pipes, faucets, etc.) first and work to the trap. If you do not have this advantage of easy access, it will be rather difficult to make the connections.

After the tub is shimmed up, mark the wall where the center of the overflow and drain holes fall. You need three measurements to locate the exact center of each hole (i.e., the distance from two walls and the height off the floor). Nail the shims in place so that the tub can be taken away and replaced without the necessity of leveling it all over again.

Remove the tub. Make whatever alterations are necessary to the floor framing to make room for the drain pipes (one from the overflow, one from the bottom of the tub). Assemble the drain pipes on the tub and screw them up tight, and then remove them as an assembly. Hold the assembly in approximate place on the waste pipe according to your measurements to get an idea of where the trap has to be. A number of ways to hook it up are possible.

The brass tub trap has a joint in it so that the "U" part can swing 180 degrees or more. This gives great flexibility for alignment. Screw the trap directly on the waste pipe. Then set the whole thing up and make up all the joints tight; adjust the trap to align the waste flange (lip) and overflow flange according to the marks and measurements you took earlier.

Use tape to hold the washers in place on the two flanges temporarily. Then put the tub in place. If you did everything properly, the two flanges will line up with the two holes in the tub. Pack plenty of stainless putty around the drain fitting and screw it in, using the handles of a large pair of pliers and a screwdriver to turn it.

If there is access to the back and bottom of the tub, all the fittings can be made up after the tub is in place. The trap can be used to make the final adjustment.

Installing a Toilet   *FAIRLY EASY* **2–5 hours**

Toilets are made in two basic shapes—elongated and round. The bowl of the elongated style is egg-shaped and bulges out in the front, while the round style is, well, round. Both styles are available as two-piece units and as one piece. The federal government mandates that all residential toilets be designed to flush only 1.6 gallons of water per flush, to reduce water consumption. The government has also established minimum trapway diameters and exposed water surface areas for each bowl design.

Colors vary (colored fixtures are more expensive than white), but toilets are usually made of vitreous china. As durable as this material is, it is subject to chipping, so be careful while you are handling the toilet—it can break.

Three different flushing actions are commonly used in toilets designed for residential use. These result in specific bowl and tank designs. Some feature pressurized vessels to move the water quickly, while others rely on gravity alone. The following descriptions of the flushing actions may help you select a bowl when renovating your bathroom.

FLUSHING MECHANISMS

The *siphon jet flush* has a large, exposed water surface, leaving less interior china surface exposed to fouling or contamination. The trapway must be large, and it is engineered to be as round as possible for the most efficient flushing action. The flush is standard. It's not loud, and the water is not necessarily fast-moving. It is available as a one-piece or a two-piece unit. These units are the most inexpensive. The Kohler Wellworth (in white) sells for $99. American Standard also sells a white unit for $99.

The *rim jet flush* style has a quieter, softer flush and is also available in one- or two-piece units. However, homeowners usually seem to pick one-piece units. Perhaps the softer flush has an appeal. These are pricier and look kind of elegant, with a low profile. A white, round Kohler one-piece sells for $289 at Home Depot.

The *power-assisted flush* toilet, though designed for the home, flushes more like a public restroom toilet. When the water is released, it means business. Inside the tank is a pressurized vessel called a sloan valve, which remains closed when nobody is using the unit. This allows pressure to build up in the tank. When somebody flushes it, those 1.6 gallons of water are put to the test by being pushed out quickly. These toilets are also available in one or two pieces, and American Cadet sells white units for $265. They are also available at Home Depot.

THE INSTALLATION

There is usually a 4-inch lead or cast-iron waste pipe coming up through the floor that is 12 inches (to the center of the pipe) from the finished wall. Sometimes the pipe is 3 inches wide. Each pipe calls for its own kind of flange. The 4-inch pipe calls for a brass flange that can be standard or offset in design. Standard is fine if the center of the waste pipe is 12 inches from the back wall. The offset flange is used to get more or less clearance from the wall if the waste pipe is not positioned exactly right.

The 3-inch pipe requires a closet flange. This is a single brass piece with a standard flange on top and the bottom tapers (with a lip on it) into the 3-inch waste pipe.

Also, if a lead pipe is not exactly right for the flange to fit, it may be dressed (bent) by tapping it gently with a dressing tool or with a hammer handle to fit. Lead is soft, so fitting should be no problem.

In any case, the flange must be positioned so that you can locate two bolts opposite each other. Once they are in position, both kinds of flanges are then screwed down to the subfloor.

Next, put the flange bolts in place and set up the bowl and tank dry, to make certain that everything fits. Set the tank aside. Place a wax ring around the horn (the toilet discharge opening) and put the bowl in place, being careful to bring the bolts through the holes in the toilet. Rock the bowl gently to compress the wax, and work the bowl so it rests solidly on the floor. You can achieve this by simply sitting on it.

The bolts will protrude through the wax and the bolt slots. Tighten gently on both sides. (Do not use too much pressure, or you may crack the bowl.) Then put the elongated washers and nuts on the bolts. Install the tank according to the manufacturer's directions, and hook up the water supply with a soft brass tank supply tubing and angle stop.

Installing Lavatories and Sinks

There is much confusion in some people's minds as to the difference between a sink and a lavatory. Actually, a lavatory is just the technical name for a bathroom sink.

Lavatories come in a wide variety of styles, colors, and sizes. Most lavatories are constructed of cast iron covered with porcelain, of vitreous china, or of steel covered with porcelain. Another popular type combines the lavatory and the countertop in a one-piece, seamless unit. Finally, vanity units have sinks fitted into the top of them (see Fig. 3.6).

The most popular styles of lavatories are the self-rimming, the under-the-counter, the wall-hung, and the flush-mount models. The flush-mount kind needs a metal framing ring to hold it in place in the countertop. It is not costly, but cleaning between the frame and the counter can be a problem.

The self-rimming type has its own rim, which rests in a sealant applied to the countertop, with the rim projecting slightly above the countertop. The wall-hung lavatory is just that—mounted to a special hanger secured on the wall. The under-the-counter type is mounted beneath an opening cut in the countertop, with the fittings mounted through the countertop.

Kitchen sinks may be stainless steel, porcelain on steel, or porcelain on cast iron. Cast iron is better but more expensive than steel. Stainless steel comes in a wide range of quality and price. The most common sink sizes are 21 × 24 inches for sinks that require a mounting rim and 22 × 25 inches for self-rimming sinks.

As with any sink (or tub or toilet, for that matter), fittings do not come with the unit and must be ordered and installed separately.

FIGURE 3.6

This vanity unit has a sink dropped into its top. The cabinet hides the water supply pipes and the trap and provides storage.

If you have a choice, install the faucet on the sink before you put the sink in place. Sinks have three holes in which the faucet is mounted. The center hole is used for the spray hose or the pop-up-drain fitting rod. Other types of faucets have both the hot and cold water supplies in the center hole, and two screws to clamp the faucet in place in the other holes.

Some faucets come with plastic or rubber pads to seal them to the sink; others require putty around the holes.

If the faucet must be installed after the sink is in place, a basin wrench is necessary. This wrench will tighten or loosen a nut according to which way the jaws are turned. There are four positions for the jaws. Two give extra leverage. Two work well if you use one hand to close the jaw and the other to turn the wrench with the slide-lever handle.

You can buy any type of faucet that goes into the drillings of the sink or basin. The most common drilling is 4-inch centers for a basin (lavatory) and 8-inch centers for a (kitchen) sink. Sinks sometimes have an extra hole for a spray. Both are commonly installed from the top with nuts underneath. However, others work in the opposite way (with fancy handles held in place by escutcheons on top). This type may also be tightened from the bottom when in place.

First, put the rubber gasket on the faucet wherever it comes into contact with the sink. Use plenty of putty if there is no gasket. Push it into place, put washers and nuts on from the underside; have a helper hold the faucet in position and tighten nuts with a basin wrench.

Next, attach the faucet supply pipe to the hot and cold water pipes. Faucet supply lines have undergone some changes in the last several years. Two different kinds will be discussed here. I've seen them both work equally well—first, the newer method (braided flexible supply tubes) and then the traditional chrome or brass tubes.

Braided, flexible supply tubing is now used to supply hot and cold water to faucets. This comes in many lengths—8, 10, 12, and 16 inches— and is said to be stronger and to last longer than straight chrome tubing. Although some tubing is made of stainless steel, most are really heavy-duty braided plastic. Their real appeal is that they are strong, easy to install (a nut on each end is tightened to the water source pipe), and they are flexible!

Traditional water supply tubes pipes are available in chrome or brass in lengths of 12, 18, 24, and 36 inches. Slip the nuts over the supply pipe and screw to the faucet. Once the pipes are attached, bend them carefully so that they are parallel to the compression fittings. At least an inch of the pipe must be straight above the point of connection, or it will not seat properly. Mark the pipe and cut off any excess so that about 1/2 inch will slip into the fitting. Slip the nuts and ferrules over the ends of the pipes, then slip the ends of the pipes into the fittings and carefully turn down on the nuts. It is important that the end of the pipe be aligned exactly in the fitting. Make certain that the nut is threaded properly before you tighten it.

Next, turn on one valve at a time and check for leaks. If the connections leak at the nuts, tighten them just enough to stop the drip; use only open-end wrenches on compression fittings, and always use another wrench to "hold against yourself" so that you do not twist the pipe.

When the water supplies are tight, turn the water on full blast to check leakage at the waste connections. If they do not leak, put the plug in the sink and allow it to fill about 10 inches deep. Then pull the plug and watch again for leaks. If there are any leaks, tighten nuts carefully. If it still leaks, disassemble the waste connection and do it over.

Installing a Strainer and Tail Piece FAIRLY EASY **2–5 hours**

A strainer and its corresponding tailpiece are used on either a tub, basin, or sink. There are several types of strainers on the market. If you examine them before installation, you will see how they work.

The most common strainer is made up with a large rubber washer and a metal washer and nut under the fitting. Inside the fitting there is a chrome flange. This section is beaded in stainless putty.

To install it, take the inside section of the strainer in hand and press a bead of putty about 1 inch thick all around the underside of the flange. Press this section down into the hole in the fixture from the inside, and put the washers and nuts on from the outside. The excess putty will squeeze out. Have an assistant use the handles of a large pair of pliers inserted between the cross in the bottom of the strainer and a large screwdriver to hold the strainer from turning while you take up on the nut from below. Make certain that the rubber washer does not become displaced while you do this. If it does, release the pressure on the nut and replace the washer (it may be necessary to remove some putty from the underside of the fixture) and take up on the nut again just tightly enough that the strainer is snugly in place and does not easily turn from the pressure of the wrench. The tailpiece is connected to the strainer with a nut; there is a special washer that fits into the end of the tailpiece.

Repairing Leaks in Pipes and Tanks

Leaks in pipes usually result from corrosion or from damage to the pipe; pipes may be damaged by freezing, vibration, or by water hammer.

Corrosion

Occasionally, waters are encountered that corrode metal pipe and tubing. (Some acid soils also corrode metal pipe and tubing.) The corrosion usually occurs, in varying degrees, along the entire length of pipe rather than at some particular point. An exception is where dissimilar metals, such as copper and steel, are joined.

Treatment of the water may solve the problem of corrosion. Otherwise, you may have to replace the pipe with a type made of material that will be less subject to the corrosive action of the water. It is good practice to get a chemical analysis of the water before selecting materials for a plumbing system. For advice on this, call your local water authority and ask where you could have your water tested.

Repairing Leaks in Pipes
EASY **1–2 hours**

Pipes that are split by freezing must be replaced. A leak at a threaded connection can often be stopped by unscrewing the fitting and applying a pipe joint compound that will seal the joint when the fitting is screwed back together.

Small leaks in a pipe can often be repaired with a rubber patch and metal clamp or sleeve. This must be considered an emergency repair job and should be followed by permanent repair as soon as practicable.

Large leaks in a pipe may require cutting out the damaged section and installing a new piece of pipe. For the beginner, this kind of job is probably best left to a professional plumber.

Repairing Leaks in Tanks
EASY **1–2 hours**

Leaks in tanks are usually caused by corrosion. Sometimes, a safety valve may fail to open and the pressure developed will spring a leak. Although a leak may occur at only one place in a tank wall, the wall may also be corroded thin in other places. Therefore, any repair should be considered as temporary, and the tank should be replaced as soon as possible.

A leak can be temporarily repaired with a toggle bolt, rubber gasket, and/or brass washer. You may have to drill or ream the hole larger to insert the toggle bolt. Draw the bolt up tight to compress the rubber gasket against the tank wall. If you are unsure about how to do this, ask a professional plumber or hire one to do it.

Water Hammer

Water hammer sometimes occurs when a faucet is closed suddenly. When the flow of water is abruptly stopped, its moving energy is expended against the walls of the piping. This causes the piping to vibrate (and knock), and leaks or other damage may result.

Water hammer may be prevented or its severity reduced by installing an air chamber just ahead of the faucet. The air chamber may be a piece of air-filled pipe or tubing, about 2 feet long, extending vertically from the pipe.

This is probably a job for a plumber. If you suspect your pipes suffer from water hammer, call a plumber, have him confirm that this is the problem, and then consider having him solve the problem for you.

Frozen Water Pipes

In cold weather, water may freeze in underground pipes laid above the frost line, in open crawl spaces under your house perhaps, or in outside walls.

When water freezes, it expands. Unless a pipe can also expand, it may rupture when the water freezes. Iron pipe and steel pipe do not expand appreciably. Copper pipe stretches to some degree, but does not resume its original dimensions when thawed out; repeated freezings will cause it to fail eventually. Flexible plastic tubing can sometimes stand repeated freezes, but it is good practice to prevent it from freezing.

PREVENTING FREEZING
FAIRLY EASY **2–5 hours**

Pipes may be insulated to prevent freezing, but this is not a completely dependable method. Insulation does not stop the loss of heat from the pipe—it merely slows it down—and the water may freeze if it stands in the pipe long enough at below-freezing temperature. Also, if the insulation becomes wet, it may lose its effectiveness.

Electric heating cable can be used to prevent pipes from freezing. The cable should be wrapped around the pipe and covered with insulation. Check your local home center for this product.

THAWING

Using electric heating cable is a good method of thawing frozen pipe, because the entire heated length of the pipe is thawed at one time. Thawing pipe with a blowtorch can be dangerous. The water may get hot enough at the point where the torch is applied to generate sufficient steam under pressure to rupture the pipe. Steam from the break could severely scald you. *This is not recommended.*

Thawing pipes with hot water is safer than thawing with a blowtorch. One method is to cover the pipe with rags and then pour the hot water over the rags. When thawing pipe with hot water, or similar methods, open a faucet and start thawing at that point. The open faucet will permit steam to escape, thus reducing the chance of the buildup of dangerous pressure. Do not allow the steam to condense and refreeze before it reaches the faucet.

Underground metal pipes can be thawed by passing a low-voltage electric current through them. The current will heat the entire length of pipe through which it passes. Both ends of the pipe must be open to prevent the buildup of steam pressure.

A word of caution: This method of thawing frozen pipe can be dangerous. It cannot be used to thaw plastic tubing or other non-electricity-conducting pipe or tubing. Be careful about how you do this. If you are unsure of how to do this or whether the pipe you are trying to thaw is right for low-voltage current, it is probably best to ask (call a plumbing supply store or home center professional for advice) questions about how to do it, or let a professional—a contractor who specializes in this kind of work—handle it.

Cleaning Clogged Drains

Drains may become clogged by objects dropped into them or by accumulations of grease, dirt, or other matter. If the obstruction is in a fixture trap, usually the trap can be removed and cleared. If the obstruction is elsewhere in the pipe, other means must be used. Cleanout augers—long, flexible, steel cables commonly called "snakes"—may be run down drain pipes to break up obstructions or to hook onto and pull out objects. Augers, including electrically powered ones, are made in various lengths and diameters and are available at hardware and plumbing supply stores.

Small obstructions can sometimes be forced down or drawn up by use of an ordinary rubber force cup (plunger).

Grease and soap clinging to a pipe can sometimes be removed by flushing with hot water for 10 minutes or so. The use of chemical cleaners is not recommended. They may not do anything for a solid blockage, and if they don't work, you will have to plunge or use a snake, exposing yourself to the water with the chemical cleaners in it.

Floor Drains

Sand, dirt, or lint sometimes clog floor drains. Remove the strainer and ladle out as much of the sediment as possible. You may have to carefully chip away some concrete or other floor material around the strainer to free it. Flush the drain with clean water. If pressure is needed, use a garden hose.

Wrap cloths around the hose where it enters the drain to prevent backflow of water. You may have to stand on this plug to keep it in place when the water is turned on. Occasional flushing of floor drains may prevent clogging. Consider it routine, preventative maintenance.

An Important Note: Garden hoses, augurs, rubber force cups, and other tools used in direct contact with sewage are subject to contamination. Do not later use them for work on your potable water supply system unless they have been properly sterilized.

Outside Lines

Roots growing through cracks or defective joints sometimes clog outside drains or sewers. You can clear the stoppage temporarily by using a root-cutting tool. Professional plumbers use these with a power auger. This is not typically a job for homeowners.

Sometimes, if lines are very old or damaged, they will need to be replaced. This is a job for a professional contractor. The contractor can re-lay a defective portion of line or replace the whole line. It is important to use sound pipe and to make sure that all joints are watertight.

If possible, sewer lines should be laid out of the reach of roots. If this is impossible or impracticable, consider using impregnated fiber pipe, which tends to repel roots. Ask a professional in a plumbing supply store or a home center about this kind of pipe.

Draining Plumbing in a Vacant House   *DIFFICULT* **5–7 hours**

If you ever need to drain the plumbing in a house that will not be occupied, perhaps in your second home or if you are a landlord and the house you rent may be vacant for some time, here's how.

Shut off the water supply at the main shutoff valve at the street; then, beginning with those on the top floor, open all faucets, and leave them open. When water stops running from these faucets, open the cap in the main pipe valve in the basement, and drain the remaining water into a pail or tub. This cap must be closed until the faucets have run dry, or the house water supply will flow from this valve and flood the basement.

Remove all water in the traps under sinks, water closets, bathtubs, and lavatories by opening the cleanout plugs at the bottom of traps and draining them into a pail. If no traps are provided, use a force pump or other method to siphon the water out. Sponge all the water out of the toilet bowls. Clean out all water in the flush tank.

Fill all the traps with antifreeze. This will seal off bad odors from waste pipes. Do not forget to fill the trap in the flood drain in the basement.

Drain all hot-water tanks. Most water tanks are equipped with a vented tube at the top which lets air in and allows the water to drain out the faucet at the bottom. Make sure that all horizontal pipes drain properly. Air pressure will get rid of trapped water in these pipes, but occasionally the piping may have to be disconnected and drained.

If the house is heated by hot water or steam, drain the heating pipes and boiler before leaving. Fires should be completely out and the main water supply turned off at the basement wall or street. Draw off the water from the boiler by opening the draw-off valve at the lowest point in the system.

Open the water supply valve to the boiler so that no water will be trapped above it. If you have a hot water system, begin with the highest radiators and open the air valve on each as fast as the water lowers. Every radiator valve must be opened on a one-pipe system to release condensation. And don't forget to lock the doors!

Electrical Systems

The electrical system in a house is the one system that all beginning do-it-yourselfers avoid like the plague. The reason is simple: fear. Fear of getting shocked, or worse. Actually, an electrical system should be respected. But once you understand it, it's about as complicated as a plumbing system. In other words, it's simple.

Just like the water in the main service line flows through a meter that records its usage, electricity flows through the wires in your house. Like water, electricity is always under pressure, ready to surge out when you turn on a light switch or plug in a toaster. It comes into your home through the electrical service line, called the *service entrance cable* (see Fig. 4.1) and goes through the electric meter (Fig. 4.2), which records how much electricity you use.

Where does the electricity in the wires start? It starts at the power company, where electricity is generated with the use of very large magnets. High-tension wires carry it from there to the service line that leads into your home. After entering your house, electricity continues to flow to the fuse box or circuit breaker panel (usually in your basement). This is where the fuses and circuit breakers are (Fig. 4.3). From there it continues through house circuit wires to switches, plugs, and outlets, where the current is tapped off by appliances, machines, and devices that use electricity.

In order to make it flow, electricity needs a *circuit*—a path to take— a closed loop that has no off-ramp. As long as this loop remains unbroken, electricity continues to flow. Break the circuit and electricity stops flowing. This is where circuits take the stage.

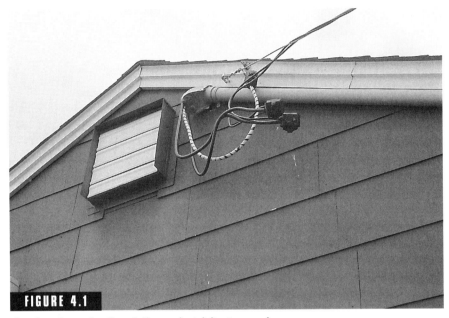

FIGURE 4.1

The electric service line delivers electricity to your home.

Circuits

Each circuit supplies power—electricity—to a given number of appliances and lights. Each circuit consists of a black wire, called the *hot* wire, on which the electricity travels out, and a white wire, which carries the electricity back to *ground.*

Each circuit is designed to supply just so much power. It is limited as to how many amperes (which is the amount of electricity that can go through a wire) it can carry and under what pressure.

Things like dryers and other big power users may have their own separate circuits. Lights and other small power users may all use one circuit. Problems arise when there are too many things drawing off one circuit. The electrical flow demand is beyond the capacity of the circuit to carry it, and suddenly everything stops working. That's good: The fuse or circuit breaker has done its job.

Circuit Breakers

Circuit breakers are safety devices (see Fig. 4.4). Instead of letting electric-hungry appliances draw too much power, and possibly filling the wire to "breaking," and maybe starting a fire, the fuse or circuit breaker breaks the circuit and stops the electrical flow.

You'll note, if you examine fuses or circuit breakers, that each has an amperage figure on it—say, 15 or 20 or 25 amperes. This indicates the capacity of the circuit protected by the particular fuse or breaker. If a fuse blows, be sure to replace it with one of the same capacity. Putting one in that is larger will let that wire fill up to breaking, and then you can really have problems that only a fire truck can solve.

When working on anything electrical, you can shut off the power—and you should—by removing the fuse that protects the circuit or tripping the circuit breaker. Or, you can turn off all the power in the house by throwing the main shut-down switch. Have an electrician look at your system and label all the various circuits for you and what they control. It won't cost you much, and from then on you can work in complete safety.

In order for a circuit to work properly, it should be designed with tolerances in mind—in other words, the amount of electricity it can handle. The way to figure this out is pretty simple. You get this by multiplying the total amperes of your system by the volts. For example, if you have a 100-ampere system, and the voltage is 240, your

FIGURE 4.2

Electric meters measure how much electricity you use. Your utility company reads these once a month.

wattage is 24,000. This means that you can use lights and appliances that draw up to but not more than 24,000 watts of electrical energy, or power.

Electrical Problems

A reminder for homeowners, and this can never be repeated often enough. If you have any doubt whatsoever about electrical problems in your home, call a licensed electrician. Remember, repairs least attempted by do-it-yourselfers are electrical ones. The reason is simple. Not only do you not want to burn the house down, more important, you want to stay safe.

It is also important to note that your homeowner's insurance policy may be invalid if it is discovered that you did electrical work that started a fire.

The fuse box door should be kept closed.

FIGURE 4.4

Circuit breakers are really safety switches that shut down dangerous amounts of electricity.

The First Electrical Customers

The first homes to have electricity delivered to them were on Pearl Street in New York City. The families in those homes were subscribers to the Edison Electrical Light Company, which ran wires through pipes that were once gas pipes. As the sun set on the evening of October 18, 1878, a worker threw a switch at a power station nearby, making this the first night in history that became day inside the rooms of those 85 houses.

Actually, many electrical repairs should be left to a pro. Indeed, all communities prohibit anyone but a licensed professional from making certain ones. Happily, though, there are some that can be made without approval and with no hazard whatsoever, and these are commonly the ones that need to be done. Following are some of them.

Outlets   *EASY* **1–2 hours**

Problems with electrical outlets are usually not with the outlet itself. Instead, problems begin with how they are connected to the stud inside the wall or connected to the wall itself. As people plug things in, they line up the metal prongs with the slots, and push hard. Over time, this repeated pushing causes the plug to become loose in its housing; eventually the socket begins to move around and may become disconnected from the wall (see Fig. 4.5).

This is a potentially dangerous situation. Even the faceplate does not offer protection from shocks if the plug is moving around or wiring becomes exposed. To repair this, make sure you cut off the power (it's best to do this during the day, when you don't need lights) to the whole house. This way, you can be sure the power that supplies the outlet is off.

Remove the faceplate. Unscrew the top and bottom screws and pull the outlet out of its housing. Check the connections on either side of the outlet and make sure the wires are secured tightly to the screws. If they aren't, loosen the screws, reposition the wires, and tighten the screws down again.

Next, check the box the outlet rests in. If it is secure and doesn't move, assemble the pieces and finish the job. Make sure you reinstall the cover (switch) plate before you turn the power back on. If the outlet moves around at all, check to see how it is secured to the stud behind the wall. You might have to replace a nail or screw that has fallen out or broken. You might need to insert additional nails or screws to secure it. As a last resort, you may want to call an electrician. Although it may seem like carpentry, this is within their work domain.

FIGURE 4.5

Standard outlets are pretty reliable and should stay secure in their wall housing—even when things are repeatedly plugged in and pulled out. However, occasionally they may need tightening.

Switch Plates   *EASY*

Saving Money

Buying electrical supplies in bulk can save you money. For instance, if you plan on remodeling your house, and you know you'll need a lot of switch plates for different rooms, it's wise to buy all of them at one time. This way, your cost per plate is reduced. The same is generally true of other electrical products you use around your home: buying in bulk will be cost-effective.

Even if all you need to do is replace or tighten a switch plate, turn off the power. It's better to be safe than sorry. Make sure you hold onto the screws that you take out when replacing switch plates. I can't tell you how many times I've been in the middle of a job and lost small screws or nails. It may not seem too important in the whole scheme of things, but when the color of the screw head is the same as the switch plate, it looks silly with new screws that don't match because you lost the originals (see Fig. 4.6).

Lastly, when you screw in the new switch plate, make sure the screws are snug but not too tight. Tightening them down too tight can cause the plate (especially plastic ones) to crack and metal ones to bend (see Fig. 4.7).

Lights Go Out or Appliances Stop Working Suddenly

EASY

Did you ever have the experience of working in the kitchen or elsewhere with a lot of appliances or other devices plugged in and when somebody turned on the TV or plugged in another appliance, everything went off?

The reason was that a fuse blew or, if you live in a fairly modern house, the circuit breaker tripped. The fuse, which serves the same purpose as the circuit breaker, is a safety device. It is part of your electrical wiring system, and when the wires are working too hard—because that extra thing was plugged in—the fuse blowing or the circuit breaker tripping stops everything. If the fuse or circuit breaker wasn't there, the wires could heat up and malfunction to the point of starting a fire.

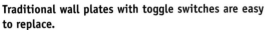

FIGURE 4.6

Traditional wall plates with toggle switches are easy to replace.

FIGURE 4.7

Plates with flat (rocker switches) should not be tightened down too hard.

The first thing to do is to unplug the extra appliance. Then find the bad fuse or tripped circuit breaker. If you live in an apartment, you'll have four or more fuses and they'll likely be in a little metal box on a wall either in the kitchen or near it. If you live in a house, they'll probably be in the basement.

Open the little door on the box and look closely at the fuses. The fuses are little round things with tiny windows. The "bad one" will have a blackened window, or a little silver strip behind the window will be broken. Compare it to the other fuses and you'll immediately see the difference.

By the way, before touching anything electrical, make sure that you are safely away from any water on the floor before you unscrew the fuse. Take the bad fuse down to your hardware store or home center and get one just like it. It may say "15 amps" on it, or "20 amps." In any case, your dealer will give you the right one. It will cost about $2.

If you have circuit breakers instead of fuses, you'll be saved from a trip to the home center. This is because circuit breakers, for the most part, don't have to be replaced; they just have to be reset. Circuit breakers will be located in the circuit panel, probably in your basement. Take a walk down to your basement and open the door to the metal box on the wall.

See how all of them have the word ON showing? Except one. The tripped circuit breaker will say OFF or be out of position with the other ones. It is important to turn the breaker all the way to OFF and then just flip it back to ON. This accomplishes the same thing as putting in a new fuse.

To avoid the problem in the future, just don't plug in that extra appliance. If you want to keep using so many appliances on one circuit breaker, you will have to get new wiring installed. This is the province of an electrician. Incidentally, if fuses blow or circuit breakers trip frequently when you have *not* plugged in extra appliances, the wiring should be checked by a licensed electrician.

Plug Keeps Coming out of Socket   *EASY*

Plugs from appliances and lamps often fall out of wall receptacles or outlets. The reason is usually that the plug prongs are bent or misshapen and can't get a grip. Or the receptacle may be a little worn. To solve the problem, simply bend the prongs outward with your fingers a little. Stick the plug in the receptacle. Gently pull on it. Does it stick? No? Bend the prongs out a little further.

Broken Plug   *EASY* **1–2 hours**

When a plug is corroded, or cracked, or damaged in some other way, it's a good idea to replace it. Indeed, it may be the reason why a lamp or small appliance doesn't work, and should be suspected immediately.

There are two kinds of plugs. One is *sealed,* so-called because the ends of the electrical wires are buried inside it. There's no way to get at the wires that go into it without cutting open and ruining the plug. The other kind is *open construction,* so-called because it has a removable fiber disk that slips over the plug prongs and snaps into place.

This disk can be removed, revealing the bare wire ends of the electrical cord. The open-construction kind are generally older in style, and sealed plugs are used on most appliances you buy today. In fact, the open-construction variety is now nearly obsolete, and sealed plugs (molded plastic) are almost always used today on nearly all appliances.

If you have an open-construction plug style that is broken, my advice is just to give it a send-off to the garbage can. It may not be worth the effort of going to an appliance store and searching for parts that aren't made any more. A new plug is inexpensive enough to get. Home improvement centers and hardware stores have them for about $1–$3.

A word of caution: do not just buy a new plug and connect it to any appliance whose plug is broken—chances are, the tolerable electrical load of the old wire and the new plug will be different. This could cause a short, a loss of power, or a fire.

Even when you are replacing new plugs, make sure they match. Some have serial or model numbers on them. If you are still uncertain about what plug to use, take the old wire and the plug to an electrical supply store and ask for help.

Appliances Don't Work   EASY **1–2 hours**

There are many reasons why refrigerators, freezers, washing machines, and other big appliances go "on the blink." There are a few things you can try before calling the repairman.

First, though it may sound obvious, check that the appliance is plugged in. Check not only the plug that goes into the wall socket, but the plug that plugs into the appliance itself.

If both plugs are in, examine the plug that goes into the wall. Does it look in good shape? It does? If the wall plug is okay, check the appliance plug. These plugs might look different from open-construction or sealed plugs, but they are really alike—and the repair is almost the same. To check the appliance plug, first pull the wall plug out of the socket. This eliminates any electrical hazard.

If the appliance plug is the sealed kind and you cannot do anything with it, clip it off and take it to an appliance repair shop or an electrical supply store. There they can sell you a new plug and tell you how it should be connected. (They can match the plug to the exact appliance you have.)

If you're game, and you have some version of an older kind of plug, follow these instructions. Split the plug into halves by either unscrewing little screws in it or, on some, simply snapping it apart. Inside you will see two wires, each attached to a little screw. If either is loose, rese-cure it under its little screws (as you did with the open-construction plug) and the problem should be solved.

Even though they may not yet have interfered with the working of an appliance, an older or damaged cord or broken plug body should be remedied immediately. For a frayed cord, first open up the plug. Each screw is attached to a little metal clip. Cut the plug off, including the frayed portion of the cord. Loosen the screws and snap out the clips. Draw the cord out and discard.

Broken Lamp   *EASY* **1–2 hours**

If a lamp flickers or doesn't go on, it could be a bad bulb. If a new bulb doesn't solve the problem, check the wall plug. Are the prongs getting a good grip in the wall? How about the plug itself? Are the wires in it securely attached under the little screws? Is the plug broken?

If the wall plug is okay, the trouble is inside the lamp. Pull the plug out of the wall and set the lamp on a table where you have a good working light. Take out the bulb, then unscrew the cap on the very top of the lamp; take off the shade and then the harp, the wire section around the bulb.

The shiny metal part that the bulb screws into is called the shell. On it, you'll see imprinted the word PRESS. Push on the word PRESS with your thumb, at the same time twisting the shell upward very hard. It will slip off. Inside the shell is a fiber liner shaped just like it. It may come off with the shell. If it doesn't, lift it off (this is easy to do).

Inside you will see two wires, each attached to a little screw, as in a plug. If either is loose, tighten it. If they are broken, cut off the cord and prepare and attach new wires, just as with a broken plug. If the socket itself is damaged, simply loosen the screws and slip out the wires. Lift the socket off and get a replacement like it at your hardware store. As with a plug, tie the wires to the screws. Finally, put the lamp back together by reversing the procedure you used to take it apart. Lamp sockets, by the way, cost about $4.

Flickering or Burnt-out Fluorescent Tube   *EASY* **1–2 hours**

Like regular lamps, fluorescent tubes indicate that something is wrong by flickering or simply not going on. A variety of simple things can cause problems. If, when you flip on the light switch, the tube blinks repeatedly before it stays lit, that may mean that it's loose. Gently grasp it at the ends and turn it away from you to see if that seats it more securely; if it doesn't, turn it toward you to try to get it in tighter.

If it still flickers after tightening—or tightening wasn't needed—the problem may be caused by loose sockets that the ends of the tube fit into. The sockets are held on by screws on the outside ends of the metal housing. Try tightening them.

If the tube still flickers, probably a defective starter is causing the difficulty. This is a little barrel-shaped device that sits in a hole in the metal housing. To see it, you have to remove the tube.

Grasp the tube near the ends and turn it gently, first in one direction, then the other, until you hear a little blip; continue to turn that way until you hear another blip. Lift out the tube. When replacing it, reverse the process.

Most starters have the word REMOVE imprinted on the end, with a little arrow pointing left or right. First press the starter in as far as you can, then turn it in the direction of the arrow and lift out. Take the starter down to your hardware store and get a replacement just like it. These go for about $3. Install it by reversing the way you took it out. Other indications of a defective starter are when the ends of the tube glow brighter than the middle part, or when the light switch has to be flipped several times before the tube stays lit. If all else fails, replace the tube. However, a bad tube is unlikely, because they're designed to last hundreds of hours.

Iron Doesn't Work

EASY **1–2 hours**

Of all the appliances in a house, the iron is one you can't really do without, especially if you need pressed clothes and the dry cleaner is closed. When you turn on the iron and it doesn't work, it's likely that one of the wires inside the iron is loose. To find out, use a little screwdriver and remove the plate where the cord disappears into the iron, in back.

Inside, you'll see that the cord splits into two wires, and that each wire has a little metal thing on the end, called a grommet, and is attached to a little screw. That is, only one grommet will be on, the other will be loose—that's the problem. So, simply slip the grommet back onto the screw shaft where it belongs and tighten the screw on it.

Many times iron cords become loose or knocked (a cut is made in the plastic) and require replacement. So, take the plate off in the back of the iron, loosen the screws holding the grommets, and take the cord to a hardware store or electrical supplies dealer and get one just like it. Then slip the grommets on the screws, tighten the screws, and replace the plate.

Heating and Cooling Systems

Heating Systems

Of all the systems in your home, the heating system is the one that it's wisest to leave alone, except for occasional routine maintenance (changing filters, etc). Working on it is really a job for a pro. A professional plumber is usually called to install any heating system that utilizes water as a heating source. Still, it's good to know something about how different systems work so your maintenance goes smoothly.

A home's heating system is simple: it's designed to transmit heat from the furnace or boiler to living areas. Designs that move warm air throughout a house are known as forced-air systems. Another design, known as a hydronic system, uses hot water or steam to create heat. Some of the common systems are described here, but before we look at them, let's look at a piece of equipment that is vital to any heating system, the thermostat.

Thermostats

The key to any heating system is the thermostat. It is a heat-sensitive device which usually can sense a temperature drop of 2°F in a room. It is from the thermostat that your furnace or boiler gets the signal that heat is needed and goes into action. When you have your heating system tuned up—and this should be done at least once a year—have the technician check the thermostats as well.

FIGURE 5.1

Oil-fired hot water heating systems are reliable when maintained properly.

Hot Water Heating Systems

Hot water heating systems consist of a boiler, pipes, and room heating units (radiators or convectors). Hot water, heated or generated in the boiler (see Fig. 5.1), is circulated through the pipes to the radiators or convectors, where the heat is transferred to the room air.

The action starts in the boiler. Boilers are made of cast iron or steel and are designed to burn coal, gas, or oil. Cast-iron boilers are more resistant to corrosion than steel ones. Although corrosive water is a primary cause of corrosion, it can be reduced with chemicals.

Proper water treatment can greatly prolong the life of steel boiler tubes. If your boiler needs replacing, and you are there when the plumbers are installing the new one, ask a question or two about it. The more you know, the better.

Buy only a certified boiler. Certified cast-iron boilers are stamped I-B-R (Institute of

Boiler and Radiator Manufacturers); steel boilers are stamped SBI (Steel Boiler Institute). Most boilers are rated (on the nameplate) for both hot water and steam.

Radiators

Conventional radiators are set on the floor or mounted on the wall. Some types may also be recessed in the wall. Insulation should be installed behind recessed radiators with either insulation board, a sheet of reflective insulation, or both.

PREVENT CLOGGED HEATING OIL LINES

If you use oil in your furnace, the next time you get a delivery, turn off your furnace for a half-hour or so. This gives the sediment at the bottom of your oil tank time to settle. Then turn it on. This sediment is the main source of oil line clogs—a headache you don't want.

Radiators may be also be partially or fully enclosed in a cabinet. The preferred locations for radiators is under a window.

Baseboard radiators are hollow or finned units that resemble and replace the conventional wooden baseboard along outside walls. Their benefit is they heat a well-insulated room uniformly, with little temperature difference between floor and ceiling.

Convectors usually consist of finned tubes enclosed in a cabinet with openings at the top and bottom. Hot water circulates through the tubes. Air comes in at the bottom of the cabinet, is heated by the tubes, and goes out the top. Some units have fans for forced air circulation. With this type of convector, summer cooling may be provided by adding a chiller and the necessary controls to the system. Convectors are installed against an outside wall or are recessed in the wall.

Forced Hot Water Heating Systems

Forced hot water heating systems are more efficient than the gravity hot water heating systems. In a forced hot water system, a small booster or circulating pump forces or circulates the hot water through the pipes to the room radiators or convectors.

In a one-pipe system, one pipe or main serves for both supply and return. It makes a complete circuit from the boiler and back again. Two risers extend from the main to each room heating unit. A two-pipe system has two pipes or mains: One carries the heated water to the room heating units; the other returns the cooled water to the boiler.

A one-pipe system, as the name indicates, takes less pipe than a two-pipe system. However, in the one-pipe system, cooled water from each radiator mixes with the hot water flowing through the main, and each succeeding radiator receives cooler water. Allowance must be made for this in sizing the radiators—larger ones may be required farther along the system for proper heating.

Because water expands when heated, an expansion tank must be provided in this system. In an *open system,* the tank is located above the highest point in the system and has an overflow pipe extending through the roof. In a *closed system,* the tank is placed anywhere in the system, usually near the boiler.

Half of the tank is filled with air, which compresses when the heated water expands. Higher water pressure can be used in a closed system than in an open one. Higher pressure raises the boiling point of the water, so higher temperatures can be maintained without steam in the radiators, and smaller radiators can be used. There is almost no difference in fuel requirements.

With heating coils installed in the boiler or in a water heater connected to the boiler, a forced hot water system can be used to heat domestic water all year.

One boiler can supply hot water for several circulation heating systems. The house can be "zoned" so that temperatures of individual rooms or areas can be controlled independently. Remote areas, such as a garage, a workshop, or a small greenhouse, can be supplied with controlled heat.

Gas and oil-fired boilers for hot water heating are compact and are designed for installation in a closet, utility room, or similar space, on the first floor.

Electrically heated hydronic (water) systems are especially compact, and the heat exchanger, expansion tank, and controls may be mounted on a wall. Some systems have thermostatically controlled electric heating components in the hydronic baseboard units, a type of installation which eliminates the central heating unit. Such a system may be a single-loop installation for circulating water by a pump, or it may be composed of individual sealed units filled with antifreeze solution.

The sealed units depend on gravity flow of the solution in the unit. Each unit may have a thermostat, or several units may be controlled from a wall thermostat. An advantage of these types of systems is that the heating capacity can be increased easily if the house is enlarged.

Steam Heating Systems

Steam heating systems are not used as much as forced hot water or warm air systems. For one thing, they are less responsive to rapid changes in heat demand. One-pipe steam heating systems cost about as much to install as one-pipe hot water systems. Two-pipe systems are more expensive.

This system uses steam to carry the heat from the furnace to the rest of the house. The steam travels from the furnace, expands, and rises through pipes into radiators. A special valve in room radiators vents the cool air left in them to allow steam to enter. Once it does, the valve shuts and traps the steam. The radiator then does what its name says: It "radiates" heat into the room.

Later, as the steam cools down, the moisture is released and condenses into water so it can make its journey back to the boiler. After you have this system tuned up by a professional, you can perform a much-needed ritual: drain a bucket of water from the system. This is needed because as steam, water, and air flow through the system, it creates sediment on the bottom of the pipes that has to be removed occasionally.

Before draining any water, though, check the sight glass to make sure there is water in the boiler. This is usually attached to the outside of the unit. Your guide as to how much water you should remove will be the halfway mark on the sight guide. If the level drops below the halfway mark, it's time to add more water.

When you have finished draining water, discard it and make sure the plug is back in its original position so that more water can't escape. If even this isn't a job you'd like to do, call a plumber and have him or her do it.

As noted above, steam heating systems are not used much any more and are most frequently found in older apartment houses.

Preventing Water Hammer   *EASY* **1–2 hours**

A common problem associated with a steam heating system is noise coming from the pipes. In fact, it has been the subject of more than one sitcom or movie (particularly in the Woody Allen and Neil Simon genre), in which tenants lament their living conditions that include those "old, loud pipes."

Water hammer, as plumbers call it, happens when cool water gets trapped in radiators and pipes and meets the steam that is rising in them. When this happens it creates a vacuum and the water naturally rushes to fill it, slamming into the pipes as it does.

The best way to prevent water hammer is to ask your plumber if the return pipes are inclined toward the boiler. If they are, you should have no problem. If not, ask what can be done. The other thing a homeowner can do is to open radiator valves fully. This is because when a valve is open halfway, it will allow steam to enter, but at the same time it will also trap the condensed water, leading to water hammer.

Bleeding a Radiator   *EASY* **1–2 hours**

Something that has to be done occasionally in this kind of a heating system is known as bleeding a radiator. It's not a difficult job. *Bleeding* refers to bleeding air from the system. Occasionally, trapped air may prevent a hot water radiator from filling up completely. As a result, the radiator will never fill completely—and will never fully heat the room. When this happens, it's a pretty simple procedure to correct the problem.

Place a pan or shallow bucket under the radiator bleed valve and open it with a radiator key. (A radiator key is available at plumbing supply stores, hardware stores, or home centers, generally for less than a dollar.) Keep the valve open until all the air escapes and only water flows out. Then close the valve.

Steam radiators do not require bleeding because trapped air doesn't actually stay trapped. Instead, it is forced out of a vent about halfway down the side. Some of the problems with these vents is that they get painted over. When this happens, the vent can't do what it was designed to do—vent air—and the system is not as efficient as it could be. If you can, clear out the opening of the vent with a wire hanger. If you can't do that, replacing these kinds of vents costs about $16–$20 per radiator.

Forced Hot Air Heating Systems

In a forced hot air system, the furnace, generally gas- or oil-fired, heats up air. The air is then transmitted, by a blower, to supply ducts and registers (vents) in rooms. Usually, the warm air is filtered by inexpensive, washable filters or by an electronic air cleaner. There is also some sort of cold air return "inlet" that draws cooled air in the room back down to the furnace for heating. A bonus with this type of system is that air conditioning can be easily added to it.

Normally, warm-air registers are located under windows in outside walls, but they may also be located in the interior walls. They can also be used to heat bathrooms (see Fig. 5.2).

In addition to keeping the filters clean, there is another job you can do to keep your system running properly. This involves maintaining the room where the hot air emerges. It may seem obvious, but it is important to keep furniture or other objects clear of the register, and to wipe them down occasionally with a moist disposable towel to prevent soot or other dirt from collecting on them.

Lastly, one of the drawbacks of this type of system is occasional complaints by homeowners about the dryness of the warm air being pushed into rooms. To solve this problem, mechanics sometimes add humidifying equipment to boilers. This adds moisture to the air and lets people breath a little easier (see Fig. 5.3).

FIGURE 5.2

Forced-air registers are mounted close to the floor, because warm air rises.

FIGURE 5.3

Humidifying chambers add moisture to the heated air inside houses.

WANT TO SAVE MONEY ON YOUR HEATING BILLS?

Stay away from electric heating—unless it's absolutely necessary. Electric heaters are a quick source of heat and easy to use, but they draw a lot of electricity and, over time, will end up costing you a lot more than other sources of heat.

Electric Heating Systems

The most common electric heating system utilizes the resistance principle. Heating elements, made of a special alloy, are heated by electricity passing through them. The systems comes in a variety of forms, including baseboard heaters. Other forms include portable units that plug into a wall outlet.

Safety precautions should be taken with portable heaters. It is widely known that these often cause unnecessary fires because of how they are used. They may be left on at night while people sleep, or used next to combustible materials such as drapes, furniture, clothing, or towels. In a word: Don't.

In addition to taking these precautions, it is important to inspect the unit itself. When you use it for the first time in the cooler weather, inspect the cord. Make sure there are no gaps in the plastic insulation and that the plug is intact.

Let the unit heat up and then feel the cord. It should be cold. If it's hot to the touch, replace it immediately. Believe it or not, let an electrician replace the cord or replace the unit. You can't use any old replacement cord you have laying around. It must be rated for heaters. This is specifically rated for this purpose.

Another maintenance tip: never, under any circumstances, use an extension cord with a portable electric heater. This is because you will be presenting a fire hazard and/or a shock hazard. As always, be careful with electric heaters around any water source.

Wood and Coal Stoves

An important part of maintaining a wood- or coal-burning stove is a decision that has to be made in the beginning: The stove should stand on a noncombustible floor such as bricks that extends beyond the stove on all sides (see Fig. 5.4). It should also be positioned away from combustible walls. Also, be sure to follow manufacturer's directions that come with the stove regarding installation and use.

Still another thing to consider is how to use the stove and what to burn in it. Do not burn trash or use any kind of liquid propellant in the stove. Even with wood fires, creosote buildup is a common problem and could, if enough builds up on the walls, start a chimney fire. Regular maintenance includes brushing out the inside of the flue and vacuuming out the stove itself. There are fire extinguishers made specifically for chimney fires, and one should be within reach at all times.

Kerosene Heaters

Although many fire codes forbid the use of kerosene heaters in your home, they are still being used. Please check with your local fire department before using one.

If you do get the go ahead to use one, use only white kerosene as fuel. This is highly refined fuel designed specifically for kerosene heaters. Only this fuel will do. Do not, under any circumstances, substitute this fuel with any other. It is called K1 or 1-K.

Use the kerosene heater fuel only according to the manufacturer's recommendations and always store it outdoors in sealed metal containers. It is important to make sure the room in which you use the heater is well ventilated. Although the purpose of the heater is to heat the room, sealing all the windows for that purpose only increases the potency of the vapors produced. Instead, open a small window a crack.

FIGURE 5.4

A wood- or coal-burning stove is a good source of heat, and adds charm to a room.

Lastly, use common sense when operating the unit. Keep it at least 3 feet from any combustible material such as blankets, pillows, clothing, or curtains.

Water Heaters

Basically, a water heater consists of a storage tank and a means of heating the water in it (see Fig. 5.5). In operation, water comes in at the top of the tank through a dip tube and is routed to the bottom, where it mixes with already heated water. This process allows it to mix gradually rather than rapidly, which would bring down the temperature of the water too quickly.

A thermostat on the tank keeps the water at a certain temperature. The water enters the hot water supply line through an opening at the top of the tank. There is also a magnesium anode rod in the tank whose purpose is to retard corrosion (by attracting it), thereby keeping other parts of the tank relatively corrosion-free.

At the bottom of the tank is a spigot for draining off water and any scale or soil buildup. For safety, a hot water heater should be equipped with a temperature/pressure relief valve; if the water temperature gets too high, this will bleed off excess pressure. The newest water heaters also have an ECO (energy cut-off) device that shuts off the fuel supply—

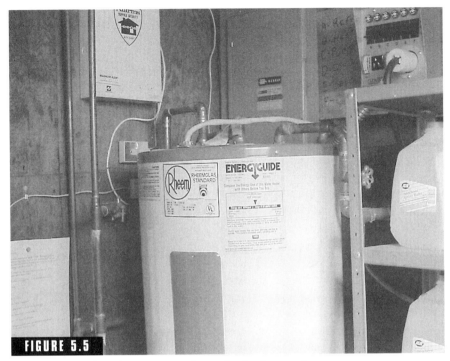

FIGURE 5.5

If you like long, hot showers, a new hot water heater may be your answer.

and therefore the fire—if the water temperature gets above 200°F. The tank itself is insulated with fiberglass or some other material.

Water heaters are commonly fueled by natural gas, liquefied petroleum gas, electricity, or oil. Let us take a look at each.

Natural Gas Water Heaters

A natural gas water heater has a flue area running through it or around it. A gas flame burns below the tank to heat the water, and the flue is vented to the outdoors.

When the thermostat calls for heat, the pilot flame ignites the burner and it runs until the water reaches the proper temperature. A safety feature of this type of heater is that if the pilot flame goes out, all gas shuts down. Without this feature (some older heaters do not have it), the gas could escape through the house.

Liquefied Petroleum Gas (LPG) Water Heaters

The LPG water heater operates essentially the same way as the natural gas heater, except that fuel and heating orifices are smaller because the gas is much more concentrated. Fuel is stored as a liquid but vaporizes to burn. This type of heater has long been equipped with a 100 percent shutoff valve.

Any gas heater should have a Blue Star certificate, which certifies that the manufacturer has made it according to recognized safety standards.

Electric Hot Water Heaters

In an electric hot water heater, the tank is heated by an insulated heating element immersed in the water. It, too, has a thermostat that calls for heat and shuts off when the water is the proper temperature. Electric heaters may also have two elements controlled by individual thermostats.

For adequate hot water, an electric heater should be wired to a 240-volt electrical service. Some electric heaters operate on 120-volt service, but they do not give much hot water. An electric heater does not require a flue, and it is normally cheaper to buy than other types. However, as electrical costs have risen markedly in recent years, careful consideration to operating cost should be given before purchasing one.

Oil-Fired Hot Water Heaters

An oil-fired hot water heater uses a pressure-fire burner like the one on a home heating oil burner. The older types use a pot-type burner. There are rather complicated controls to start and stop the fire safely.

Choosing a Water Heater

There are a number of things to look for when shopping for a water heater. Usually the best kinds are glass-lined. This keeps the water from eating into the sides of the tank. However, their usefulness really depends on the kind of water used, and is something that should be checked out with a dealer.

Another criterion of quality is the willingness of the manufacturer to stand behind the heater. Top-quality ones are guaranteed for 10 years. Electric and gas heaters come in a variety of shapes, including ones that can fit under a counter if space is at a premium. However, most units are stand-alone ones that will be installed near the boiler or on the first floor of your house.

Home water heaters are available in sizes from 10- to 80-gallon capacities. However, mere size is not the crucial factor. What engineers call the *recovery rate* is far more important. A nontechnical definition of this term is the ability of the heater to deliver water with the tap left wide open. Another way of putting it is to say that the recovery rate is how many gallons of water a heater will raise 100°F in temperature in an hour. For example, if cold water enters the heater at 50°F and is heated to 150°F at the rate of 60 gallons per hour, the heater's recovery rate is 60 gallons per hour. Make certain when checking the recovery rate, however, that you are not comparing apples with oranges: Some manufacturers list a 60°F rather than a 100°F recovery rate.

Now, the actual amount of water that can be drawn from a heater in an hour equals the recovery rate plus about 70 percent of its storage capacity. When more than 70 percent of the stored water is drawn, cold water mixing with it lowers the temperature.

Installing a Water Heater

There are many ways to install a water heater; the method of installation depends to a large degree on local codes (see Fig. 5.6). If possible, both the hot and cold water lines and the gas piping, if any, should be put in with corrugated brass connectors. These are 1–1½ feet long, come with appropriate connectors, and are very easy to handle. Gas used for heat should shut off when the water is the proper temperature. Electric heaters may also have two elements controlled by individual thermostats.

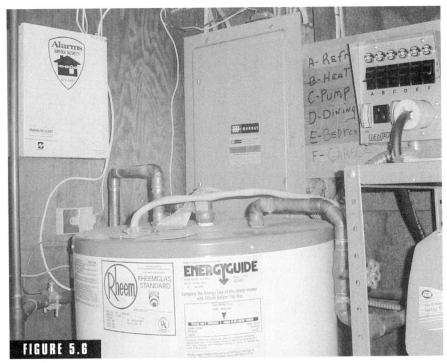

FIGURE 5.6

The method of installing a hot water heater is important. It is also a job for a licensed plumber.

Installing a water heater is definitely a job for a licensed plumber. Make sure the plumber is licensed and insured. Finally, be sure and let him know what your water heating needs are; he can advise you about the water heater you should get.

Water Heater Maintenance

EASY **1–2 hours**

The first rule for proper maintenance of a water heater is to set the temperature of the water properly. The manufacturer will recommend a figure, but an average temperature range for a home water heating unit is from 160 to 180°F. Be sure this is set accurately. Too high a setting will result in your paying for hot water that you do not need and will shorten the life of the tank.

Once a month, the heater should be drained by turning the petcock valve at the bottom of the tank. Draining draws off sediment in the tank and prevents buildup inside, which can interfere with the heater's functioning. It is also a good idea to lift the lever on the temperature and pressure valve to bleed off some water to check for safe operation.

If a heater is more than three years old, the magnesium anode rod in it should be checked. If it has seen better days (i.e., if it is covered with scale), get a new one. The same goes for an electric heater. Its element should be periodically unscrewed and checked visually for scale. Scaling usually occurs in hard-water areas.

An oil heater should be cleaned and adjusted when it is dirty or every few years. When a fired heater is checked, the flue should be examined for efficiency. This examination can be made by holding a lighted match in the draft diverter or draft regulator and seeing if the flame is drawn by suction.

Troubleshooting Your Water Heater

Though a water heater is a relatively stable appliance, some problems may develop. Following are symptoms of problems and possible solutions.

- If the heater makes a "cooking" sound, scale may have drifted down and built up a crust on the bottom of the tank. Droplets of water get under this crust and make the sound when they flash into steam. It is nothing to be concerned about.

- If a faucet is turned on and there is a long wait for water, the problem usually is in the heating system and can be cured with a circulating hot water system. Though originally expensive, it can be worth the expenditure in the long run. If there never seems to be enough hot water, it could be that the heater is too small, the thermostat is at too low a setting, the thermostat is defective, or the pipes are too small or improperly installed. The simplest solution here is to set the thermostat higher and see how it works.

■ If the water looks rusty, it usually means that mud or silt has gotten into the tank and colored the water. (The tank is not rusting.) This quite commonly occurs when a city periodically turns on the hydrants in a particular area. The way to get rid of this is to turn the heat off and try draining the tank.

■ If there is a sizzling noise when the heater is on, it could mean that the tank is leaking or a nearby pipe is. If the tank is leaking, you can try to repair it: or simply shop for a new heater.

■ If the T and P relief valve keeps popping, there may be a valve somewhere in the plumbing that is defective and is allowing excess pressure to build up when the heated water is expanded. To correct this problem, you can install an expansion chamber. Another possible cause is too high a temperature setting or a bad relief valve. For a temporary cure, lower the thermostat.

Faucets and Valves

Faucets and globe valves, the type of shutoff valves commonly used in home water systems, are similar in construction, and repair instructions given apply to both. Faucets or valves may differ somewhat in general design because both come in a wide variety of styles. Some have handles that simply turn the water off or on (Fig 5.7).

Mixing faucets, which are found on sinks, laundry trays, and bathtubs, are actually two separate units with a common spout. Each unit is repaired independently (see Fig. 5.7).

If a faucet drips when closed or vibrates ("sings" or "flutters") when opened, the trouble is usually the washer at the lower end of the spindle. Water, which is constantly flowing up under pressure, is not completely sealed off. A little gets by and causes the drip. If it leaks around the spindle when the faucet is opened, new packing is needed.

Replacing Washers   *FAIRLY EASY* **2–5 hours**

Shut off the water at the shutoff valve nearest the particular faucet. Next, disassemble the faucet—the handle, packing nut, packing, and spindle, in that order. You may have to set the handle back on the spindle and use it to unscrew and remove the spindle.

Remove the screw and worn washer from the spindle. Scrape all the worn washer parts from the cup and install a new washer of the proper size. Examine the seat on the faucet body. If it is nicked or

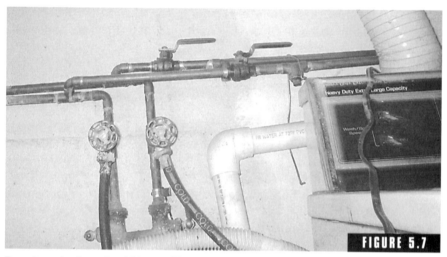

FIGURE 5.7

Faucets and valves should be readily accessible.

rough, reface it with a seat dressing tool. Hold the tool vertically when refacing the seat (instructions come with the unit).

If refacing fails, you may be able to unscrew the faucet seat with an Allen wrench and replace it with one of the same size. Reassemble the faucet. Handles of mixing faucets should be in matched positions. If this is something you aren't comfortable with, have your plumber do it—it's what he gets paid for.

Replacing Valves
FAIRLY EASY **2–5 hours**

After extended use and several repairs, some valves will no longer give tight shutoff and must be replaced. When replacement becomes necessary, it may be advisable to upgrade the quality with equipment having better flow characteristics and longer-life design and materials.

In some cases, ball valves will deliver more water than globe valves. Some globe valves deliver more flow than others for identical pipe sizes. Y-pattern globe valves, in straight runs of pipe, have better flow characteristics than straight stop valves. You can verify this by visiting a plumbing supply house, or you can ask questions at the plumbing department of your local home center.

Frostproof Hydrants

Frostproof hydrants are basically faucets, although they may look somewhat different in design from ordinary faucets. Two important features of a frostproof hydrant are that the valve is installed under ground—below the frost line—to prevent freezing, and that the valve is designed to drain the water from the hydrant when the valve is closed.

Frostproof hydrants work as follows: When the handle is raised, the piston rises, opening the valve. Water flows from the supply pipe into the cylinder, up through the riser, and out the spout. When the handle is pushed down, the piston goes down, closing the valve and stopping the flow of water.

Water left in the hydrant flows out the drain tube into a small gravel-filled dry well or drain pit. As with ordinary faucets, leakage will probably be the most common trouble encountered. Worn packing, gaskets, and washers can all cause leakage. If this happens, disassemble the hydrant as necessary to replace or repair these and other parts. Again, if this job is beyond your scope of skills or you would rather watch the ball game, hire a plumber.

Frostproof yard hydrants that have buried drains can be health hazards. The vacuum created by water flowing from the hydrant may draw in contaminated water standing above the hydrant drain level. Such hydrants should be used only where positive drainage can be provided. For this reason, frostproof wall hydrants are the preferred type.

Maintaining Air Conditioners   EASY 1–2 hours

Inspecting and maintaining an air conditioner is not a hard job but is one that must be done. Start by unplugging the unit. Next, remove the unit from its protective sleeve and remove the front grill and filter.

Cleaning the grill and, in particular, the filter, will ensure that the unit runs efficiently and maintains the right amount of air circulation. If the filter is simply dirty but intact, wash it gently with soap and water. If it is in pretty bad shape (torn, with holes or runs), replace it with a new one. Make sure you get the exact same type. If you are not sure which one to get, take the old one with you. You may want to take a measurement of your unit with you to the home center so you can be sure you get the right size.

Vacuum the inside and all the crevices you can find. Next, wipe the unit down with a rag and get off all the dirt that you can see. Next, use a paintbrush dipped in warm, soapy water to clean the coils, fan blades, and any other surface that needs it.

Rinse the unit down with a fine spray. You don't want to get loads of water inside the unit or allow the water to pool anywhere. After it is totally dry, lubricate the fan motor with a few drops of motor oil.

Lastly, use a fin comb (available at most hardware stores) to straighten out the condenser fans. After a final look for anything missed, slide the unit back into its sleeve and back to its original position, and plug it in. Job well done.

Floors

Floors are the most abused and often the most neglected parts of the house. Think about it: we walk over them, spill things on them, drop things on them, and then cover them with carpet or furniture. Depending on what kind of flooring you have, and what you use it for, some kind of maintenance will be required.

Hardwood Floors

Hardwood floors are a thing of beauty and add warmth and texture to rooms (see Fig. 6.1). In fact, most realtors list them as amenities in their ads, knowing they are sought after among homebuyers. As charming as they are, they do require some kind of maintenance in order to retain their original appearance.

Assuming your hardwood floor is in good shape, frequent vacuuming is required. Dust particles in the air land on it and accumulate, and believe it or not, in time can act as an abrasive and scratch your floor. Frequent dusting is also essential.

Use a dry mop (of wool or synthetic fibers) to pick up dirt and grit before feet walking on the floor embed it into the cracks. These materials (wool dry mops and synthetic fibers) actually create a static charge that attracts dust particles. What a concept—you are sweeping and vacuuming at the same time!

If the floor has a polyurethane finish, use a damp mop for general cleaning and mopping up spills.

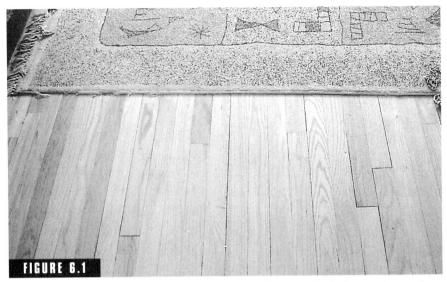

FIGURE 6.1

Hardwood floors add warmth and charm to homes. They are relatively easy to care for.

Still Not Clean?

DIFFICULT **5–7 hours**

Floors that don't come clean probably have one of two different problems. One is that there is no protective finish at all on the floor, and the wood is stained. The other is that the protective coating, either polyurethane, wax, varnish, or Swedish wax, has not been embedded into the floor long enough and remains kind of sticky.

How do you test for either one? Simple. Pick a small area that's not noticeable and drop a few drops of water on it. If it soaks into the wood, you have no protective coating. If it slowly turns white, there is some wax on the wood. If the drops bead up, the floor has a coating of polyurethane or varnish on it.

If the wood is stained badly enough, it may be time to rent a commercial wood floor cleaner to strip away wax and/or oil finishes. If you go this route, ask your dealer or rental center what pads and products to use. They can advise you. Sometimes, this is all you have to do. After stripping away the dirty coating, it may just be a matter of applying a new coating of the same material. Again, if you are unsure what to use or how to go about it, ask your floor dealer.

If the floor is too dirty, you may have to have a professional floor sander remove the topcoat entirely and refinish it. This also may be an option if you have a very large area to do, or you have several levels in a house.

Damaged beyond Repair

EASY **1–2 hours**

Pieces of flooring that are damaged beyond repair (rotten, broken, or warped) should be removed and replaced immediately to avoid potential injury and further damage. This means you have to cut out the damaged section (carefully, to avoid further damage) and nail or glue down replacement boards.

It is important to pay attention to how the damaged pieces come out and to inspect the subflooring (the material under the floor). This is because you will attach the new pieces to this, and it should be in good condition to support the floor you'll see and walk on.

Once you have the new pieces in, the remaining work is often the most important: filling in cracks with wood putty, then sanding and refinishing the surface so it matches the rest of the floor. If you think this is too daunting, it probably is. Hire a wood floor specialist who will guarantee the work.

Squeaky Floors

EASY **1–2 hours**

Squeaky floors are caused by one or more loose floorboards, usually just one. When you step on the board, it bends more than it should and rubs against adjacent boards. The rubbing produces the squeak. Or one board is bowed (warped).

The answer is to nail the board down tightly so it can't move. You can use a $2^{1}/_{2}$-inch finishing nail or, for an even tighter job, a special nail called a *spiral-fluted flooring nail*. This has a surface that is partially fluted, or grooved, and has greater holding power. If it wants out, it has to twist itself out.

First press on the various boards to find out which one is squeaking. When you discover it, drive a nail in at the approximate point

HOW TO SAVE MONEY ON HARDWOOD FLOORING

Homeowners can save money on hardwood flooring by cutting out the middleman and shopping direct from the mill. Unlike some retailers, mills have the flexibility to sell a few or a lot of pieces. There's another benefit for homeowners: Many retailers sell pieces from 10 inches to 7 feet long, with the average piece being 3.25 feet long and $3/_4$ inch thick. Mills can sell wood with pieces averaging 7.5 feet long and $13/_{16}$ inch thick. The boards are nearly twice as long and thicker. This means fewer seams in the finished floor and more rigidity and savings.

where you figure it's bending. (If you don't get it exactly, no sweat.) For greater holding power, drive the nail in at about a 20-degree angle.

Step on the board. Still squeaks? Okay, drive another nail in a little way (2 inches) from the other, also angling it. Test for squeaking again. *Still* squeak? If so, drive another nail, also angled, about 2 inches from the first nail you drove in.

With the nails in, take a nail set (a tool that looks like an extra thick nail with a small, blunt end) and drive the heads of the nails a little bit below the surface. Then fill the space with wood putty and sand smooth. This will hide the nail heads. Of course, if you have a rug or other covering on the floor, this won't be necessary.

(Incidentally, when using the hammer, hold it down near the end and, every time you hit the nail, flip your wrist as if you were cracking a whip. Your arm has very little to do with the force you can apply to the nail. I learned how to hold a hammer the hard way, years ago when I was doing construction work. The job foreman, a laconic Southerner, observed me holding a hammer several inches from the end. He asked me for the hammer, drew a rule mark on it a couple of inches from the end, and asked for my saw. As he was poised to cut off the end of the hammer I said, "Wait, why are you doing that?" "Shoot, boy," he answered, "you don't need this last 2 inches. You held the hammer up here." Then everybody roared. Except me. I reddened.)

There's another way you might be able to solve this problem. You may be able to silence the squeak without nails. Just squirt some powdered graphite between the boards. When the board rubs, the lubrication prevents it from making noise.

Shallow Scratches   EASY 1–2 hours

The best way to repair shallow scratches is to fill the scratch with material that matches the surrounding wood. Wood putty works well. It comes in several colors and is easily workable. Using a small putty knife, work it into the scratch and scrape off any extra material. When it dries, sand it smooth.

If you are concerned about matching the color of the wood putty to your floor, take a color picture of the floor and bring it to a home center or a hardware store. Another possibility is to bring a sample piece of the floor to the store. There you can match up the colors.

Another way to fix scratches is to buff them away with steel wool or sandpaper. The idea here is to use some old-fashioned elbow grease. If the area is small, simply restrict your sanding to the area and rub the wood in the direction of the grain in the wood. This will prevent scratches where you don't want them.

If your floor has a polyurethane finish, try a scouring pad (highly abrasive) dipped in mineral spirits. Rub the area with the scratch until you see it disappear. Try and gently feather the sanding away from the scratch. Stop when you see the scratch disappear.

Deep Scratches   *EASY* **1–2 hours**

Filling, as with shallow scratches, is also a good method for deep ones. Various fillers can be used. For a fast job, buy Plastic Wood in the color of your floor (it dries in 15 minutes). Using a putty knife, work it into the scratch and scrape it flush. Let it dry, sand it smooth with fine sandpaper, then touch it up with whatever floor finish is already there.

If the scratch is especially deep, do the repair in two stages—fill the hole halfway, let it dry, then fill it the rest of the way. If you want a near-perfect match on the floor, make your own filler. Obtain a piece of wood that matches your floor wood. Sand or saw it to create sawdust, then mix the sawdust with white glue and work it into a thick paste. Fill the scratch, let it dry, sand it, and touch it up.

Squeaky Stairs   *EASY* **1–2 hours**

Stairs squeak because the tread, the part you step on, is loose, and when it is pressed down it rubs against the board called the riser, which supports it. The repair is the same, essentially, as for a loose floor board. Have an adult stand on the loose tread to bring it into close contact with the riser. Drive nails through the tread into the riser. You can tell that the nail is going into the riser if you encounter resistance. If the nail suddenly gets easy to drive, you know you've missed it.

Drive the nails even with the tread surface. To hide the holes, tap the nails a little ($1/16$ inch) below the surface, using a nail set. Then fill the little holes with wood putty the color of the tread wood. If the tread is covered by carpeting, you needn't drive the nails below the surface. In fact, if appearance isn't important, you can completely forget this step (no pun intended).

Tile Floors

Damaged Ceramic Tile   *DIFFICULT* **5–7 hours**

Replacing damaged ceramic tiles on floors starts with an inspection and a decision. Start by inspecting what is underneath the tiles: this will affect your decision about how to fix it. Tiles on floors are installed in one of two ways. One way is with an adhesive attached to a subfloor (usually of wood); the other is what is known as a "mud job," placing the tiles in concrete.

Regardless of what type of installation you have, taking out the damaged tile is done the same way. Use a cold chisel and a hammer to chip away at the material under a part of the tile, until you have created a space to insert the chisel blade. Do this and pry the whole tile up. It will usually come up without a problem.

Clean the area by removing the old adhesive with a putty knife or something stronger—say a cold chisel. Buy new adhesive (or new cement in the event of a mud job—check with your flooring supplier about what kind to use and how to do it).

Armstrong makes a good epoxy adhesive. A 1-gallon bucket covers about 350 square feet and sells for about $12. Spread it around the edges and in the middle of the replacement tile and set it in place. Push it in so it's level with the surrounding tiles and until it has an equal amount of space around its edges.

If you don't want to use epoxy, you can just mix up some plaster of Paris and set the tile in this. When the adhesive or plaster of Paris is dry, use your finger to fill in around the tile with a ready-mixed grout (available in cans for about $5 at hardware stores). Smooth it out with your finger so it (the grout) is shaped like the grout between the other tiles. Finally, take a wet sponge and clean off all grout smeared on the tiles.

The grout needed is usually white. If you need it colored, get the "universal" kind that can be tinted with colors. These are available in small tubes at paint stores and home centers.

Worn Resilient Tile
DIFFICULT **5–7 hours**

Resilient tile gets its name from the fact that it has some "give"—it depresses when you step on it. If a tile gets badly worn, cracked, or chipped, you should replace it. There are six or seven different kinds, and repair methods vary according to the type being replaced. If you don't know what kind you have, you can try several methods until one works.

Your first job, of course, is to remove the bad tile. If you have vinyl asbestos or asphalt tile, you can do this pretty easily with heat. First, put a damp rag on the tile, then place an iron, at its hottest setting, on the rag. As you apply heat, pry up the tile at the edges with a putty knife. Usually the tile will curl up and can be removed easily.

Apply the new tile. The existing adhesive may still be good. All you need to do is lay the new tile in place and roll it on securely with a rolling pin. If you can't use the old adhesive, use epoxy.

Vinyl and rubber tiles are removed without heat. Using a curved linoleum knife, a single-edge razor blade, or a utility knife, cut deeply around the edge of the tile, in the seams between it and adjacent tiles.

Using a chisel (a cold chisel is good) and a hammer, start removing the damaged tile. Take care not to damage the edges of adjacent tiles. If necessary, you can chop into the center of the tile and work toward the edges. When you have all the pieces out, take off any adhesive remaining on the floor, and high spots of any sort. Also, fill any holes with wood putty. The goal is to get a level surface so the new tile will be level with surrounding tiles.

If you don't have a spare replacement tile around—and you probably don't—you may have a problem. You may not be able to get a matching replacement tile, because the existing ones may have become discolored. If this is the case, consider taking up four or five tiles in a row, or four tiles in adjacent rows, and installing tiles of a contrasting color as an accent touch. It may be more work, but it will solve the color-matching problem. This works well in front of a kitchen sink or in the middle of a room.

Cleaning Tile Floors

RESILIENT FLOORING

- *Acids.* Wash with plain water, rub gently with steel wool, rinse with water, dry, wax.

- *Ink.* For washable inks: if the ink is still wet, blot as much as possible with a dry rag, flush with water, and dry; if the ink has dried, wash and dry. For permanent inks: if wet, blot as much as possible with a dry rag, flush with water, dry; if dried, use fine steel wool with water or dry powder cleanser that has no bleach in it, wipe clean, wax.

- *Pet stains.* Sponge with lukewarm water, mop up with a soft cloth.

- *Rust.* Wash with plain water and cleanser with no chlorine or bleach, dry.

- *Paint, chewing gum, varnish, shellac.* Scrape up as much staining material as possible with a knife; then use fine steel wool, wash with water, dry, wax.

- *Shoe polish, tar, oil, grease, heel marks.* Rub with steel wool and soap, rinse, dry, and wax.

VINYL AND VINYL ASBESTOS TILES

- *Alkali, lye, drain cleaner.* Wash with diluted solution of water and vinegar. Rinse and dry.

- *Shoe polish, tar, oil, grease, heel marks.* Clean with floor-mark remover pad (available at supermarkets) or rub with fine steel wool dipped in mild detergent. Rinse with warm water, then dry.

- *Cigarette burns, dye, mildew, blood, grass, or rust stains.* Rub with fine steel wool dipped in mild detergent. Rinse with water.

- *Nail polish, paint, lacquer, chewing gum, varnish, shellac.* Scrape up as much of the staining material as possible with a putty knife. Rub with fine steel wool dipped in mild detergent. Rinse.

- *Coffee, alcohol, fruit juice, ink.* Try washing with mild detergent. If this doesn't work, rub with fine steel wool dipped in mild detergent. Rinse.

- *Burn marks.* Scrape away the charred portion with a single-edge razor blade. Clean with cotton swab soaked in naphtha (available at paint stores). Follow method for scratches.

- *Paint.* If wet, wipe up immediately with a rag dipped in solvent you are using (water or mineral spirits). Wipe dry. If the paint is dry, scrape off as much as you can with a putty knife, and remove the rest with fine-grade steel wool dipped in solvent. Wipe dry and touch up.

- *Milk, fruit, ink.* It is important when any substance spills on the floor to wipe it up immediately. To remove the stain that remains (or any type of dry stain), rub it off with an abrasive. For this, get some pumice (at paint stores), an inexpensive gray powder that feels smooth to the touch but has remarkable abrasive power. Put the pumice in one saucer and water in another. Fold a small piece of felt or flannel into a small pad. Dip it in water, then pumice, and rub the stain. Wipe clean and check. Repeat procedure until stain is gone.

Rug and Carpet Care
EASY **1–2 hours**

In general, vacuum rugs and carpets frequently to remove the loose soil, which otherwise can dig in and damage the fibers. Occasionally you can dry-clean your rugs and carpets. This will remove the accumulation of greasy film. To dry-clean, buy a commercial product.

SAVE ON CARPET AND LINOLEUM REMNANTS

A good way to save on linoleum and carpet is to watch for "remnants sales" at home improvement centers and carpet stores. These kinds of flooring come in giant rolls, and a remnant is the end of the roll—usually a section that is 20 square yards or less. That means a section of about 12 × 15 feet is reduced in price as much as 25 percent for a limited time, so the dealer can get rid of it. Remnants are great for small sections of bedrooms, staircases, hallways, or closets.

These are made from absorbent powders or fine sawdust saturated with fat solvents. As they are brushed into the pile, they dissolve and absorb the greasy soil, which is carried away with the powder as you vacuum. (An upright vacuum gives the best results.) The product you select should be recommended for the carpet fibers you intend to clean; check the label. Some of these cleaners are combustible, and all of them should be used only in well-ventilated rooms.

For deep cleaning, you can shampoo a rug with a commercial shampoo machine and a rented shampooer or, if the area is not too large, with a sponge mop or brush.

Carpet Spots and Stains   *EASY* **1–2 hours**

High on the alarm list of household traumas is a stained carpet. However, the spot can usually be removed by the nonprofessional. If you don't know what the stain is from, gently blot on a nonflammable dry-cleaning fluid, working from the stain edges toward the center. If this works, dry the carpet quickly and thoroughly by blowing air on the wet area with a vacuum cleaner hose, hair dryer, or electric fan. If you can lift the carpet off the floor, this will help it dry faster.

If the dry cleaner doesn't remove the stain, use a clean cloth and blot on a carpet-cleaning detergent. Every now and then, blot up excess fluid with a dry rag. The wetter you get the carpet, the harder it is to dry. Dry the area again and check. If some stain still remains, use the dry cleaner or detergent again, whichever worked best the first time.

Spot Removal

Immediate treatment of spots is always most successful. If you can't dab up a stain with a wet and/or dry cloth, it might be wise to use a professional spot-removing product. There are products to choose from at your local home center. Read the labels carefully, and follow all directions. For specific types of stains, try the following.

- *Pet stain.* Sponge stain with lukewarm water, then blot up as much water as possible with a soft cloth. Pat on detergent carpet cleaner, let stand for 15 minutes. Blot up remaining solution, then sponge the area with a cloth dipped in lukewarm water. Air-blow to dry. If the stain doesn't come off, the rug must be re-dyed, or it might be possible to get it spot-dyed. Replacement is the last option.

- *Nail polish.* If the polish is wet, apply a few drops of nail polish remover. Let this mix with the polish, then blot it up with a dry rag. Repeat as needed, air-blow dry. If the polish is dry, apply a few drops of remover. Wait 5 minutes or so until the polish softens. Then gently scrape off as much as you can with a dull spoon. Apply fresh remover, blot. Repeat as needed, air-blow dry.

- *Cigarette burns.* Cut off the charred ends, then blot on carpet cleaning detergent. If necessary, you can get the bad spot rewoven or retufted.

- *Alcohol, wine, beer.* Apply a solution of a tablespoon of ammonia and a half-cup water to the spill, in small amounts. Blot frequently until stain is no longer transferred to the blotter. Follow with a solution of one-third cup white vinegar and two-thirds cup of water. Dab on small amounts, blotting frequently until the stain is gone. Remove as much moisture as possible. Then place a half-inch layer of absorbent material on the dampened area, weigh it down, and let it dry about 6 hours.

- *Unknown.* Do you have a mystery stain? Working from the stain edges to the center, gently blot on a nonflammable dry-cleaning fluid. Dry the carpet quickly by blowing air on it with a machine such as a hair dryer. Lifting the carpet helps drying. Repeat the removal procedure as needed. If cleaning fluid doesn't work, blot on carpet cleaning detergent, occasionally blotting up excess detergent with a dry rag. Repeat as needed.

Thresholds

Metal strips called Vinderbar are one kind of product used to hold down the edges of carpets between rooms in houses. Silver and gold are popular colors, and they are held down with spiral style nails (so they sit flat—the nails have to twist to come out).

These are particularly popular between bedrooms and living rooms that are carpeted and between hardwood floor hallways and/or linoleum in kitchens. An important part of maintaining them is to be sure the edges don't curl up (they could catch socks or cut bare feet) and that no bounce develops in them—a sure sign the nails haven't done their job (Fig. 6-2).

Linoleum Floors

Once linoleum flooring is in need of repair, there's not much you can do with it. If it is installed as 1-foot squares, and you need to replace some of them because they are ripped, torn, or discolored, chances are you won't find others to match the old ones. This is because different batches of tiles (groups manufactured together) can sometimes appear

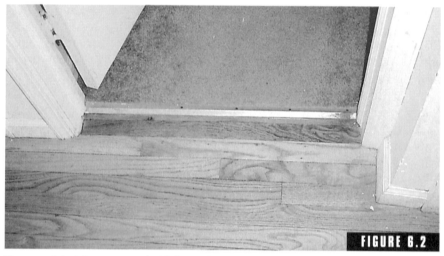

FIGURE 6.2

These metal strips serve to hold down the edge of carpeting and serves as a thrshold between two rooms.

FIGURE 6.3

Linoleum is a strong and long-lasting floor covering that is easy to clean and maintain.

a slightly different color. More often than not, though, the reason is that they are out of style. (Linoleum floors last a long time.) See Fig. 6.3.

If you have a whole sheet, and part of it is damaged, you'll most likely have to replace the whole sheet. If that's the case, tear up the old linoleum and remove all the old adhesive or old nails. Fill in any holes with wood putty, sand them smooth, and make sure the subfloor is free of oils, grease, or dirt. Make sure it is completely flat and smooth. Vacuum the surface to remove any unseen debris.

Install smooth luan over the subfloor. Use flat-head screws or flat-headed nails and make sure they don't protrude above the surface. Flash-patch any seams and sand them smooth if you have to, to make sure the surface is absolutely level. You are now ready to install the new linoleum. See your supplier for directions on this important job.

Once the new linoleum is installed, it is important to keep it clean. Linoleum can be cleaned with any mild detergent. Use a damp mop with a mild detergent for day-to-day cleaning. A tip for preserving a linoleum floor: Add baby oil to the mop water. It provides it with a sheen and helps keep the floor cleaner, longer.

Slate Floors

EASY **1–2 hours**

The rugged beauty of a slate floor is appealing to some people (see Fig. 6.4). I happen to love it. My basement has a slate floor, and taking care of it is really simple.

First, slate is a porous material, so it should be sealed so it's protected. Sealers work by penetrating the top surface of the stone, protecting it from dirt, grit, scratches, or anything else that spills on them.

Floor cleaning supply stores or home centers usually carry sealers that are designed specifically for stone floors. They can also answer your questions about how to apply sealer. Directions are usually on the product and should mention what you should use (a sponge mop or brush) to apply it.

FIGURE 6.4

Slate floors are rugged, natural, and fairly simple to clean and maintain.

Simply cleaning slate is another job. Slate floors can be washed with a solution of detergent and water. The key is to rinse it well. Strong cleaners are not recommended for these kinds of floors. Instead, you can use alkali cleaners (check the label of your product).

Mopping with a damp mop every week or so will also keep the floor clean. When you are finished, you can apply a water-based, self-polishing wax over a dry, clean floor that has been sealed. This will add a shine to the floor.

The extra work to maintain slate floors is worth it. The rugged beauty is worth preserving.

Walls and Doors

Doors in your house are in constant use, and walls are often assaulted. If you have many people living in your house, including children and pets, you know what I mean. Dirty walls, loose doorknobs, and cracked plaster are just some of the problems covered in this chapter.

Repairing Walls

Dirty Walls
EASY **1–2 hours**

In this day and age, walls can get very dirty, very quickly. To save yourself a good deal of elbow grease in washing them, start at the bottom of the wall and work up. If you wash from the top, dirty water can streak down, and it will be difficult to remove the streak marks. If you are washing plasterboard walls, don't use a lot of water. Plasterboard has a paper covering, and it could lift.

It's pretty simple to maintain the clean appearance of your walls. To wash an area, use a good-quality cellulose sponge and a solution of dish detergent (liquid soap) and water. Don't apply much pressure. Instead, let the sponge and soap and water do the cleaning. To finish, rinse the wall with clear water and a clean sponge.

Holes in Wallboard
FAIRLY EASY **2–5 hours**

Wallboard, also known as Sheetrock and plasterboard, is the most popular wall and ceiling material in new houses built within the last

30 years or so. When holes are made in it, there are several ways you can fix them. Figure 7.1 shows the materials you may need.

First, the traditional method: Obtain a small piece of plasterboard (at a building supply store or lumberyard), the same thickness as the existing material (bring a waste piece to show to your dealer). This is important, because the board is available in varying thicknesses, including $3/8$, $5/8$, $1/4$, and $1/2$ inch. Cut more material around the hole to form a hole in the shape of a rectangle (see Fig. 7.2). Cut a new piece (as a patch) to fit the rectangle, this time slanting the edges so they fit snugly into the edges of the rectangle in the wall. Install metal, serrated clips on each side of the hole, as shown in Fig. 7.3. Set the patch in place and, using drywall screws (ones designed for sheetrock), secure it to the clips (see Figs. 7.4). Be sure to use a screw on each side of the patch. Use mesh tape (with the sticky side) to cover the seams (see Fig. 7.5).

Mix up a batch of joint compound or spackle (available at hardware stores) and use a scraper or putty knife or spatula to smear compound on the seams, as if you were buttering bread (see Fig. 7.6).

This coat should also be very thin and as smooth as you can make it. When it dries, sand it smooth—gently (see Fig. 7.7). If it's bumpy, the patch will be noticeable.

FIGURE 7.1

All the supplies you may need to fix damaged Sheetrock walls in your house.

FIGURE 7.2

Start the wall repair by cutting out a rectangle.

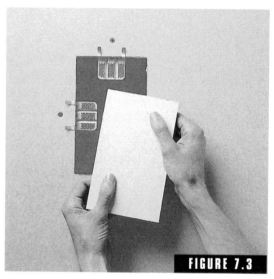

FIGURE 7.3

Install serrated metal clips.

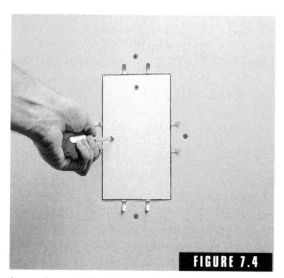

FIGURE 7.4

Screw the patch in place to the clips.

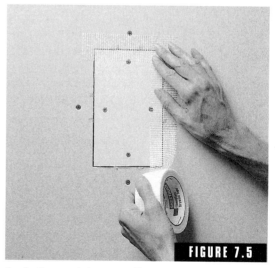

FIGURE 7.5

Apply the mesh tape on all seams.

If the wall is painted, first touch up the patch with a coat of the finish paint you are going to use, let it dry, then paint the entire wall. If you just paint the patch, it will stand out like a sore thumb, even if you use the same paint that was originally used.

Now, for the latest way to fix walls: The latest development in drywall repair is a kit available in hardware and home improvement centers.

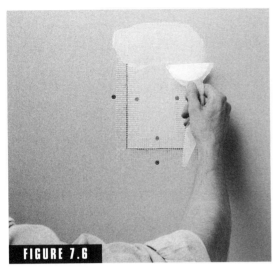

FIGURE 7.6

Spackle the edges with compound.

FIGURE 7.7

Sand it smooth on all sides.

It includes a mesh material and/or a perforated, thin metal sheet that is placed over the hole. They are available in square sheets 2 × 2 inches and 8 × 8 inches. One side has an adhesive so it sticks to the wall. Simply press the patch over the hole and spread compound over the patch. Let it dry and sand smooth.

The above repair is for holes that are, say, up to 6 or 7 inches wide. If you have larger holes than that, some home centers will sell you half a sheet or so—a 4 × 4 foot piece of wallboard for a reduced price, because they sometimes break. For this size hole, repeat the procedure described as the "traditional" method.

If you have an even bigger problem, it is better to take the whole panel down and replace it. If you do this, be careful to replace the board next to the existing one the correct way. The panels have long edges tapered on the face side to form a shallow recess to receive joint compound and tape. However, I think this is probably a bit too much for someone new to the plasterboard game. It might be smarter to hire a professional. There's an art to taping and spackling—the pro feathers the spackle and works it to remove air bubbles—for a beautiful finish that is ready to be primed or painted (see Fig. 7.8).

Holes in Plaster

EASY **1–2 hours**

Plaster is a popular material in apartments, especially older ones. Unlike wallboard, which is applied in solid sheets, plaster is applied wet with a trowel. If you don't know what you have, here's a simple, kind of primitive test you can conduct: Rap on a wall with your knuckles. Wallboard sounds hollow, plaster solid. Plaster commonly develops cracks and holes. The repair and maintenance techniques depend on what you are dealing with.

If a wall or ceiling has "hairline" cracks—they look like veins—the first step is to widen and deepen them so the repair filler used can get a better grip. Use a wallboard knife or a razor blade. Draw the sharp part of the blade along inside the crack, digging deeply as you go.

For filler, use plaster of Paris. A 5-pound bag (enough for all the rooms in the average house) costs about $6. Pour some plaster in an empty coffee can or similar container and add a little water. Using a scraper, mix it up. Gradually add more until the plaster is soft and workable without being soupy. To every coffee can full you mix, add a teaspoon of ordinary vinegar. This will triple the setting (hardening) time of the plaster, which ordinarily would be only about 10 minutes. This will let you work with that much longer.

FIGURE 7.8

The art of taping and spackling makes the difference in replacing boards and new construction.

Wet the crack(s) down by sponging water in with a soaking wet rag. Using a 3$\frac{1}{2}$-inch-wide scraper with a flexible blade (a good scraper costs around $5 in paint stores), force the plaster into the crack and smooth it out level with the surrounding wall.

Try to get the plaster perfectly smooth with the scraper. If you try to sandpaper it smooth later, you won't succeed. After smoothing with the scraper (try to use as few strokes as possible), draw a folded, soaking wet rag across it as a final smoothing process.

If you have a hole to repair that's less than 2 inches wide, follow this procedure. First, remove all loose crumbly material with a scraper. Slop a soaking rag into the hole, wetting it completely.

Mix plaster (don't forget the vinegar) and pack it into the hole until it's three-quarters full. Let it dry completely, then fill the hole the rest of the way. Smooth it level with the surrounding wall and wipe extra-smooth with a wet rag.

If a hole is more than 2 inches wide, clean it out as described above, then fill it three-quarters full with ordinary steel wool, wedging it in tightly. (This is done because plaster walls commonly have no backing material to which the new plaster can stick—the steel wool becomes the backing.) Apply a coat of plaster in the hole that fills it about three-quarters of the way; be sure to cover the hole edges. When this dries, fill the hole the rest of the way, smoothing it out as before.

Mildew

EASY **1–2 hours**

You may find mildew on the inside or outside of your house, commonly in damp areas. The purpose of this section is to explain how to tackle the problem inside your house. Mildew is a fungus and should be removed for good looks and to stop it from discoloring the surface it's on, particularly walls.

Many people mistake mildew for dirt (see Fig. 7.9). To tell the difference, do a little test. Dab a little pure bleach on the discoloration. If the stain disappears, it's probably mildew; if not, it's dirt. Usually, mildew is gray and has a cobweb-like appearance.

You can remove mildew with a homemade solution. To every 3 quarts of warm water, add $2/3$ cup of Soilax, $1/3$ cup of detergent, and 1 quart of household bleach. Another (and many say better) way to remove mildew is with straight bleach and water. In either case, use a scrub brush and wear rubber gloves.

PLASTER WALLS AND PLANES

Older houses suffer more than just being haunted by ghosts. Before Sheetrock came along, houses were made with plaster walls. They are rigid and more apt to develop cracks than Sheetrock—especially houses near airports. Believe it or not, the continued roar of aircraft engines causes these plaster walls to crack over the years, calling for repairs.

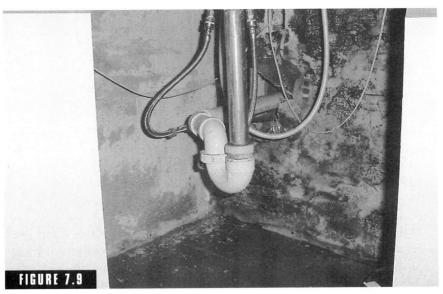

FIGURE 7.9

Mildew can stain and permanently damage walls.

MILDEW—THE HIDDEN ENEMY

It's sometimes hard to tell if you have a mildew problem—especially if it's hidden from sight. I found out I had the problem—my nose told me before I saw it. I walked downstairs to my basement one morning and smelled how wet it was—sure enough, a pipe under a kitchen sink had sprung a small, quiet leak—not enough to flood, but enough for mildew to grow and cause the smell. Learn from my experience—your nose knows.

Fixing Water Damage

DIFFICULT **5–7 hours**

If water collects anywhere inside your house (from a burst pipe or leaky roof, perhaps), chances are it will affect the walls and doors as well as the floor. If there is enough water, it will damage the bottom of doors and the bottom parts of walls will be affected. Even with the best paint on walls, they will suck up water and damage the wallboard. This may call for removing the damaged wallboard and installing new pieces (see Fig. 7.10). Plaster is also damaged by water. (See Fig. 7.10.)

After removing the water (use a wet/dry shop vacuum for this), inspect the wall and determine how far up the damage is. Chances are you will have to replace whole panels of wallboard or large sections of plaster (see "Holes in Wallboard" and "Holes in Plaster").

Damaged Ceramic Wall Tiles

FAIRLY EASY **2–5 hours**

Ceramic tile is one of the toughest building materials available. That's why it's often used for bathroom walls. However, it is not impervious to damage. It can be scratched, broken, or chipped, and it can fall out. For good looks and to keep moisture from sneaking behind the tiles, any that are damaged should be replaced.

This is sometimes easier said than done. You can buy replacement tiles at tile stores, but if the tiles have been up a fair amount of time, their original color will have changed slightly and you may not be able to get ones that match. Then again, you might be in luck and get ones that do match—or match well enough. At any rate, if you do make the replacement, the main thing to remember is not to damage adjacent tiles.

To get a damaged tile out, use a $3/4$-inch cold chisel (available at hardware stores for about $5) and a hammer. Chip away at the corners of the tile. Usually there's a little space under them.

When all the corners have been chipped out, slip the chisel under one and lift. The tile should come out easily. Scrape away all the adhesive on the wall. When it's all off, apply fresh epoxy adhesive around the edges and in the middle of the replacement tile and set it in place.

FIGURE 7.10

This basement ceiling was replaced after a burst pipe from the bathtub drain, above it, leaked, and destroyed the wallboard.

Push it in so it's level with surrounding tiles and has an equal amount of space around its edges.

Or, even easier and cheaper, just mix up some plaster of Paris and set the tile in this. When the adhesive or plaster of Paris is dry, use your finger to fill in around the tile with a ready-mixed grout (available in cans for about $4 at hardware stores). Smooth it out with your finger so it (the grout) is shaped like the grout between the other tiles. Finally, after it dries, take a wet sponge and clean off all grout smeared on the tiles.

Usually, the grout required is white. If you need a colored grout, get the "universal" kind that can be tinted with colors. These are available in small tubes at paint stores.

Crooked Pictures   *EASY*

This may seem like a simple and obvious repair, but it matters—crooked pictures say your house is in disrepair to visitors. When a picture falls out of line, it usually means that it was not made properly—one side is heavier than the other. Or, it simply needs to be adjusted—slid back to level. You should, of course, straighten it out—but fix it so it can't move again.

First, straighten the picture on the wall; note the point on the wire or cord where it balances. If a wire is used, crimp it at the balance point. If you use cord, make a little loop at this point.

Also, cut a pencil eraser in half and glue one piece (use rubber cement) to each bottom back corner of the frame. This will help stop the frame from moving and will allow free air circulation—when you take the picture down there won't be a dirty outline of it on the wall.

Cleaning Wallpaper

EASY **1–2 hours**

If wallpaper is torn or it curls up at the seams, this can be repaired easily. If you're careful, you can reglue these so they look like new. Wallpaper repair kits are available at home centers and paint stores. They include glue and all the tools you'll need to repair wallpaper. They are pretty straightforward, and directions are included.

A time-proven method for cleaning washable paper is to use a light-duty detergent and cool water solution. Apply it with a soft, sudsy sponge (use as little water as possible) and wash a small area at a time, proceeding with a very light touch. Rinse with a clean sponge. Pat it dry with a clean, soft cloth. Don't rub. It's best to start cleaning on a small, inconspicuous area to see how effective it is.

Stains are never easy to remove, but immediate treatment will be more successful than after the material has penetrated the paper. Here's how to treat and/or clean some common stains.

- *Grease.* Cover fresh grease spots immediately with two thicknesses of paper towel or facial tissue; press with an iron. This will remove some of the grease. Then use any dry-cleaning fluid and an absorbent powder such as talcum powder or cornstarch. Cover the spot with the paste and, after it has dried, brush away the powder. If the paper is washable, wash the spot gently after this treatment.

- *Crayon.* Scrape off as much of the crayon as possible with a spatula. Sponge lightly with a cloth dampened in a dry-cleaning fluid. Repeat treatment as needed. If a ring remains after the crayon has been removed, make and apply a paste as for grease spots.

- *Pencil marks and smudges.* An art gum or ordinary pencil eraser will remove many marks that appear on wallpaper. Rub gently so you don't roughen or tear the paper.

- *Ink.* Blot the ink quickly, being careful not to smear it. Apply an absorbent powder such as cornstarch or talcum powder. Brush off as fast as it takes up the ink and repeat the application. A commercial ink eradicator may be used. A fine, light application is better than a heavy dose. You can sometimes use chlorine bleach on washable paper, but check for color fastness. If it is safe, pat the ink spot. Get it dampened in the bleach. Rinse with clear water.

Painting

Paints and Primers

Not all interior paint jobs can be done with one coat of paint. For example, if paint is peeling extensively, good painting procedure calls for removing all the peeling paint and applying at least two coats of paint. If you are going to change from one color to another—from a dark to a light color—a two-coat job is also needed.

The first coat is called the primer, and for this job you should use one of the special paints called primers. It will do a number of things. First, it will provide a smooth base for the finish paint. Second, it will ensure that the finish paint does not penetrate the surface unevenly, creating a spotty effect. And, finally, it will provide good "tooth" for the finish paint—it will be able to get a better grip.

There are a wide variety of primers available, each formulated for specific surfaces—wood, new plasterboard, iron, what-have-you. Since expert opinion is that the primer is more important than the finish coat, buy a good-quality product and follow label directions.

You use the primer the same way as you would a finish paint with regard to mixing. Follow directions. To make things easier, it's best to tint the primer to the approximate color of the finish paint. You can do this with so-called universal colorants; directions for use are on the tubes. You can also have primers custom-colored, like finish paints, at home improvement centers and at most paint stores.

Tables 7.1 and 7.2 will help answer any questions you might have in deciding what kinds of primers and paints you should use in your house.

Painting Ceilings
EASY **1–2 hours**

Here are some helpful hints for painting ceilings.

Move as much furniture as you can to the center of the room. It's always best to work around it. You can work around it freely with a

TABLE 7.1 Interior Primers

Product	Use on
Alkyd primer-sealer	New, dry plaster or painted plaster.
Enamel undercoater	Bare wood or metal to be finished with gloss or semi-gloss paint.
Latex primer-sealer	Bare drywall (plasterboard) or plaster, new or old.
Pigmented shellac primer	New woods such as mahogany and cedar (e.g., new hand rails on stairs).

TABLE 7.2 Interior Paints

Product	Use on
Latex glossy	Walls. It dries to a glossy surface and cleans up very easily with soap and water.
Latex semigloss	Walls. It dries to a partially shiny surface and cleans up pretty easily with soap and water.
Latex pearl	Walls. It dries to a flat surface with a small shine to it and cleans up easily most of the time with soap and water.
Latex eggshell	Walls and Ceiling. This takes some muscle power to clean up with soap and water. In other words, it's harder to clean than glossy paints. It dries to a flat finish.
Latex flat	Ceilings. It dries to a flat surface and cleanup is easy with soap and water.

roller while standing where you expect to walk. Cover the furniture in the middle of the room and the surrounding area with drop cloths.

It's best to also cover fixtures and appliances in kitchens when working there. Start by patching any holes or damaged parts where needed (see "Holes in Wallboard"). Next, if your vacuum cleaner hose is long enough, vacuum up any cobwebs in the corners and make sure the surface is free of dirt and any kind of grease.

If you are painting a new ceiling, you will have to prime it first. New wallboard is thirsty, and primer is a good base for the finished coat. If the ceiling has already been painted, one coat of latex flat paint will do the trick. Flat paint is traditionally used for ceilings because of its durability.

Use a long handle attached to a quality roller. Fill the paint tray halfway up with paint. This will prevent spills and dripping. Start at the highest part of the ceiling (the peak in cathedral ceilings). When the roller approaches a wall, be careful the roller frame doesn't scratch the wall. You can get this area (where the ceiling meets the wall) later with a brush. Foam brushes designed to roll in this

SAVE ON OOPS! PAINT AND PRIMERS

A good way to buy primers and paints is to wait until your local home center and/or paint store has some on sale or they have some reduced in price because it can't be sold to anyone else. Sometimes paints are mixed for customers and mistakes are made or minds have changed—and the store has paint on their hands. It might be perfect for you—and they're happy to sell it—at a discount. Ask when you shop. You never know what bargains might be out there.

crevice are suggested. They are pretty cheap and you can buy them with your paint.

Be careful to stop using the roller when you near fixtures such as lights or ceiling fans. You can get these later with a brush. You don't want to spend your time wiping off paint from sloppy work.

Be sure to use long, steady passes with the roller and do a section at a time. However, you'll want to block out enough time to do the whole ceiling in one day. That way, it will dry uniformly.

Painting Walls

FAIRLY EASY **2–5 hours**

Now you're ready to attack the walls.

Preparation for painting walls is the same as for painting ceilings. Again, before you paint, even if you are adding another coat, make sure the surface is free of dirt and grease of any kind. Also, a recently repaired wall should be sanded thoroughly (see Fig. 7.11). You may want to use a long handle attached to the roller, but working in narrow hallways may prevent this.

Unlike ceilings, you have some choices about what kind of paint to use. To help you make your choice, see Tables 7.1 and 7.2. Before you start, be sure and remove light switchplates and outlet covers. Also, be careful around doorknobs and other hanging items on walls, such as door bell chimes and the like. As you apply the paint, use floor-to-ceiling smoothing strokes. This will allow you to work steadily, without having to go back to get parts you may skip.

FIGURE 7.11

This wall is ready to be washed and painted.

Later, you can use a brush to finish the corners and the sides of molding and trim around windows and near doors. It's best to use small foam brushes here. They can help you get into small areas that are not accessible with brushes.

Also, paint windows working from the inside out. Don't be afraid of getting paint on the glass. If you do, wipe it off immediately with a rag moistened with water. Latex cleans up pretty well if you catch it fast enough, before it can dry. Finish other trim areas—doors and frames, molding, and the like—with a brush.

Spray Painting   *DIFFICULT* **5–7 hours**

Spray painting is a technique which, if used correctly, can save you a lot of time and trouble. Believe it or not, it is suitable for inside work, and is particularly useful for painting rough surfaces such as stucco, which are hard to paint with a brush. On wood it gives a finished, even feel and look (to moldings, handrails, or balusters).

The kind of paint you are planning to use should be thinned according to the manufacturer's instructions. Most conventional paints are suitable for spraying. Gloss paint sprays well but requires care to avoid getting sags and runs all over the surface.

Masking and Protection   *DIFFICULT* **5–7 hours**

Sprayed paint gets everywhere. Anything that you do not wish to be sprayed must be masked thoroughly before you begin—and *thoroughly* is the operative word. It is no good just hanging a sheet of newspaper in front of an object, because the fine mist of paint will easily float around the back of the paper. The object must be properly wrapped in newspaper and the edges of the paper stuck down all the way around with masking tape. Proper masking takes quite a long time and uses a lot of paper and tape, but it's worth the time and effort.

Fortunately, masking tape is not expensive—but do not try to save money by buying cheap tape. Inferior grades of tape do not stick too well and pull the paint off the things they are stuck to. Good masking tape will save you a lot of trouble. Buy two widths: thicker for holding down newspaper, and thinner for covering small objects such as door handles and pipes.

Particular care should be taken to protect the floor, especially if there is wall-to-wall carpeting. Furniture that cannot be taken out of the room should be stacked in the middle and well covered with drop cloths. A quick way is to use plastic sheets held to the floor with a stapler. The staples come out easily when the job is done. Make sure there are no gaps that paint mist can float through.

Whenever you paint indoors, take care to give the room proper ventilation. Mask windows in the open position. You should also protect your lungs by buying a painter's mask and plenty of replaceable pads for it, because the paint clogs pads quickly. Do not laugh at this precaution; it is really necessary. Paint spray can be harmful to your respiratory system.

Also, wear old clothes for spray painting. This applies to garments that would not be touched by ordinary painting, such as socks. Remember, although it may not be something you think about in the beginning, take off your wristwatch and any rings or bracelets while operating spraying equipment.

Spraying Techniques

All types of paint must be diluted with the appropriate thinner to make them suitable for spraying. Ask your paint dealer about this. He can advise you properly. Many paints should be thinned with water; and gloss paints with turpentine, or a substitute. Most of these are very flammable, so *do not smoke* when spraying, and turn off all pilot lights when spraying any type of flammable paint.

The exact amount of thinner to add to any type of paint can best be found by experience, but follow the manufacturer's instructions. Too little makes the paint too thick, so that the nozzle clogs in a few seconds. Too much makes the paint so thin that it does not cover the surface properly. Experiment on scrap material until you get it right. Even when the paint is the right consistency, the spray nozzle will probably clog occasionally. It should be cleaned out with a suitable solvent.

Spray the wall with horizontal strokes of the gun, holding it 12 to 18 inches away from the surface. Move the gun back and forth parallel to the wall, rather than sweeping it in an arc. Spray on only a thin coat of the paint or it will run; you may have to put two or three coats on the surface, but spraying is so quick that you will not waste much time doing this. Here, again, follow the manufacturer's instructions.

Every time you stop spraying, even for a few minutes, clean the gun thoroughly with the appropriate solvent (the same as you use for diluting the paint).

When you are finished, look around. Did you get any paint on any surface other than what you wanted to paint? If not, after cleaning the equipment, take off the tarps and coverings, and consider it a job well done.

Caulk and Weather Stripping

Caulking

EASY 1–2 hours

Caulk is usually associated with outside work—around windows and vents, to seal out moisture, wind, and anything else mother nature throws at houses. However, it is used inside, for generally the same purpose: to block out drafts and seal out moisture. After visually inspecting caulk around windows, air conditioners, and the like (making sure it retains its rubbery consistency), replace any parts that are dry and cracked.

It's best to get a latex caulk for replacement. Your local hardware store or home center has this available, and they can recommend which kind to use for indoor projects.

Weather Stripping
EASY **1–2 hours**

Weather stripping serves the same purpose as caulk, but it is used most often as a seal where a door closes or a window opens. It is stationary and usually has a sticky side to it so it can be pressed in place and/or glued or stapled around the surfaces of door and window jams. Again, your local hardware dealer or home center has a variety of weather stripping products and directions for installing them and replacing them.

Both caulk and weather stripping are important. Using them correctly and maintaining them keeps heat in your house and the elements out. This goes a long way in energy savings and lower utility bills.

Hardware

The best way to maintain hardware such as hinges, doorknobs, and the like is to inspect the items and give them some attention before they break and you have to replace them. This includes simply tightening hinges on doors or the screws on doorknobs if you feel them getting loose. It's also important to keep moving parts well lubricated.

It's important to take a moment and do this before the problem gets worse. Doing so may save you a trip to the hardware store. However, if it does come down to that, and you have to replace pieces, take the hardware with you if you are in doubt about what you need. This way, a hardware or home center professional can help you replace something with the exact item you need.

Sticking Door
EASY **1–2 hours**

If a regular door sticks when you try to close it, chances are that the top hinge is loose—the door sags and its bottom rubs against the floor. You'll probably see scuff marks on the floor. A loose hinge means loose screws. Tighten them up and the problem's solved.

First, open the door all the way and stick as many thin books as you can under the outer door edge. This keeps it steady while you work and stops the door from pulling on the screws as you try to tighten them.

Tighten all the screws you can see—even the ones that don't look loose—as tight as you can (you turn the screws clockwise to tighten them). This will include the screws that go through the hinge into the door and those that go into the door opening framework (technically known as the jamb). Take away the books and try the door. It should work. If it still sticks, it's a job for a carpenter or handyman to fix.

Sometimes you won't be able to tighten the screws well because the screw holes on the wall framework are too chewed up—there isn't enough solid wood left for the screws to bite into. Screw holes in the door itself usually stay good.

To handle this problem, first wedge up the door with thin books again (or one fairly thick book). Take out all the screws in the hinge and turn back the hinge leaf. Pack Plastic Wood (available at hardware stores for about $2) into the bad holes. (You'll know which ones these are because you'll never quite succeed in tightening up the screws in them. The screws will just keep turning, even though the heads are all the way in; if you look closely, you will also see how chewed up they are.)

Pack the Plastic Wood into each hole with a finger, poking at it with the tip of a screwdriver to eliminate air pockets. Fill each hole all the way and smooth it off with your finger. Let the Plastic Wood dry according to label directions.

Finally, drive in new screws where needed, the same kind as were used before but 1/2 inch longer. (Show the old screws to your hardware store dealer.) Take your time and drive the screws all the way in. The combination of Plastic Wood and the extra length of the screws—enabling them to bite into new wood—should solve the problem once and for all.

Believe it or not, if you wish, you can pack white glue-coated wooden match sticks (without the heads) into the screw holes. This serves the same purpose as the Plastic Wood.

Loose Doorknob   *EASY* **1–2 hours**

Doorknobs have an annoying way of coming loose, making it difficult and sometimes impossible to open doors.

To fix the condition, first look for a little screw on the neck (the narrow part) of the doorknob. Using a screwdriver, turn the little screw two or three full turns to the left to loosen it. Have someone hold the knob on the other side of the door so it can't move (or hold it yourself) and turn the knob on your side all the way to the right, pushing it forward as you do, until the front of the neck contacts the plate on the door. This may require a little muscle. When the neck is snug against the plate, turn the knob back and forth to see how it works. If it's too tight (the latch won't come out after going in), turn the knob to your left about a quarter turn to loosen it. Then tighten up the little screw. That's it.

If you don't see screws on the neck of the doorknob, they may be hiding behind a decorative sleeve where the neck goes into the door. In this case, pry off the decorative sleeve with a narrow, straight-edged screwdriver, repeat the procedure (tightening the screws), and snap it back in place.

Cabinet Door Won't Shut

EASY **1–2 hours**

Many cabinet doors have two parts: a pronglike affair on the door and the part on the shelf that the prong fits into when you close the door. When the door doesn't shut, it's because repeated door closings have knocked the shelf part (the catch) out of line and the prong isn't fitting into it.

To get the door to shut properly, all you have to do is reposition the shelf part. On close inspection, you'll see that it's held on by two screws that go through a slot (rather than a hole). Loosen each of the screws a half turn to the left so you can slide the catch forward. As you do, straighten it out. Try the door. Does it stay closed? No?

Then reposition the catch until it does. Tighten the screws. To prevent a recurrence, drive another little screw against the back of the slot. That should do it.

Windows

If the eyes are the window to the soul, windows offer a glimpse into your life. Maintaining them is important for energy efficiency, security, aesthetic beauty, and for your piece of mind. While most windows work well for a long time—long enough not to think about them often—they do require some maintenance.

Window Troubles

The two main problems with windows are that they become stuck and the glass breaks. Both problems are fairly easily fixed.

Stuck Windows

EASY **1–2 hours**

Double-hung windows have a top section you lower and a bottom section you raise (see Figs. 8.1 and 8.2). If you can't open (or close) a wooden window, a likely reason is that dried paint has stuck it to the track it rides in.

To free the window, stick a knife in where the window meets the framework. Run the knife up and down until it cuts the dried paint. Here's another way: Take a hammer and carefully tap all around the window frame, using a little wood block or a folded towel to protect the window finish. This vibrates the window and breaks the paint seal.

Once you get a window moving, open and close it 10 or 15 times. Then apply a liberal amount of lubrication in the track. You can use a silicone spray or WD40, another lubricant. Sears sells an 8-ounce can

FIGURE 8.1

Keep double-hung windows well lubricated for ease of use.

FIGURE 8.2

Pull-down shades work well with double-hung windows because they have no hardware or turning cranks that stick out.

of silicone spray for around $3. A small can of WD40 goes for about $2.50. The investment is well worth it.

Another reason for a wooden window to stick is that it's lopsided in its track. This can be the case in newer, vinyl windows that you don't paint. You pull up, or down, and the one side jams against the track.

The cure here is to get the window level before you attempt to move it. Pull along the bottom to get it level, then carefully keep it level every time you raise or lower it. Also, lubricate the track. A repair involves taking the window out, and this is outside the scope of this book. It's really a job for a professional. If the window is stuck or sticking for no apparent reason, apply lubrication and try to get it moving.

Casement windows—ones that open by turning a little crank handle—can also become stuck (see Fig. 8.3). Paint builds up on the bottom edge, or the hinge screws come loose, allowing the window to sag—and stick. The cure in the first case is to scrape off the paint from the bottom edge with a scraper or a butter knife. Tightening the screws should solve the second problem.

When sliding windows stick, it's usually because the lower tracks they slide in get clogged with soil or debris (see Fig. 8.4). Brushing out the dirt should solve the problem. Follow this by spraying a silicone spray into the track. That should do the trick.

Double hung windows suffer the same maladies (see Fig. 8.5). Keeping them well lubricated and clean (not only the glass but most

FIGURE 8.3

Casement windows are closed manually with hand cranks.

FIGURE 8.4

The tracks in sliding windows must be kept clean and lubricated.

FIGURE 8.5

Windows that are kept clean and well lubricated stay attractive for years.

importantly the hardware) should keep them working well for years without any significant problems.

Broken Windows   *EASY* **1–2 hours**

The hardest part of fixing broken windows is cutting a new piece of glass to fit into the window frame. But you don't have to do it. You can get a piece cut to size free by a professional at the glass shop where you get the new glass. (See the Yellow Pages, under "Glass.") And you can get the glass cheaply. I recently bought a 14-by-20-inch piece of single-strength glass for $5. We're talking here about replacing glass in a wooden frame window, either little panes or big ones, so prices will vary. Either way, glass of this kind is very reasonably priced.

WOODEN FRAME WINDOWS   *FAIRLY EASY* **2–5 hours**

With the glass out, scrape away all the old putty from the window frame. Do a good job, going down to clean, bare wood. When the scraping is complete, brush out, or use a rag to wipe out all putty crumbs.

As you remove the putty, you'll notice little triangular pieces of metal sticking into the frame. These are called glazier's points, and their job is to hold the glass in place—it's not the putty that does this. Remove them with a pair of pliers or a screwdriver. Note the places they were removed from. You can mark them with a pencil or crayon.

When the frame is clean, apply a coat of exterior paint to it. The wood is likely to be dry and will suck up the paint.

Measure from edge to edge inside the frame, both horizontally and vertically. When you have the dimensions, subtract $1/8$ inch from each. For example, if your vertical measurement is 12 inches, subtract the $1/8$ inch and you get $11^7/8$ inches. Order the glass in this size. The smaller glass gives you more space and allows the framework to expand and contract with cold and warm weather. To be sure you are measuring accurately, it's a good idea to do it a few times at different points on the window.

If you are replacing glass in a little (multipaned) window, order single-strength glass. For a large (single-pane) window, order double-strength.

You will need a little tub of glazing compound, which is the modern counterpart of putty. Glazing compound is a little more expensive than putty, but it is easier to work with and is more flexible—it doesn't dry out like putty. One brand is Dap; a can costs about $2.50.

First, mix the compound in the can with a narrow putty knife. Scoop out a little on the end of your knife and apply a cardboard-thin layer of it all around the window frame wood where the glass will rest.

Place the new glass all the way inside the frame. Push the glazier's points into the frame in their original holes. Each point should go in about halfway. For pushing you can use the end of a chisel, a screwdriver, or a putty knife.

Now apply the glazing compound to the window where it meets the frame. Do this by scooping out small globs of it, pressing them along on the frame in the approximate finish shape you want it to have. It's probably best to check the putty on other windows for this. When one frame side is done, smooth the compound out into final shape by drawing the putty knife along it.

Then, proceed to the other sides of each window, one by one, as just described. Let the compound dry for half a day, then paint it and the rest of the window.

OLDER STEEL-FRAMED WINDOWS

DIFFICULT **5–7 hours**

Replacing glass in an older, steel window frame is a pretty simple job, but one that requires some care. First, don heavy work gloves. Next, take out the broken glass. Get a grip on a broken section and gently rock it back and forth until it comes out. Repeat for other broken sections. If the glass isn't broken enough to get a grip on it, gently tap it with a hammer until it is. It's a good idea here to wear glasses or goggles—something to protect your eyes as you work.

Put the frame into a vice so that it doesn't move. Work some glazier's compound into a ball on a flat surface and roll it out into a long string. Work this string into the frame (a little off-center to make room for the glass).

Set the new glass into the frame and let it rest against the glazier's points. Work the bead of glazing compound into the other side. Mold it against the glass and set it aside. Just like the wooden frames, it should take about half a day to set and be ready to paint.

Temporary Repairs

EASY **1–2 hours**

If glass breaks on a Sunday or another time when you can't replace it, you can make a temporary repair with a piece of cardboard or plastic wrap. Simply tape the material over the window for the time being—it's better than having nothing there.

Repairing and Replacing Screening

Screening is fairly delicate stuff, and it's the rare home indeed that can go an entire summer without one or more being damaged. Two types of screening are common: aluminum and plastic (fiberglass). What you do to correct the damage depends on which type you have, and the degree of damage.

Holes in Screening

EASY **1–2 hours**

Hail to the genius who invented screening! He made the openings in the screening small enough so bugs can't get in but big enough so cooling breezes can, and you can see through the screen. Frequently, however, holes show up that weren't part of the original design. And before you know it, you've got tiny, unwelcome visitors.

The repair depends on whether you have aluminum or plastic screening, and the extent of the damage. If wires in an aluminum screen are misaligned, making a "hole," push them back into position with the point of an awl or ice pick.

A small hole—less than $1/4$ inch wide—in either type of screening can be plugged with a drop of airplane glue or household cement. For this repair there's no need to take the screen down or out of its frame.

For a bigger hole in aluminum screening, you can buy a ready-to-use patch (available at hardware stores). This is simply a small rectangle of screening with hooks on the ends.

Take the screen down and place it on a flat surface. Place the hole over a small block of wood and tap the hole edges with a hammer to flatten them. Next, place the patch over the hole and thread the hooked ends through the screening. Turn the screen over, placing the patch on the small wood block (or a book). Tap the patch hooks with a hammer so they flatten and grip the screening. That's it.

For a hole in plastic screening, you need to obtain a piece of scrap screening. If you don't have a piece, try a hardware store; they sell it loose.

Once you have a piece of screening, cut a patch about $1/4$ inch larger than the hole. Squeeze out a line of household cement around the edge of the patch. Press the patch in place over the hole and hold it there for a few minutes, then release it and let it dry completely.

WHEN YOU'VE SCREENED ENOUGH

When I was growing up, our family dog used to run through screens in doors—often. It seemed like every weekend they had to be repaired. If you've got the same problem, it may be time to switch doors and move screens to the tops of doors instead of the bottom—or simply keep screens in windows. Screens are lovely for summer breezes, but with little kids and pets, they sometimes become fragile inconveniences that need a lot of attention.

Small Holes in Aluminum Screens   EASY **1–2 hours**

Some holes in aluminum screens aren't really holes, but simply screen wires that are pushed far enough apart to form a hole. If close inspection reveals this is the problem, simply take an awl, nail, or another sharply pointed item and push the wires back into correct position.

If there actually is a hole, but it is very small, you can sometimes fill it by squirting a blob of clear glue over it, effectively filling it.

Larger Holes   EASY **1–2 hours**

If the hole is too large for this kind of treatment, a patch is the answer. If you want to save a little money, and have some scrap screening handy, cut a square patch with a utility knife or tin snips, then sew the patch over the hole with individual strands of screen wire.

Easier, though, is to buy a small package of patches at a hardware store. These come with hooked edges and are simple to install. You just position the patch over the hole, bend it slightly, and make sure the hooked edges are threaded into the screening, and let go. It snaps in place.

Replacing Screening   EASY **1–2 hours**

If the hole is too large to be handled by a patch, your best bet is to replace the screening. Kits for the job, containing screening and hardware, are available, but this is not the way to save money. Less costly is to buy the screening loose. Hardware stores and home centers carry rolls of it—they'll cut off whatever size piece you need. You'll also need one basic tool, called a splining tool. It has a handle with a convex wheel attached to one end, and a concave wheel on the other. At around 40 cents a square foot for screening, and $4 or $5 for the tool, replacing one screen is still cheaper than buying a kit or getting it done professionally.

First, remove the old screening. On metal frames, the screening is commonly held on by rubber or plastic strips, called spline, which wedges it down into grooves. Pry one end of the spline up with a screwdriver or knife tip. Once you can grab it—carefully, so as not to break it—pull it free. It may be in one piece, or there may be separate pieces on each of the four frame sides.

Examine the spline. If it is not corroded or brittle, you may be able to use it for installing the new screening. If it is in poor shape, get new spline. Since it comes in various sizes, your best bet is to show the dealer the old spline and buy exactly the same size.

CUT SCREENING

Cut a piece of screening an inch larger all around than the frame. Set it squarely on the frame and smooth it flat. Clamp it on with two C-clamps on any side. Begin working on the side opposite that. Using the concave wheel on the splining tool, make short back and forth strokes to force the screening into the groove—don't try to force it down with one pass. As you do, use your free hand to pull it tight across the frame.

INSERTING SPLINE

EASY **1–2 hours**

When a professional installs screening, he uses one long uncut spline piece, working it down into side after side, and rounding corners with ease. For the beginner, though, the best bet is to cut the spline into a separate piece for each side.

Place the spline against any side of the frame and cut it to the length needed. Lay the spline over the groove, then use the convex wheel on the roller to work it snugly into place. Use the concave wheel on the tool to force screening into the groove on the side opposite the clamped side. Pull it taut as you do. To make the spline pliable and easy to work with, first wash it in warm soapy water.

Start from any end and work your way to the other end, using short strokes to force the screening into the groove—don't try to force it down in one pass. As you work, use your free hand to pull it tight across the frame.

SECURE OPPOSITE SIDE

With the screen secured on one side, go to the opposite side. Remove the C-clamps, and repeat the procedure used on the first side. Then do the remaining two sides as you did the first two.

Finally, trim any excess screening. Use a sharp utility knife, or a razor blade, holding it at an angle to the edge of the frame, and use the frame as a guide.

Some metal screens in metal frames are secured with rigid strips of metal rather than flexible spline. In this case, first remove the spline carefully with a screwdriver. Try not to bend it as you do. If it does bend, you'll have to straighten it out before reinserting it.

Then, proceed as above to replace the screen. To get each strip back into its groove, gently tap along its length using a narrow wedge-shaped board and hammer angle to the edge of the frame, using the frame as a guide.

Metal Screening in Wood Frame

EASY **1–2 hours**

If you have the older-type wood frame screens, installation depends on the way the screening is held on. If the frame is the type with a spline in a groove, you can proceed as for a metal-frame screen. If you have the type where the screening edges are stapled or tacked to recesses all around the screen, and the edges are covered with a thin molding, proceed as follows.

Gently pry the molding loose and unfasten the screen. Square a piece of screening as large as the frame over the frame. Fasten the screening to any side with C-clamps. On the opposite side, pull the screening taut and staple it on, using a staple every 2 inches. Trim any excess with a utility knife. Once one side is done, release the other side, and staple this in place. Repeat the procedure for the remaining two sides.

Fiberglass Screening

EASY **1–2 hours**

Repair of fiberglass screens is slightly different than for metal. For one thing, the fiberglass strands don't pull apart—they're fused together. But holes are as common as in aluminum screens.

For small up to fairly large holes, you can use a homemade fiberglass patch. Cut a piece of screening about $1/4$ inch larger all around than the hole. Secure it over the hole with a bit of plastic adhesive and the job's done.

If the hole is extra large, it's best to replace the entire screen. As with metal screens, the "how to" depends on the type of frame. If it is metal with a flexible spline, proceed as follows.

First, remove the spline. Place a piece of screening, about the same size as the frame, over the frame. Clamp down any side. On the opposite side, pull the screening taut. Use your roller to wedge the screen and the spline into the groove simultaneously. Trim excess. Repeat the procedure on the other sides, trimming excess screening as you go. If the spline is rigid, proceed the same way but use a wedge-shaped board and hammer to get the spline in place.

Wood Frames

EASY **1–2 hours**

If you have wood frames with a flexible spline, you can follow the same procedure as for metal frames. If the screening is tacked to recesses on the frame, follow this procedure. Place a frame-size piece of screening on the frame. Clamp one side. On the other side, fold the edge of the screening over into a sort of hem and, as you pull it taut, staple it down, setting the staples about 2 inches apart. Loosen the clamps and repeat the procedure on the opposite side, then do the other two sides. Replace the molding.

Painting Screens

Metal door and window screens will last longer—and look better—if they are kept well painted. For this, you can get special thin screen paints that won't clog the mesh. (Tip: A coat of thinned white paint applied to the screen wire makes the interior of the house less visible from the outside. If this is your purpose, I hope you can use this tip.)

How Often?

Frequency of painting depends on screen quality. A cheap grade will probably require painting every year, while galvanized screening may show signs of rust only after a long time and may then require only a light coat of paint. Copper or bronze screen wire will not deteriorate if not painted, but corrosion from weathering makes it advisable to paint or varnish copper or bronze screens to avoid them staining the trim and siding.

Paint can be applied to screens evenly and economically with a special screen applicator. Most paint dealers carry these applicators, but, if not available, they are not hard to make. Cover a block of wood $1 \times 3 \times 8$ inches with thick felt or carpet attached to the face side of the block with the fiber out. Nail a cleat of wood for a handle along the center of the opposite side of the block. The carpet may be fastened by glue or tacks, but if tacks are used, the heads should be well embedded so that they will not catch on the wire mesh when the paint is applied.

Place Screen Flat

The screen should be placed on a level surface such as a table, then cleaned of all dust, soot, and loose rust with a bristle brush. If more thorough cleaning is necessary, wash the screen with soap and warm water (apply with a brush), then rinse with clear water and dry with a cloth. After the screen has been cleaned on both sides and dried thoroughly, rub paint on, using small amounts of paint at one time, avoiding clogging the mesh.

Frames should not require painting more than once every 3 to 5 years. If the screens are cleaned and painted as described, they'll last longer and look better.

Basements

Basements are in daily, direct contact with a home's worst natural enemy: moisture. Because they are in direct contact with the earth (soil), the potential for moisture to show up and leach through the walls of the basement in your home is very high. This is why moisture is a constant threat, and often a problem, in basements.

Although you can handle minor problems yourself, major repairs are best left to foundation and waterproofing professionals. There are a number of things you can do to maintain them.

Leaks in Basement Wall or Floor

EASY **1–2 hours**

On a rainy day, you may notice that your basement wall or floor has some leaks. If this happens, no sweat. There is actually a product that, when applied to a crack or hole from which water is flowing, stops the leak in minutes!

The material is called hydraulic cement. There are various brands. One good one I've used is made by the Rutland Co., of Rutland, Vermont. They call it Hydraulic Cement (of all things).

To use the material to stop a flowing leak, mix it with water until it has the consistency of putty. Wait a few minutes until it stiffens a little. Then, using a trowel or putty knife, force it into the crack or hole and hold it there with the tool for a few minutes until it stays by itself. Add more cement the same way until the water stops flowing. When this occurs, shave the material even with the rest of the wall or floor.

Hydraulic cement is not pretty. It's gray, and the patches will show on the wall or floor. And it's expensive; a ½-pound can costs around $5–$6. But a half-hour after you apply it, it will be as hard as a rock, with nary a drop of water in sight. Controlling moisture in your basement is vital if you want to "finish" it—make it suitable as living space—perhaps as an apartment or as another living space (see Figs. 9.1 and 9.2).

Installing a Sump Pump

VERY DIFFICULT **7–10 hours**

Installing a sump pump is not for the faint of heart. What follows are directions for doing the job, but if it's not for you, and you'd like to have a professional do the job, this information will still be of value to you. Knowing how a sump pump works is important because you'll know what to look for if there's trouble and you'll have a better understanding of how it operates.

A sump pump consists of a motor which powers a vertical drive shaft connected to a pump set in a hole you make in the basement floor. The hole is lined with a material that is like a piece of chimney flue lining. The pump has a float mechanism. When the water table

FIGURE 9.1

Controlling moisture in basements can add living space in your home.

rises, the hole fills with water. The float mechanism senses this, starts the motor, and the water is pumped out through a discharge tube which terminates some-place outside the house. In effect, the pump lowers the level of the water table under the house.

The first step is to dig the hole for the sump pump. The hole should be as close to the center of the cellar as you can make it. Also, dig the hole when the water table is down. Otherwise the hole will keep fill-ing with water as you dig.

Hole size is based on the size of the flue lining, which should be 12 inches square by 2 feet long, on the average. You should dig slightly deeper and larger than the lining so you can slip the lining in place easily. The lining should have a series of holes drilled in it through which water can pass. Drill these carefully.

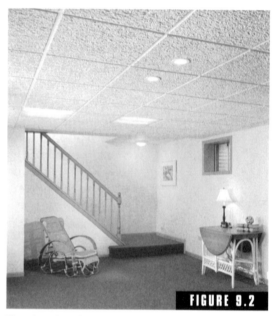

FIGURE 9.2

There's only a few ways to control moisture—but lots of ways to decorate the space in your basement once the moisture problem is solved.

Step 1. To break through concrete, use a sledgehammer (the 8-pound size is usually best, but you can get larger or smaller sizes), hitting the middle of the hole first, then chipping away at the edges. You can use a manual posthole digger to get dirt out, but a shovel and a square-edge spade to define hole sides are also good.

Step 2. When the hole is dug, fill the bot-tom of it with gravel, enough so that the water will flow freely into the hole to the pump. On top of this put a piece of slate just big enough to stand your pump on (say, 8 inches × 8 inches). Anchor the motor to any convenient support, perhaps a pipe or a board.

OLD-TIME ROOT CELLARS

Remember when Grandma stored perish-able food in the cellar? The reason base-ments were so great for this is the subject of this chapter: humidity and moisture. Years ago, it wasn't important to home-owners to keep basements dry—in fact, it was the opposite—and the natural mois-ture smelled, but it worked charms for storing food. People don't react as well to such high moisture—staying dry is better for your health.

Step 3. You also need a discharge pipe. The easiest thing to hook up is flexible plastic pipe or, if you want a better-looking job, you can use rigid plastic pipe. The diameter of the pipe will depend on the manufacturer's recommendations.

As mentioned, the tubing has to terminate outside the house. Depending on your house, you may be able to run it out a window without any problems.

Step 4. Or you may have to go through the foundation wall. For this, make a hole with a sledgehammer and star drill, chisel, or electric hammer you rent. The hole in the wall should be $1/8$–$1/16$ inch larger than the pipe diameter.

The water should be routed where it can run downhill on a cement or asphalt surface. In most cases, running it down the driveway is best. In some localities it may be necessary to install a drywell. If you do, keep it at least 12 feet away from the house and install it to your particular town's codes and specifications.

For power you need an electrical connection in the vicinity of the pump. You shouldn't have the switch on the pump. The pump goes on and off automatically. Just have the pump plugged into the wall. To shut off power, simply pull the plug.

Even if you choose to do the work yourself, it's best to have an electrician or plumber (certainly a professional tradesman) look over the work and make sure you've taken all the necessary precautions to make it as safe as possible.

Mildew Control

EASY **1–2 hours**

If you have mildew in your basement, you have too much moisture that you can't get rid of. I've already mentioned the obvious source of

THE BEST TIME TO CALL CONTRACTORS

If you live in a part of the country that has sharp seasonal changes in weather and you need a basement contractor, call one before the spring season starts. Floods and spring thaws keep them very busy, and they may be too busy to get to you.

CHECK YOUR WATER TABLE

Before buying a home, particularly near the water, be sure and ask how high the water table is. If the homeowner or real estate agent doesn't know, check with the local town government. If the water table is really high, and you don't have the proper equipment in the basement, such as a sump pump, you could be walking into potential basement moisture problems.

moisture that leads to mildew. The sump pump takes care of the problem and gets rid of the water as it arrives. In order to solve your mildew problem, however, you should ask yourself some questions.

What other sources of water are invading your basement? Leaky gutters on the outside of the house and poor drainage can cause water to seep through the basement walls.

Another source could be from inside: leaking or "sweating" water pipes, an improperly vented clothes dryer, a leaking clothes washer, or a basement shower could all produce enough moisture to cause mildew.

The answer to these problems is to not just stop the source of the leak, but to increase the amount of ventilation in your basement (perhaps keeping a window open during the day in warm months) or installing a dehumidifier. New dehumidifiers are very efficient and have time-controlled on and off switches, so they don't have to be watched all the time. They also have automatic shutoff switches for when the containers are full. They will go a long way in drying out your basement, thereby solving mildew problems.

Another way to solve the problem temporarily is simply to open the basement door (if you have an outside entrance) during the summer months and allow air to circulate (see Fig. 9.3).

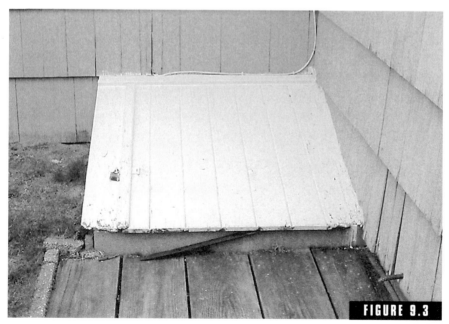

FIGURE 9.3

An outside basement entrance door can be opened to allow air to circulate.

Pest Control

The best way to control pests in your basement is to make sure the floor and walls are clutter-free to begin with. Mice and crawling insects love to hide, and clothes, toys, rags, and any other small items give them incentive.

The other thing is to control moisture. Any water source is going to attract insects and other small animals who want a drink. See the mildew section of this chapter. You may want to set mice traps and insect traps you can buy at home centers.

Also, make sure that if you store food in the basement, store only dry goods and canned goods. Any packaging that can be chewed through or torn open is essentially inviting small critters to dinner. Lastly, if the problem is pervasive and continues, call an exterminator. These professionals have specialized knowledge and products for basement pest problems.

Driveways, Walkways, and Patios

Some parts of your home and property take more abuse then others. They are simply used more, will wear out faster, and as a result, require more maintenance. Driveways, walkways, and patios are just such examples. They are always exposed to the wind, baking sun, rain, and snow. They are walked on, driven on, and used every day. Maintaining them is not that difficult. It's well worth the effort, because a home's value is partially dependent on how good the property looks.

Repairing Brickwork

Crumbling Brick Mortar

FAIRLY EASY **2–5 hours**

Patios are often made of bricks. Walkways and driveways are often lined with bricks. Their natural, rustic beauty, particularly as they weather, adds charm to any landscape. However, as time passes, some maintenance is required.

Over time, mortar—the stuff between bricks—loosens and crumbles. The holes should be filled for good looks and to stop further deterioration.

To do the job, five tools are required, all available at hardware stores or building supply dealers (see your Yellow Pages): a pointing trowel (about $4); a hammer; a wire brush (about $3); a jointer (about $3.50), which is a special tool (it looks like a very thin trowel) for smoothing the mortar out after it is applied; and a ³/₄-inch cold chisel (about $6).

For the hole filler, a premixed mortar is best. This is a powder that comes in 10- to 80-pound bags. All you do is add water in the amount specified on the label, and mix. Sakrete is one brand name.

First, use the cold chisel and hammer to chip out all unsound mortar—the stuff that's barely hanging on. To protect your eyes against flying chips, wear a pair of plastic sunglasses or those plastic goggles you wore in your high school science class.

Follow this by wire-brushing out all loose, crumbly material. Next, open up the bag of mortar mix and pour the powder out on a piece of plywood, cardboard, or into a wheelbarrow. (You can also mix the mortar in a plastic pail.) Thoroughly mix it with the trowel, as if you were blending flour and sugar. When it is all the same color, shape it into a little hill and make a hole in the center. Add a little water. Mix this thoroughly with the powder. Gradually add more water until you have added all that is specified on the label.

Carry the fresh mortar to the bricks in a pail or pan. Plop a soaking rag against the holey area to get it good and wet, then scoop out some mortar on the tip of the trowel and force it into a hole. Keep putting mortar in until the hole is overfilled a fraction of an inch; while filling, poke at the mortar to remove air pockets.

Let the mortar alone for about 5 minutes, then draw the jointer over it to shape and smooth it so it looks like the surrounding mortar.

If you smear any mortar on the bricks, clean it off right away, using the wire brush and water.

Every day for a week or so after the job, give the patches a half-minute light spray from your garden hose. This enables the mortar to "cure" properly.

Incidentally, you won't know how much mortar you'll need until you start the job. So buy a 40-pound bag at first. Hardware stores and building supply dealers carry it. A 40-pound bag costs about $6.

Tuck Pointing Brick
EASY 1–2 hours

The most common problem with brick is that the mortar that holds it together falls out in spots. The solution is to replace with fresh mortar, a process known as *tuck pointing.* For this job, you can use one of the premixed mortars or paste patchers. The latter come in cartridges and are available in various colors to match mortar colors.

First, clean out any loose or cracked mortar with a cold chisel. Get all the smaller pieces out by flushing the area with a hose, or use a stiff bristle brush and water.

Prepare the mortar mix, then wet the joints again and press the mortar into the crack with a jointer. When filled, use the jointer to finish the mortar to match joints on the rest of the bricks. After 5 minutes, clean the faces of bricks of excess mortar with a brush, then finish with the jointer.

Repairing Concrete

Cracks in Concrete

EASY **1–2 hours**

Concrete steps, walks, driveways, and patios commonly develop cracks (see Fig. 10.1). Indeed, sometimes it seems as if there is no such thing as concrete without cracks. At any rate, the repair is as easy as filling mortar holes. You should use the same tools, except you don't need the jointer.

Start by digging out all unsound (loose) material with your cold chisel and hammer. Brush out as much material as you can with a wire brush. Douse the crack with a fine spray from the hose. Fill the crack immediately.

The best filler for concrete is sand mix. Like mortar mix, it comes in a premixed form to which you add water. Start with a 20-pound bag. (Cost is about $4.50.)

Pour the mix onto a piece of plywood, cardboard, or into a wheelbarrow. Or, as with mortar, you can use a pail. Blend it with the trowel, make a little hill, poke a hole in the middle, and add a little water. Blend this water in, then the rest as specified on the bag.

Force the fresh mix down into the crack, poking it frequently to remove air pockets. Fill the crack completely, then smooth it level

FIGURE 10.1

Fixing cracks in concrete (patios in particular) is important if you don't want them to get bigger.

with the surrounding concrete by drawing the bottom of the trowel across it.

Place a piece of cloth or an old towel on the patch. Wet the cloth with a fine spray from your garden hose. Each day for a couple of days, wet it down the same way. A loose brick or board will hold the cloth or towel in place. Anything heavy will do.

The purpose of the moisture is to cure the mix gradually. If it is allowed to dry quickly, it stands a good chance of cracking and weakening, and you'll have to redo the job.

If you have a large-area cementing job, it may well be necessary to hire a professional to do it if you are very much concerned with appearance. The real skill that a mason brings to a job is the ability to smooth cement well, something that takes a long time to learn.

NARROW CRACKS

EASY **1–2 hours**

Driveways, steps, walks, walls, and other things made of concrete commonly develop hairline (narrow) cracks. While usually not serious in themselves unless they're in supporting walls, they should be repaired promptly because, left alone, they will get bigger and may necessitate a large job where an entire segment of material—say, a section of sidewalk—needs replacement.

For this job you can use a premixed sand mix, such as Sakrete makes, or a masonry paste patcher that comes in a cartridge, such as made by United Gilsonite or Red Devil. The premix is a powder that you mix with water; the paste comes ready for use. Unless you have lots of cracks, the paste will be more convenient.

Before using anything, first clean out the crack thoroughly. Repair material won't stick to a crack that is filled with soil and debris; it has to bond to concrete. For this you can use a stiff bristle brush, or a wire brush, or you can dig debris out with an old screwdriver, putty knife, or scraper.

To use the cartridge, first clip off the plastic nozzle at a 45-degree angle with a sharp knife. The wider the bead you want, the closer to the cartridge itself you should cut. Then break the cartridge seal by sticking a long nail down into the nozzle until it penetrates the heavy foil seal.

Rest the nozzle tip on the crack and squeeze the gun it sits in; the repair material will flow out in a neat bead. Move the tip along, pressing down to get the material as deeply into the crack as you can, and also to remove air bubbles.

When the crack is filled, use a putty knife or scraper to smooth the material. As you smooth, frequently dip the blade into a dish of water. This will make the material spread easier. Then, simply let it dry.

LARGER CRACKS
FAIRLY EASY **2–5 hours**

If you have a large crack to repair, one of the premixed cements is best. First, use a brush, scraper, and your fingers to remove all loose, crumbling material and soil. Examine the edges of the crack. Are they sound? If not, use a cold chisel and hammer to remove hanging parts. You want a solid, clean base to apply the premix to. Following the directions on the bag, mix a batch of the sand mix. Premix comes in various sizes—20, 45, and 80 pounds—and is not expensive. A 20-pound bag costs about $4.

The best way to mix a large batch is to dump the dry ingredients on a piece of plywood, a piece of plastic, or into a wheelbarrow. Stir them thoroughly with a shovel. Then, form the mix into a pile with a hole in the middle. Pour water in the hole and fold in the mix with the shovel. Mix thoroughly, adding water as needed, but don't exceed the amount specified on the bag unless the mix is too stiff. It's too easy to have, at one moment, a mix that is too stiff, and the next, a mix that is soupy. Go slowly as it will pay in the long run.

Before using the mix, douse the crack with water. The dry concrete will suck in this moisture rather than the water in the sand mix, which would weaken it. Then, pack the mix into the crack with a trowel, poking at it to remove all air pockets. Level it with a square trowel or board and then come back an hour or so later and give it a final smoothing with your square trowel. You can buy an inexpensive trowel at hardware stores. Smooth with sweeping strokes, keeping the front, or leading edge, of the trowel raised as you do.

That same day, and for a couple of days thereafter, spray the patch with a fine spray from a hose, or cover it with some sort of cloth, and keep that wet. This lets the concrete cure, or dry gradually, and prevents cracking.

Blacktop (Asphalt) Driveways

Holes in a Blacktop Driveway
FAIRLY EASY **2–5 hours**

If you have some holes in your blacktop driveway, you can repair them easily. The job is done with ready-to-use cold-mix asphalt patching compound, which comes in various-size heavy bags. Unless you've taken up weight lifting, however, you should have the store (hardware store or building materials supply) deliver it to your driveway where you're going to use it. Sakrete is one good brand. The cost is about $4.50 for a 40-pound bag.

First, shovel out all loose rocks and debris from the hole. If the hole is more than 6 inches wide and 4 inches deep, place a large rock at the bottom (you might get one at a local lot or from nearby woods). This will serve as your base.

Open the blacktop bag and scoop out a shovelful. Pour it into the hole. Do this until the hole is filled to within about an inch of the top. Use the end of a hefty board or the back of the shovel to compact (pat down hard) the blacktop; it's fairly soft, so you shouldn't have any trouble. When it seems thoroughly compacted, add more blacktop mix, this time filling a half-inch higher than the surrounding driveway surface.

Now compact some more. You can do this with a board or shovel, but it's easier and you'll do a better job with your car. Simply drive one wheel back and forth over it until the patch is level with the rest of the driveway.

Resealing a Driveway   *FAIRLY EASY* **2–5 hours**

Asphalt driveways should be resealed every year (see Fig. 10.2). This is not a particularly difficult job, but it should be done with care. Doing so will add years to the life of your driveway. *Sealcoating* is the process of applying a coat of liquid sealer to the surface of the driveway, sealing and protecting it from the cycle of melting and freezing water: the death knell of driveways.

How do you know if your driveway needs sealcoating? Simple. If you see cracks developing and dry, smaller pieces (bits of gravel that have come loose from the tarlike mixture), it needs to be sealcoated.

FIGURE 10.2

Blacktop driveways will serve you well if you take care of them.

HOW MUCH DO I NEED?

Measure your driveway. Multiply the length by the width. When you have the total square feet, figure that you'll get about 80 square feet of coverage for every gallon of sealer. It's available in 5-gallon buckets and costs about $20 (see Fig. 10.3). Velvetop and Weatherbeater are good brands of sealer.

DRESS FOR SUCCESS

Another important part of the job is dressing for it. Sealcoating is messy work, and wearing older, loose-fitting clothes—that you don't mind slopping up—is best. It's also a good idea to wear the right footwear for this kind of job. Heavy-soled shoes that you don't mind getting dirty are recommended (see Fig. 10.4). The final criterion is that the weather be at least 50°F and that there is no rain in the forecast for the next day and a half.

PREPARING THE SURFACE *EASY 1–2 HOURS*

Before starting any work, make sure you have repaired any large cracks or holes (usually over $1/4$ inch, as described in this chapter). Cracks or small holes (less than $1/4$ inch) can be filled with sealcoating. Also, sweep or blow off the driveway to remove any loose material from the surface.

Next, spray the entire driveway with water to remove any dust that's left on it. Finally, clean any oil spots with a commercial detergent (see Fig. 10.5). Do the best you can and follow the directions on the package. This is done with a stiff-bristled brush. You should scrub the stain and put some muscle power into it for the best results. You can get the detergent at your local home center (where you bought the driveway sealer), along with an applicator.

You may also want to cover these oil spots with a blacktop primer that is designed

FIGURE 10.3

Blacktop sealer is available in 5-gallon buckets— enough to cover about 400 square feet of driveway.

FIGURE 10.4

Workboots with heavy soles are best used when sealing driveways.

FIGURE 10.5

Scrubbing oil stains away before you seal the driveway will produce the best results.

FIGURE 10.6

Carefully pour the sealer where you think you'll need it to start.

FIGURE 10.7

Use an applicator to spread the sealer evenly.

to cover stains before you apply the sealcoat. It is available where you buy the sealer. Now let the surface dry, completely.

When you are ready to start sealing, mix the coating mixture thoroughly, because the heavier material sinks to the bottom when it is stored. You can mix it in the bucket with a clean stick, and it's best to mix it every so often as you apply it to maintain consistency.

Pour some of the sealer in the corner of the driveway, about 5 feet from the house (see Fig. 10.6). You can expect to spread about a 15- to 20-square-foot section at a time as you move down the driveway. Start with less than you'll need. That way, you won't have to rush to get it spread out. You can always add more.

Using the applicator, spread the sealcoating across the driveway with slightly overlapping strokes. Try to spread a thin layer and feather it out. It's important to spread it evenly, and not too thick, so it dries evenly (see Fig. 10.7).

When you are finished, mark or block off the driveway and stay off it for 24–48 hours. Allow it to dry thoroughly before you drive on it.

Powerwashing

FAIRLY EASY **2–5 hours**

People who want nearly instant gratification enjoy working with powerwashers. With this equipment you can wipe away years of dirt and filth in minutes. Although powerwashing is effective on asphalt driveways, it is even more effective on concrete. This is because concrete starts out lighter in color and is also more durable—it can withstand the powerful jets of water required to clean it. Be very careful with asphalt driveways. If you're not, bits and pieces can begin to come up. They get dislodged by the pressure of the water.

Start at the top of your driveway, holding the head of the washer about 8 inches from the driveway. You can adjust the height by watching the effect the water has on the driveway. If it seems to clean it pretty easily, work this way and use even strokes so you get one section done at a time. This way, you know what you've done and what you still have to do. It's important to spray toward the grade—that is, make sure the water runs downhill or to one side of the driveway. Slowly work away from the house, toward the street.

An important tip: keep an eye on the water and where it's going. Make sure it's draining properly and isn't pooling up somewhere on the driveway or elsewhere on your property. Let the driveway dry thoroughly before working on it any more.

Retaining Walls   *VERY DIFFICULT* **2 days**

Houses on steep, hilly terrain prove challenging for homeowners and contractors they employ. Places where people walk (walkways and patios) aren't necessarily enjoyable if they have to climb steps that resemble those in the Empire State Building.

To solve this problem, many contractors and homeowners install railroad tie walls to hold back earth so grading can be done to make flat surfaces on the property. This is popular on the north shore of Long Island, where I live.

However, a movement in the last few years has replaced two things: the materials used to build these walls and the people who build them. Now, more and more homeowners are choosing to do the work themselves using decorative blocks (instead of railroad ties) to build walls along driveways, walkways, and patios.

The Benefits of Blocks

Decorative cement blocks don't require mortar, cement (mixing and measuring can be daunting enough for homeowners), or forms used to pour foundations. Instead, using a level, string, and a strong back, a weekend warrior can build a 4-foot-high retaining wall in a weekend and save hundreds of dollars in labor costs. (Two-thirds of the cost of landscape construction jobs is for labor alone.)

The materials for block walls are about the same price as railroad ties, are much easier to work with, can be installed more quickly (blocks don't have to be cribbed, using extra ties to anchor the wall to hillsides), and are environmentally friendlier than railroad ties (arsenic is used to treat the ties, for a long life and to prevent rot). The following tips will help the ambitious homeowner.

Preparation—The Key to Success   *DIFFICULT* **5–7 hours**

Start by excavating the soil with a flat, square-end shovel. Dig a trench with neat, vertical walls and a flat, level bottom (see Fig. 10.8). The trench should be approximately 18 inches wide and 12 inches deep.

FIGURE 10.8

The trench should have a smooth, flat bottom and straight, vertical walls.

Next, line the bottom of the trench with 6 inches of recycled concrete. This material should be tamped solid. You can do this by nailing a 2 × 6 piece of wood (approximately 18 inches long) to a 2 × 4 × 6. Using the flat surface of the 2 × 6, pound the recycled concrete in the trench until it is solid. This material can be delivered by the yard and should be placed close to where you need it. Next, drive stakes into the ground at each end of the trench. Tie easily visible string between the stakes. This will serve to guide the first row of blocks to ensure that they are installed in a straight line.

Installing the Blocks

DIFFICULT **5–7 hours**

If your finished wall will be a straight line, you can start installing the blocks on either end of the trench. Lay the first block in the trench with the face of the block just touching the string. Next, grasp the block on both ends and wiggle it back and forth until it rests snugly in the crushed concrete mix. The blocks will sit square because of their design. They measure 18 inches across and are 8 inches high. The rear of the block is shaped like a standard cinder block, and the face is a concave, rough surface (available in gray or rose-tan color). Each block could weigh up to 80 pounds. It is certainly not going anywhere once it is installed.

Next, using a standard level, check to be sure that the block is level (right to left and back to front). You may have to scoop small amounts of base material under the blocks or remove some as you go. Repeat the pattern for each block until you have completed the whole row.

It is critically important to achieve a straight and strong first row of blocks that is resting on a firm, solid base, because this row will support the rest of the wall (see Fig. 10.9). Taking time and care at this stage will have tremendous benefits later!

Backfill for Strength and Drainage   *DIFFICULT* **5–7 hours**

When the first row is complete, backfill the trench behind the blocks with ³⁄₄-inch rocks (bluestone or other rocks are available at your local

FIGURE 10.9

The first row of blocks is critical, because it will support the rest of the wall.

THE BENEFITS OF BACKFILLING

Backfilling, the act of replacing and/or installing material (dirt, rocks, etc.) behind walls, is vital. A neighbor of mine years ago built a similar wall. He was in a hurry and didn't bother to backfill the blocks before moving to the next level. After a month, the wall (three levels and about 12 feet high) was on the ground, in heaps of broken blocks. A strong rainstorm had dumped water behind the blocks. Without any stones to dissipate the water and help it drain, the water pooled and swept away the foundation—causing the whole wall to come down. Thank goodness nobody was hurt. Lesson learned: backfill properly—even if it takes a long time.

nursery). Again, having this material delivered close at hand is smart, because it is very heavy and half a wheelbarrel at a time is par for the course. Be sure to shovel the rocks behind the blocks (leave 6–10 inches for rocks) and inside the holes in the blocks themselves. This will serve to shore up each level of the wall and provide adequate water drainage behind the wall.

Stagger Each Row for Strength and Beauty   *DIFFICULT* **5–7 hours**

Each block should be placed over the seam where two blocks meet in the previous row (see Fig. 10.10). Round fiberglass pins that resemble an 8-inch piece of white chalk should be placed inside holes on the tops of blocks. The next row of blocks should be placed so their holes slip over the exposed edge of the pins from the previous row. This will prevent the blocks from sliding forward, back, or from side to side.

Be sure to remember to backfill each row of blocks as you build. It is a good idea to tamp the backfill material as you work, to ensure that the rock serves its purpose of strength and dissipation of water.

Capping the Job   *FAIRLY EASY* **2–5 hours**

When you have reached the desired height for your wall, capping the structure is one of the last things to install before you clean up the

FIGURE 10.10

Each row of blocks should be added carefully, with each block over the seam where two meet below it.

worksite. Capping material is similar in appearance to the blocks but they are half the thickness, and they do not have a cinder block back. These caps are much lighter and easier to work with than the blocks. They should be installed over pins just like the previous row of blocks and set in place with the right and left sides butting up against the neighboring caps on the right and left (see Fig. 10.11). The caps give the wall a finished appearance and provide an aesthetically pleasing border to the top (see Fig. 10.12).

Final Backfill and Job Cleanup   *FAIRLY EASY* **2–5 hours**

After all the rocks have been backfilled behind the wall, the dirt from the embankment should be backfilled behind the wall. A good grading job above and behind the wall is important because it shapes the slope of the ground that the wall is holding back and serves to define and highlight the beauty and effectiveness of the wall itself. Lastly, hose down the wall to remove concrete and rock dust that inevitably accumulates on the jobsite. By doing this, you will reveal the original luster and beauty of the blocks. And don't worry if you see scratches and imperfections in the blocks. The material is processed, but made from a natural material. This natural material is not supposed to be perfect. That's the rugged beauty of it! Enjoy it!

FIGURE 10.11

Caps on the top of the wall provide a neat, finished look.

FIGURE 10.12

The finished wall is attractive and functional.

Siding

Maintaining the outside of your house is very important for several reasons. First, for most people, their homes are their most valuable asset. Protecting your house from the ravages of wind, rain, snow, and anything else is protecting your investment. Second, keeping your house attractive and looking new (with a fresh coat of paint or siding) is aesthetically pleasing and adds a lot of curb appeal—a potential buyer's (and your neighbors') first impression of your house.

Painting the Outside of Your House

Doing your own exterior house painting can save you a lot of money. Labor normally is about 80 to 85 percent of the cost of the job, and jobs start at around $1000. Also, you don't need great skills to do a good job. If you take your time, and give the job some tender, loving care, you can do quite well indeed.

Unlike interior painting, though, many people don't like to do exterior painting. Perhaps you're one. It is more tiring than doing an interior job (those trips up and down a ladder do add up), and if a house has more than one story, you have to spend some time high on a ladder. If the view up there is not worth the nail biting you may do while you're up there, I suggest that you do the lower, easily reached portions of the house and hire a contractor to do the top. You can still save a good deal of cash.

Paint

There are two basic kinds of paint that can be used for painting the exterior of your home: latex, which thins and cleans up with water; and oil-based, which uses mineral spirits as the solvent (see Table 11.1).

One advantage of latex is that it can be applied when the siding is damp, such as after a light rain. Another is that you can touch up missed spots later, without the touch-up showing. But its big plus is using water as the solvent. This makes it much easier to work with than oil-based paint.

It's a good idea to save the oil-based paint for metal surfaces. Oil-based paint is more effective in preventing rust and staving off mildew.

In general, latex paint for siding (asbestos and cedar shingles) is available in flat or low-luster finishes, though a few manufacturers do make high-gloss exterior latex paints. Oil-based paint is available in a gloss finish only. For trim work, you can get latex and oil-based paints in semigloss and high-gloss finishes. Some companies make paints that are good for both siding and trim. Also, even some low-luster paints have enough of a shine to them to allow rain to wash off their surfaces. This is an obvious plus when painting the outside of your house.

BUY GOOD PAINT

No matter what type of paint you get, make sure it's a good paint. Bargain-basement paint gives bargain-basement results. It doesn't hide well, fades quickly, is difficult to apply, and—the final indictment against it—it doesn't give as much coverage per gallon (sometimes only half as much) as quality paint.

One way to get good paint is to buy only brand names, but you have to take care: Even top brands have lines of varying quality, and the lowest on the totem pole can be little better than bargain paint. The criterion I have always used is price. If a gallon of siding paint doesn't

TABLE 11.1 Exterior Paints

Product	Inscription
Oil paint	Also commonly called house paint. Cleans up with mineral spirits. Dries to a high gloss. Good covering power.
Latex paint	Dries and cleans up with water. Can be applied to damp surface. Less prone to fading than oil-based paint. Low sheen. Good covering power. Coats to a high gloss.

cost at least $18, and a gallon of trim $15, better stay away from it, unless it's a legitimate sale.

Behr or Gliddon are good-quality paints. A gallon of satin-finish exterior paint will run you about $20 a gallon, and you'll get about 400 square feet of coverage from it.

If your house requires two coats, either because you're changing from a dark to a light color or because the surface is badly weathered, or you are painting it for the first time, use a primer.

Primers are formulated to penetrate deeply into siding and trim, providing a smooth base for your finishing coat and good "tooth"—the new paint will adhere better. A variety of types are available for painting everything from wood siding to older, flat asbestos shingles. My advice is to ask a knowledgeable paint dealer what would be best for your situation.

A great all-around primer is made by a company called Zinsser. The product is simply called 1-2-3 and costs about $18 a gallon. Depending on the porosity of the surface you are priming, you'll get up to 400 square feet of coverage. When working with a primer, tint it slightly to the approximate finish color. Covering will be easier.

One caution about finish paint: Don't be misled by claims of manufacturers about their paint being able to cover any color—say, to cite an extreme example, white over black. Sometimes the paint really will cover in one coat, but you have to be a magician (or a professional) with a brush. Most times the paint simply won't cover. Manufacturers know this, but they gamble that their paint (at a much higher price than normally, of course) will cover most colors; meanwhile, they are able to wave dramatic "one coat covers!" ads.

COLOR

Color is, of course, an important consideration. You can get finish paint in both custom-mixed and a wide variety of standard colors. In recent years, custom-mixed colors have been priced the same as stock colors, so you can get exactly what you want at no extra charge. Be aware, though, that the shade of a color on a chip card will not be exactly the same as on your house. Different surfaces absorb the paint to different degrees, and this, among other things, affects final color.

HOW MUCH PAINT?

There are involved, Einstein-like formulas for calculating how much paint you will need to cover a house. These have always struck me as a bit of overkill. Rule of thumb is less taxing. The average house will take about 10 gallons of siding paint and 3 gallons of trim (assuming one coat). If you need more, you can always pick it up. If you need less,

MONEY-SAVING TIP

Tell your paint supplier that you are going to buy a lot of paint, enough for your whole house. Chances are, he'll discount brand names 10 to 15 percent.

While you're in the store, pick up a few inexpensive, large plastic buckets for mixing. The dealer will also give you free painting hats and mixing sticks.

the dealer will usually take back unused gallons and refund your money—but clear this with him beforehand. Of course, he won't do this with custom-mixed paint.

Brushes

The kind of tools you use to paint with depends on what you are painting. For siding it is usually best to avoid rollers. The reason: The time it takes to cut in—paint places where the roller can't reach—cancels out the time saved by using the roller on flat areas. Nylon brushes will work fine with both latex and oil-based paints. Figure on using a 4-inch brush for siding, a $2^1/_2$-inch brush for general trim, and a 2-incher for windows.

BUY QUALITY BRUSHES

As with paint, you can get stuck by buying bargain-basement brushes. Bristles may be too short, tips blunted instead of flagged (split), handles too short. Again, like paint, price is a good indicator of quality. Figure to spend about $10 for a 4-incher and half that for your $2^1/_2$ and 2-inchers.

With proper care, good brushes will last for many years. For shakes, which have vertical striations, or grooves, a cut-down old brush is good. Don't use a good brush—you'll kill it. Or, you can use any of the many pad-type painters on the market. With these, you dip the pad into the paint and wipe it on. They work well.

MASONRY ROLLERS

Rollers do have their place when surfaces are extra rough, such as for masonry, whose textured surface has many minute hills and valleys. A roller with a long nap or fiber works well. Loaded with paint, it gets into those hills and valleys. A long-nap of $1^1/_2$ inches or more works pretty well on the rough surface of bricks and cement.

Preparation

DIFFICULT **5–7 hours**

You've likely heard it before, but it's worth repeating: The key to a good paint job is preparation. The better you prepare surfaces for painting, the longer the job will last and the better the result will be.

The most common siding problem most people have is peeling paint. For heavy peeling, a hook-type scraper and wire brush will do nicely (see Fig. 11.1). When all unsound paint is off, use a medium sandpaper to feather or smooth the edges of the resulting craters so they don't advertise themselves after you paint (see Fig. 11.2).

Be sure to scrape off all loose paint and wear goggles to protect your eyes.

After scraping off peeling paint, sand it smooth with sandpaper.

If your house is peeling or blistering heavily, you might have a moisture problem: Water vapor, migrating through the siding to the outside air, literally pushes the paint off the siding. You can remove the loose paint with high-heat devices of various kinds, but I favor an electric sanding tool that you can rent. High heat can be dangerous.

The sanding tool has a sanding disc and legs which keep the disc in contact with the wall at the exact depth required, without the danger of gouging—something you should be alert to if you use a regular portable sander or a drill with a sanding attachment. You can rent these special sanding tools for very little money at almost any rental outfit. See your Yellow Pages for a location near you.

All loose paint must be removed. Just as important, if you have a big problem, though, is to diagnose and correct the cause of the symptom.

REMOVING DIRT

FAIRLY EASY **2–5 hours**

All heavy accumulations of soil must be removed. A soft bristle brush and a strong cleaning solution followed by a rinse with clear water will do the job. Wash from the bottom up to avoid streak marks from water dripping down. Before doing anything, though, make sure you are dealing with dirt, not mildew. Mildew is a fungus that does not respond to ordinary cleaning. To test, dab pure bleach on the suspect area. If the soil comes off, you have mildew.

Ordinary soil will not come off. All mildew must be taken off, or it will grow right through your paint. To do this, mix pure bleach with water and have at it with a sturdy scrub brush (use one part bleach to three parts water). If you have hard-to-reach areas, you can use a push broom. Or, if the problem is really extensive, you can rent an electric brush. After removing mildew, wash down the areas with clear water and let dry before painting.

CAULKING
EASY **1–2 hours**

Proper preparation also includes caulking the seams of your house. That is, caulk all the areas where there are potential or actual openings: around window frames, between the siding and the foundation, at house corners, wherever different materials meet (brick and siding, for example). (See Fig. 11.3.)

A variety of different caulks are available, some of which will last 10 years and more. However, these latter types are relatively expensive and make sense only if you intend to thoroughly clean out all old, deteriorated caulking, because the new material will last only as long as whatever is beneath it. A total clean-out is a large job; if you don't want to do it, your best bet is inexpensive, oil-based caulk. This will last just as long as the expensive varieties when all old material is not removed.

LEAVE SOME OPENINGS
EASY **1–2 hours**

FIGURE 11.3

Caulking in gaps and between small spaces keeps moisture and cold out of your home.

It is not required—nor desirable—to button up every seam in the house. You should allow some openings to let moisture vapor inside walls escape. Any spots where water can't run in are fine, such as where the bottom of windowsills join the siding.

If siding is damaged, now is the time to minister to it. For help, it's best to take a picture of it and bring the picture to a home center or siding supplier. If you still need help, have a contractor give you an estimate and perhaps you can pick his brain at the same time.

If window putty has dried out and cracked, it should be replaced. Use glazing compound instead of putty, which is passé now. Glazing compound stays flexible indefinitely and normally doesn't crack or dry out as putty does.

COVERING UP   *EASY* **1–2 house**

Before you start wielding a brush, cover all areas where paint can spatter, such as driveways, walks, shrubbery, and screens. The best covers you can buy are 9- × 12-foot canvas ones. Though expensive, they will last a lifetime. Cheaper are various fabric and heavy plastic coverings. Very inexpensive are drop cloths made of super-thin plastic. These are very light and susceptible to being blown away, so anchor them at the edges with boards or bricks. The cheapest drop cloth of all is overlapping sheets of newspaper, also weighted down. Screens that are left up may be covered with newspaper secured with masking tape. Also, paint that gets on concrete or screening is not simple to remove, so be careful. To save time painting screens, remove them and paint them separately. Just lay them on a couple of sawhorses or boxes.

Priming   *VERY DIFFICULT* **7–10 hours**

Not all exterior paint jobs can be done with one coat of paint. For example, if paint is peeling extensively, good painting procedure calls for removing all the peeling paint and applying at least two coats of paint. At the risk of repeating myself, it's important to know which steps come first when painting: if you're going to change from one color to another—that is, from a dark color to a light color—a two-coat job is also needed.

The first coat is called the primer, and for this job you should use one of the special paints called primers. It will do a number of things. First, it will provide a smooth base for the finish paint. Second, it will ensure that the finish paint does not penetrate the surface unevenly, creating a spotty effect. And, finally, it will provide good "tooth" for the finish paint—the paint will be able to get a better grip.

There are a wide variety of primers available, each formulated for specific surfaces—wood, shingles, what have you. Since many of the experts believe the primer is more important than the finish coat, buy a good-quality product and follow label directions exactly. Table 11.2 may help answer some questions you might have about what kind of primer to use.

You use the primer the same way as you would a finish paint; just follow label directions for mixing. To make things easier, it's best to tint the primer to the approximate color of the finish paint. You can do this with so-called universal colorants; directions for use are on the tubes. Also, you can have your primer tinted at the paint store or home improvement center where you shop.

Painting   *VERY DIFFICULT* **7–10 hours**

Follow label directions for mixing and applying paint. Most have restrictions about at what temperature to paint, if the wind is strong, and

TABLE 11.2 Exterior Primers

Product	Use on
Alkyd or oil-based	Previously painted wood, especially where caulking is a problem, and on new wood.
Rust-inhibiting primer, alkyd or latex	All metal, especially rusting metal.
Latex primer	Masonry and cement-composition shingles, where alkali is a natural product which might "burn" through the paint.

the like. Also, try to schedule your work so you don't have to paint in direct sunlight. This is tiresome on the painter and can lead to paint problems you can live without.

The best way to mix the paint is to box it, as the professionals say: Pour it repeatedly back and forth between two containers until it is all the same consistency and color. If you buy it fresh, your mixing job will be easier. Indeed, if you get paint that is lumpy or in which there is a thick residue on the bottom, take it back. Otherwise, you won't be getting the quality you're paying for.

PAINTING SEQUENCE　　　　　*VERY DIFFICULT* **7–10 hours**

Paint the siding first, then the trim—windows, eaves, etc. This way, if paint drips, it will not mar finished work. To save time on trim, cut in the entire perimeter framing of all windows with siding paint rather than trim paint (see Fig. 11.4). The reverse, cutting in with trim paint, is harder to do. It's best to start on the second story and work your way down. Let gravity be your friend when it comes to paint.

You can use a standard rung ladder for the job, suspending your paint bucket (and it should have a mouth wide enough to let you get the brush in and out easily) from a hook. Also useful are ladder jacks, which you can rent cheaply. These attach to two halves of a rung ladder. A wide, stout board is laid between them to give you a platform to work from. In general, when painting, follow these rules:

■ *Use plenty of paint.* Not using enough paint is the mistake most beginners make, and skimping leads to missed spots and much more difficult work. Just dip the brush bristles about one-third or halfway into the paint, tap it once on each side of the can, and lay it on. Don't mash the bristles. Hold the brush lightly, like something that is alive, letting it and the paint—not your arm— do the work.

- *Paint from the dry into the wet.* This is the description pros use, whereby you start each stroke about a foot and a half from the wet edge of the previously applied paint and paint back toward it. This covers the maximum dry area per each stroke. Once the paint is on, as it were, give it a few light, long strokes, lifting the brush at the end of each stroke to feather or blend areas in, rather than leaving blobs.

- *Paint small areas at one time.* Just paint what you can easily see and reach. It doesn't pay to stretch. This can lead to missed spots and a very fatigued painter very quickly.

FIGURE 11.4

Watch your work carefully when painting trim.

- *Paint windows from proper angles.* When painting narrow parts of windows, just dip the tip of the brush in the paint, stand, and apply at an angle that lets you see the wood well. For example, don't approach the framework that crosshatches the glass (called muntins) head-on. If you move to the side a little, you'll be able to see more of the wood; this will help you keep your brush on the wood. If you get paint on the glass, wipe it off with a solvent-dampened cloth wrapped around a forefinger.

Painting Siding

DIFFICULT **5–7 hours**

If you are right-handed, start painting the siding at the right side of the house, working your way across to the left. Reverse the procedure if you are left-handed. From a ladder, the average person can paint a 3-foot-square area from one ladder position. When this area is done, move the ladder and paint to an adjacent 3-foot-square area (or whatever you can easily see and reach), overlapping smoothly into the first. Work your way across, painting a horizontal band of the house, then come back and start a new band.

Depending on the kind of siding you have, slightly different brush techniques are required. On clapboard (smooth boards), first paint the bottom edge of the boards, then paint the face (see Fig. 11.5). Remember to use plenty of paint and go from the dry into the wet. If you are painting smooth shingles, follow the same basic technique as for clapboard. Paint the edges of the shingles, then the face, but make the final, smoothing strokes vertical. When painting shakes (vertically grooved

FIGURE 11.5

Painting the bottom edge of clapboard before painting the face saves time and effort.

material), hit the edge, then apply paint with either a cut-down brush or a pad painter with vertical strokes.

Painting Problems

Following are some common exterior painting problems and ways to solve them.

BLISTERING

There are two causes of blistering: temperature and moisture. Blisters caused by temperature usually occur when paint is applied in direct sunlight, or when the surface is too hot. Temperature blisters usually form quickly—within an hour or two (sometimes several days) after painting. However, wait a few weeks to be sure that all blisters have appeared, then remove them with a rented siding sander and repaint. Avoid painting in sun or high heat.

Moisture blisters can usually be distinguished if you puncture one—a little water will run out. You can install miniature vents (available from paint and hardware stores) in the siding to bleed off water vapor that gets trapped between walls and migrates outside to form blisters. Also, try to cut down on water vapor inside the house; a dehumidifier helps.

ALLIGATORING

Alligatoring is characterized by paint breaking up into segments which resemble alligator skin. The most common cause is that incompatible paints were applied. If you have alligatoring, take the paint off to bare wood, then repaint. If the problem is slight, you can take a chance and repaint over the alligator-like surface.

CHALKING

Chalking is characterized by staining. Pigment in paint washes out and stains whatever is below—such as a brick wall. Three causes are common: (1) badly weathered wood that was not primed properly; (2) cheap paint was used; or (3) paint was applied below the recommended temperature level on the can. One point: Some oil-based paints are formulated to chalk gradually to keep the paint job fresh looking. But if it's excessive, you've got a problem. If you do, wash the affected areas clean and apply primer to the offending paint. Then repaint.

CRAWLING

Crawling occurs right when you apply the paint. Paint puddles up, like water would on a greasy plate. The culprit is usually a heavy accumulation of oily dirt. If this happens, clean the area and repaint.

SPOTTING

Sometimes, sections of paint lose glossiness or color. The cause is usually skimpy application. There is no real solution for spotting. In time the bad spots will blend in with the rest of the job. Don't apply another coat of paint right away: This can lead to too quick an accumulation of paint, which leads to wrinkling. The term wrinkling is used to characterize alligatoring in its very early stages. If you get wrinkling, wait, then paint over it.

CRACKLING/WRINKLING

The symptom is that the applied paint looks like aluminum foil that has been wrinkled, then spread flat. The cause: The paint was applied too quickly. The solution: Use sandpaper in a power sander to smooth out spots.

Cleanup and Storage   *EASY* **1–2 hour**

If you are just going to be storing brushes or rollers overnight, all you need to do is wrap them in some air-tight clinging plastic wrap. If you are going to be storing the tools for a long time, they should first be thoroughly cleaned.

To clean a roller, first squeeze out as much paint as possible by running your mixing stick or scraper along the height of the roller all around, letting the paint run into the can. Then, wash the roller thoroughly. If you used latex, do this with warm water and detergent—don't forget the detergent, it's the key to easier cleaning. Then, rinse under warm water, squeeze water out with your hands, and store the roller wrapped in newspaper.

To clean a roller used with oil-based paint, squeeze out the paint, then wash in a can filled with the solvent you used. Do this for 5 minutes, then discard the solvent and rinse the roller for another few minutes in fresh solvent.

To clean a brush, place it flat on a sheet of newspaper. Squeeze out excess paint with your scraper or putty knife, working on the bristles from the ferrule, or metal part, to the tips. If latex paint was used, wash the brush in warm sudsy water, wrap, and store.

If you used oil-based paint, you can first squeeze out excess paint as above, then wash the brush thoroughly in solvent, and store.

A good trick for storing any kind of paint for just overnight is to pour a little thinner into the paint, forming a film that air can't penetrate. There's no need to put the lid on. If paint is to be stored for long periods, first clean the lip of the paint can, then hammer the lid on securely.

To clean yourself, the best thing I've found is a lanolin-based cream (designed to clean hands). You just wipe it on, let it work for a minute, then wipe it and the paint off with a paper towel. It leaves your skin in better shape than before you painted.

Spray Painting

DIFFICULT **5–7 hours**

The state of the weather will affect spray painting outdoors. Obviously, it must be prevailingly dry. No exterior painting, by any method, can be done if it keeps raining. But spraying is also affected by wind. If it is a windy time of year in your part of the world, do not use a spray gun outside the house.

Apart from this difficulty, exterior spray painting is easier than interior spray work. There is less to mask, for one thing. Doors and windows must be masked, but drainpipes, for example, can be left unmasked and brush-painted, afterwards, on top of the sprayed coat, in the color of your choice. Lawns, flower beds, and paving can simply be covered with a tarpaulin or weighted-down polyethylene sheet.

Hard surfaces such as paving can be masked with a thin layer of earth, which is brushed off afterwards. Holes and cracks in the wood (if your siding is wood) should be filled and, if necessary, the surface should be primed. The primer can be sprayed on also, if necessary, but mask the areas not to be painted.

Be sure to check what kind of spraying equipment you should use if you have questions. What you're spraying will dictate what kind of paint you should use. What kind of paint you use, in turn, will dictate what kind of equipment, particularly spray nozzles, you should use.

For instance, masonry paints, as used for the outside of houses, can be sprayed only with special equipment including an extra-wide nozzle (to let the stone particles through) and an automatic stirrer (to stop them from settling). Sometimes, if it seems a little too complicated, it's best to head down to your paint supply store or rental store and simply ask questions.

Siding Repairs

Depending on what kind of siding you have on your house, it will be more or less susceptible to damage. Wood siding develops cracks and can warp; asbestos siding, which is brittle, cracks; aluminum siding dents; and vinyl siding can become pushed in or misshapen. No matter what the problem, it is usually within the scope of the beginner's skills to make the necessary repairs.

Asbestos Shingles
FAIRLY EASY **2–5 hours**

One of the problems with asbestos shingles—in fact, with any kind of siding—is that nails sometimes come loose. But making the repair is something that should be approached gingerly. As mentioned, this type of shingle is brittle, and can crack very easily.

If the nail is still there, gently tap it back in place almost flush. For the last 1/2 inch or so, use a nail set—a thin, rodlike device that looks like an oversized nail—to tap it in the rest of the way. This lessens your chances of giving the shingle an errant tap. A tap is all you need to break it. Just drive the nail flush, no more.

If there are no existing nails, or the ones you reset are still loose, use some extra nails. Drill small holes through the shingle, an inch or two from where the existing ones are, then set the new nails in. Nails should be an annular ring type and of galvanized steel or some other metal that doesn't rust.

CRACKED ASBESTOS SHINGLES
FAIRLY EASY **2–5 hours**

If a shingle is cracked but both pieces are in place, you don't have to replace it. Just slide a sheet of roofing felt under the shingle (you will probably have to pull nails part way out first) so that it is completely beneath the crack. Then drive new nails in, at the bottom edge of the shingle, after first drilling small holes for the nails.

If a shingle is in really bad shape, then replacement is called for. Home improvement centers and hardware stores sell them in batches. Bring some muscles to the store though, as they are heavy. Shingles are nailed to the house at the top and bottom, with the top nails going through the bottom of the course above. To remove the shingle, you have a variety of methods at your disposal. Since shingles are brittle, you can simply demolish the bad one in place with a hammer, taking care not to hit good ones, and remove it piece by piece. Another way is to slip a hacksaw blade between the shingle and overlapping course above and cut the nails; also cut nails at the bottom this way. Use pliers to replace the shingle; simply slide the new one up in place so it is aligned with adjacent shingles, then nail it in place. Shingles come with predrilled holes. If you can align these with the ones on the other shingles, fine; if not, drill new ones.

The asbestos shingles that are most vulnerable are those installed at the bottom of the house. Often, the tarpaper rips after a shingle is damaged because the paper is exposed, and it must also be replaced.

Wood Shingles

Repairing wood shingles is similar to repairing asbestos ones. First, hammer all nails in flush with the surface. If a shingle is cracked in one spot, you can insert a piece of roofing felt underneath, then nail the shingle tight at the bottom.

If the shingle requires replacement, nails, of course, must also be removed. Wood shingles are commonly nailed through the bottom and the top. There may be strips of wood under the shingles at the bottom, which raise them for a shadow effect (see Fig. 11.6).

To remove the nails you can insert a hacksaw blade under the shingle and cut the nails. Or you can chisel a little space around the exposed nails to create a space for pulling the nails out with pliers. The latter method is slower, but will work if the hacksaw blade doesn't (sometimes shingles are nailed on so tightly you can't slip the blade in). Then pry the shingle out, install the new one, and nail it in place. Ask your dealer about the best nails to use if you are uncertain.

Clapboard

Wood siding also comes in long-board form; if it is tapered at the top, it's called *bevel siding*. But if it is locked together at top and bottom, with one board fitting into the slots of the other (tongue and groove), it's called *drop siding*.

FIGURE 11.6

Wood shingles are beautiful and effective when they are maintained.

There is also a siding made up of "1-by" (1 × 8, 1 × 10, 1 × 12), made of boards that are not tapered at the top but are overlapped. This and bevel siding are often called *clapboard.*

If these boards are slightly cracked, you can fill them with caulking compound or wood putty. The latter is a fibrous wood material that comes in paste form and is easy to apply with a putty knife. When it is dry, it can be sanded, sawed, or drilled just like wood. Work it into the cracks well with a putty knife. It will go a long way to help with repairs (see Fig. 11.7).

FIGURE 11.7

Sanding, sealing, and painting clapboard siding goes a long way.

BAD CRACKS

FAIRLY EASY **2–5 hours**

If the clapboard siding or "1-by" is badly cracked or rotted, complete replacement is called for. If the particular length of clapboard is short, then you may be able to buy and replace it with a new board. However, if the board is long, then you can get by with a patch.

Clapboard is nailed at the bottom and the top. Always use galvanized nails for this job. Top nails go through the bottom of the boards above. The repair is made by cutting out the bad section with a backsaw, or small handsaw, and nailing in a new piece. To do this, first insert two tapered wedges an inch or so to either side of the bad section, and three-fourths up the width of the board—far enough to create space beneath it and the board below. This will provide room for the saw to cut. If you wish, you can protect the boards beneath the bad one by wedging slim blocks of wood beneath your saw lines.

TAKE OUT NAILS

EASY **1–2 hours**

When you have cut through on both sides, drive the wedges a little higher, underneath the board above, and proceed to take out the bad section. Sometimes you can do this by hand; sometimes you will require a chisel and hammer. Take care not to tear the tar paper if you are using a chisel.

If most of the piece breaks off but some is left under the board above, slip a hacksaw up there and cut the nails out. If the whole piece comes out, you can depress the board enough so you can grip the nail with a hammer and pull it out. You can then pry the strip out with a screwdriver.

EXAMINE TAR PAPER

When the piece is out, examine the tar paper. If it is cut or torn, patch it with a glob of roofing cement. If it is ripped rather extensively, use large-headed galvanized nails to secure a patch made of tar paper over it, and seal the edges with roofing cement.

Carefully measure the gap you have to fill and cut a new piece of clapboard to fit as well as possible. Place it under the board, then tap it in place with a hammer, using a block of wood as a cushion against denting the board edge. With the new piece in place, nail it down permanently at the top and bottom. If the top board is old and dried out, it's best to drill pilot holes for the nails. Sink nail heads—you should use finishing nails—slightly below the surface and fill the depressions above with glazing compound or wood putty.

Apply a primer coat of paint, then fill the edges of the patch with caulking compound and fill nail-head depressions with wood putty. A final coat of paint can then be applied. Assuming you are painting the entire house, the patch should blend in quite nicely.

Drop Siding
FAIRLY EASY **2–5 hours**

Drop siding, because of the way it is nailed, can only be broken out with a hammer and chisel, piece by piece. Then you cut a board to fit, first trimming the tongue off the top piece to make it fit in. But this makes for a difficult repair, and you'd be better off to try and patch the bad board with wood putty.

Aluminum Siding
DIFFICULT **5–7 hours**

Aluminum siding is effective for keeping the elements out, but it has some drawbacks—if it's hit, it dents. It's difficult to get those dents out and straighten the metal. It also gets scratched and if left, can start to develop some problems.

ALUMINUM SIDING—A RICH HISTORY

Aluminum siding for houses was developed way back in 1945, by a company owned by the same family that produced Reynolds Wrap. The company predicted there would be a growing demand for aluminum in peacetime, after the war. They predicted wisely. The housing boom that followed when soldiers returned from the war saw a surge in demand for houses, and aluminum siding to protect them. It's still in use today.

To repair scratches, sand the area down to bare metal with a medium-grit sandpaper. Apply primer specifically made for aluminum, then apply latex exterior paint (colored to match your siding).

For small dents, drill a $\frac{1}{8}$-inch hole in the deepest part of the dent, install a self-tapping sheet-metal screw, grip the head of it with a pair of pliers, and pull until the dent disappears. Remove the screws. Next, sand or file down the area until smooth. Fill the holes with epoxy. You can buy this at an automotive store or home improvement center. Smear the mixture over the holes, let dry, and sand smooth. Apply an aluminum primer and then you're ready to paint it with latex house paint.

If the damage is too severe, it's best to replace a whole sheet. This is better than cutting a sheet in half and having to deal with seams. When you take the damaged panel off, look at how it is attached to the house and follow the same pattern when you install the new section. To be sure you are getting the right piece, with the correct hardware, it's probably best to bring samples with you to your supplier.

You may have to remove other sections (temporarily) to install the new one. To reinstall these sections, follow the same nail patterns you saw when you took them off.

Again, if it seems like the job isn't for you, consult a contractor and let him look at what you've got. Sometimes, it might be best to simply pick his brain on how to do a job.

Vinyl Siding

DIFFICULT **5–7 hours**

Although vinyl siding is nearly indestructible—it's sold as maintenance free, with little or no bending, breaking, warping, or discoloring—it occasionally does need some maintenance. Other than simply washing it off or scrubbing it with a sponge (with water and detergent) and rinsing it, it can crack.

A special tool that is essential for working on vinyl siding is a zip tool—a hand tool for separating and repositioning the interlocking bottom parts of sections on your house. If you don't have one, you risk slicing up your fingers. Nobody wants that.

The zip tool has a handle on one end and is a thin steel blade that looks like a hacksaw blade on the other. This end is bent to form a hook, and it's this part that you use to pry up a section of siding (particularly horizontal sections).

If you have to remove a section that is cracked, say, start by inserting the tip, with the hook up, into the side of a section. Once it's in position, pull the tool down and away from the wall to separate the edges. Slide the tool along the length and repeat the process. Once the bottom flap is up, be careful not to bend the sheet too far up, because it could break.

Slide a pry bar under the sheet and pry up the nails that are holding it on. To match broken pieces, use a piece that you might have saved from the original job. If you had the job done by a contractor, perhaps they left you some extra material to use for just such an emergency.

To attach pieces, you can use PVC cement—the kind used by plumbers to attach plastic plumbing parts together. It is strong and waterproof. Before this, you should use PVC cleaner/primer (which comes with the cement) to clean the patch and the spot that needs to receive the patch. After this, put glue on each piece and hold the patch on the siding for about 30 seconds or so, until it hardens.

To replace whole sections, reverse the removal process described before.

Decks

Most decks these days are made of pressure-treated pine, redwood, cedar, or other moisture and/or rot-resistant woods. Another popular decking material is a man-made composite that looks like wood, is available in several colors, but is virtually indestructible and immune to rot, warping, fading, or breaking. In fact, besides an occasional cleaning, it's also virtually maintenance-free. Nexwood Industries is one company that manufactures this material (see Figs. 12.1 and 12.2).

Eventually, though, foot traffic and relentless rain, wind, and baking sun all take their toll, and all decks require periodic maintenance. This may include securing and/or replacing boards or other parts (stair treads and weak railings), or cleaning and treating with sealers, stains, and preservatives.

Before treating them, decks need to be cleaned. This can be done by scrubbing the deck with a mild bleach solution or by powerwashing.

Powerwashing

FAIRLY EASY **2–5 hours**

Powerwashing is a quick way to remove old sealers, stains (bird droppings, barbecue tidbits, sap from trees, mildew, etc.) mold, and discolorations (boards that fade with age), and reveal a new layer of wood beneath (see Fig. 12.3). The results can be quite dramatic. I've seen decks 10 years old appear like new after being powerwashed.

FIGURE 12.1

Decks made of composite material resist rot, warping, and wood-boring insects. They stay beautiful with little care. *(Courtesy of Nexwood Industries.)*

FIGURE 12.2

Decks provide outdoor living space and, if you're lucky, great views. *(Courtesy of Nexwood Industries.)*

FIGURE 12.3

Powerwashing is a quick and sure way of cleaning decks.

The job is done with a powerwasher (a tank, compressor, and applicator) and a garden hose (see Figs. 12.4 and 12.5). The water enters the unit (usually portable) through the garden hose, is pressurized, and exits through a nozzle at the end of the applicator, which you can direct. If you don't have one, you can rent it for a half day. Most models will fit into a car or small truck.

The force of the water (which can be adjusted) literally blasts away a layer of wood and any stain that remains on it. It is important to carefully regulate the pressure of the water coming through the applicator and hold the nozzle at a constant distance from the wood. If you do not, the water jet will pit and/or gouge holes in the wood or, if not held close enough, not be effective.

Starting

EASY **1–2 hours**

Start by removing everything from the deck, and place a waterproof tarp or cover over the outside edges of the deck to protect objects nearby. Water splashes around, and the force of it, although directed by you, can be damaging. Also, it is important to wear clothes and shoes that you don't mind getting wet and dirty.

Next, it's a good idea to sweep the surface of the deck or blow it off with a power blower. This will remove any debris while it's still dry. When dirt, sand, or other matter gets wet, it just creates more of a mess to clean up.

Finally, when you're ready to power wash and you've turned on the machine, select a remote corner of the deck to test. Direct a blast of water on this area and watch the wood. Remember, you should see the deck in this area brighten immediately.

Experiment with the height and angle of the trigger until you develop a pattern. Work at your own pace and make ever-widening strokes from left to right, stepping backwards as you go. A good indicator of success is leaving a uniform, lighter color of wood ahead of you. Be sure to pay attention to small areas you may have missed, such as rails, stair treads, and posts.

Once the surface is powerwashed, let it dry, and it's ready to be sealed again with another coat of preservative or stain.

FIGURE 12.4

Smaller, portable powerwashers can be used on small decks.

Scrubbing the Deck

DIFFICULT **5–7 hours**

Another way to clean the deck of old sealers and assorted debris (such as mildew in damp environments) is to scrub it with a stiff bristle brush and a mild bleach solution. Deck wash, as it is sometimes called, is good for this, and is available at your local home center. Any solution that has some small part of bleach is good for this job. It's important to wear rubber gloves to protect your hands from the bleach.

In addition, it's probably a good idea to use a long handle attached to the brush. Not only will it give you leverage (for exerting more force on the brush), it will save your back.

After scrubbing, rinse off the deck with clear water. Be sure to rinse it thoroughly to remove all the bleach residue. Let it dry thoroughly.

Larger models of powerwashers can be used for tougher or larger jobs.

Sealing the Deck

DIFFICULT **5–7 hours**

Before sealing the deck, conduct a very simple experiment. Test the surface of the wood by sprinkling a little water on it. If it absorbs the water quickly, it is ready to be sealed (see Fig. 12.6). If it does not, let it dry for a week or so before sealing it.

There are several different ways you can apply sealer to your deck. Before starting any of them, be sure you have a relatively calm day. Wind will not help the job and will end up frustrating you—and perhaps cover you with a sealer mist that's not always easy to get out of your hair or clothes.

Pressure Sprayers

One way to apply a sealer is with a pressure sprayer. These tanks are usually made of plastic and are durable and lightweight. (They are small, portable, and cheap—maybe $8 to $12.) Just start at one corner (to test an area), and be sure to adjust the nozzle of the spraying wand so you don't apply too much or too little. Spray enough to cover the wood, but not enough to puddle in one area.

It is important to spray not only the top boards (the surface where you walk), but also the handrails, the underside (it it's accessible), the

FIGURE 12.6

This deck is ready to be sealed—without the kids, of course.

joists, beams, and posts. Next, use a paintbrush to work the sealer into cracks and narrow spaces you couldn't reach with the spraying wand.

Once you have the nozzle adjusted, the job should go pretty quickly. Make sure you start in a corner and work your way out with wide, sweeping strokes. When you are finished, let it dry. Read the empty container for instructions on how long it should be left to dry.

A good product to use is called Clear Wood Finish (CWF). It's not cheap, but it's worth using to preserve your deck every year or so. It costs about $18.00 per gallon and is available in 1-gallon and 5-gallon buckets. If you buy the larger container, the price per gallon drops by a dollar or so. Each gallon should cover approximately 250 square feet. However, this could change slightly, depending on the porosity of the wood.

CWF is also available in tints. Sometimes these are yellowish or orange-like and they can be mixed to match wood. For instance, if you have a deck made from pressure-treated lumber and it fades to a silvery gray over time, after you clean it, you can use a sealer that has been tinted to look yellowish-orange—the color of cedar.

Another good product is Thompson's Water Seal. This product is about the same price as CWF and covers approximately the same amount of space. When shopping, you may want to read the labels on both brands and ask some questions. Your decision may come down to a personal preference.

SAVING ON REPLACEMENT LUMBER

If the parts of your deck that need replacing are from the underside of it—and won't be seen—look for wood that is at the bottom of the rack in home improvement warehouse stores or lumber yards. It may not be the best looking, but it will be hidden, and it will serve your purpose. Sometimes the store will even give you this kind of wood, just to get rid of it. Either way, ask for a discount—you'll get it.

Paint Pads

Another effective way of applying sealer is with a paint pad. This method offers an advantage in that you can load up the pad with the sealer and push it into the grain of the wood.

Staining a deck is essentially the same process as sealing it. The only difference is in the materials used. To stain a deck, you first have to decide what shade or color you would like the deck to be when it's finished. Instead of leaving this decision to chance and guesswork, it's a good idea to either take a picture of your deck or take a small piece of the actual deck (a sample of the wood) and bring it to a home center or paint store for advice. There they can mix stains to match your personal preferences or to match the color of your house.

Replacing Boards

A deck that is damaged is not only ugly but could be potentially dangerous. More often than not, wood rot, over time, is the killer of most decks. Although earlier parts of this chapter addressed the prevention of rot by sealing the deck, damage and neglect do happen.

Wood rot can spread, especially if it isn't noticed. It can silently creep along and quietly affect good wood. It's a good idea to be thorough here. Use a flashlight when you do your initial inspection, if you have to, to see what's going on under the deck. Rot can be illusive, but finding it before it spreads is a smart start in curing the problem.

The other great enemy of wood is insects and termites. Again, during your inspection, look for certain signs. One is small mounds of what look like wood shavings. Others are holes and what appear to be tunnels in the wood. Pieces may even seem to be missing. Some ants and other insects enjoy stealing bits and chunks as raw materials for their nests. In fact, if you believe the damage might be extensive, and you suspect it's insects or termites, it might be wise to make a preemptive call to an exterminator and/or contractor to confirm your suspicions and ask for recommendations.

Removing the Rot

FAIRLY EASY **2–5 hours**

When you remove damaged wood, it doesn't pay to be slow or meticulous about it. You'll throw away the old decking anyway. If screws or nails are impossible to get out, take a saw to the rotten part of the wood. If you have to, cut the damaged piece into pieces with a chisel or a saw, then pry up the pieces.

In fact, I've been in a tight spot (unable to get to a damaged portion to remove the board) and had to remove two pieces of good wood to provide enough room to work around the damaged piece. Another thing to consider is where to cut out a damaged piece. Here's where it's important to be careful. Remember, before cutting completely through a damaged piece of wood, make certain it's fully supported on either side. You don't want the deck to collapse or find yourself falling through it.

> ## CONSIDER 5/4 STOCK FOR A GREAT LOOK
>
> If you choose cedar or pressure-treated wood for the top boards of your deck, consider using 5/4 stock. Ask your dealer about it. It's got a somewhat smooth surface, it's a little thinner than regular boards, and it has beveled edges, so when pieces are laid side by side, it forms a great-looking pattern. It also looks great as a handrail. Heck, that's just one man's opinion.

Replacing the Wood

DIFFICULT **5–7 hours**

If the wood that has to be replaced is structural (wood that is supporting the deck) or is not from the top of the deck, you can use treated lumber. This is lumber that has been chemically treated to resist rot. Ask your lumber dealer or home center employees about this product. They can answer questions about where and when you can use this treated wood. Note: Wear gloves and do not breath the dust when you cut this wood. And wash your hands (even though you wore gloves) when you have finished working with this type of lumber.

After you cut new pieces to fit, attach them with the same kind of hardware that is already in the deck. In other words, if floor boards are attached with screws, use screws for the new piece. If nails were used originally, use nails for the new piece. In fact, it's a good idea to take a sample screw or nail to a home center or hardware store to match it up with existing ones. Finally, make sure the heads of all nails and screws are flush with the top of the deck.

To replace wood that can be seen, use the same kind of wood as surrounds the replacement piece. Even so, the new pieces probably still won't match the surrounding wood very well. However, there are some things you can do to improve the look.

First, you can do nothing, and let the deck weather naturally; the new and old parts will eventually blend. You can also seal the entire deck with the same color-tinted stain after scrubbing the entire deck with deck brightener. This will provide a somewhat uniform appearance when you are finished. Lastly, you can prematurely "weather" the new part with chemicals. Visit the paint department of a home center or a paint store for advice on how to do this.

Bracing

EASY **1–2 hours**

Bracing a deck is simply reinforcing existing parts so they stay strong and last longer. A good way to start is to cut a new piece that matches the dimensions of a piece that needs reinforcing. This way, you can lay it against the original and attach it with nails. Generally, it's best to use 16d (16-penny) galvanized nails for this job. Nails should be driven about every 18 inches, and eye protection should be worn.

Sistering

EASY **1–2 hours**

Sistering wood is a process whereby a new piece of wood is laid flat against another—sandwiched really—to strengthen and lengthen the original. It's often used in floor joists and decks that extend beyond outside walls. Again, 16d galvanized nails should be used to attach the pieces.

Repairing Stair Treads

FAIRLY EASY **2–5 hours**

Steps that show any signs of damage beyond normal wear and tear should be replaced immediately. Start by cutting the damaged stair into pieces and/or prying up the pieces. You can do this with a pry bar or the claws of a hammer. Replace the step with pressure-treated cedar, or redwood that matches the existing stairs. Select lumber that is straight and strong.

When you cut the piece to fit (measure the width of the stair treads or use the old piece as a stencil), hold it where it will be installed to check for a nice fit. Make sure it will fit in its final location and it will match the rise (elevation between steps) and run (the width of each step) of existing steps.

Attach the piece with either 16d galvanized nails or screws. Place at least two on each side of the step and make sure the heads are flush with the top of the board. Before putting any weight on a new stair, make sure it's securely in place (see Fig.12.7).

FIGURE 12.7

Make sure stair treads are always secure. *(Photo courtesy of Nexwood Industries.)*

The Property

Pools

o ensure season-long swimming fun, a minimal amount of time has to be devoted to the nonfun aspects of swimming pools—namely, the care and maintenance of the pool (see Fig. 13.1). It is a simple job if it is done properly and at the required intervals. It is when these routine tasks are neglected that trouble begins.

Pool Chemicals

EASY **1–2 hours**

One of the most important aspects of pool care is maintaining proper chemical balance of the water. A glass of water coming out of the tap looks and (usually) tastes clean and clear. Put the same water in a 20- × 40-foot pool and it may have a different look entirely.

That's why you shouldn't use your pool the first day you fill it up, regardless of how tempting it is and how hot the weather. The first thing you should do is turn the filter on and let it run for a day. The filter will remove minerals and other solids that are present in most water. The water should look sparkling clear after the first day.

From the very first day you fill your pool, its purity must be guarded by a chemical disinfectant. Some purifying agent—whether it be chlorine, bromine, or iodine—must be in there to kill disease-carrying bacteria brought into the water by bathers.

FIGURE 13.1

Maintain your pool for hours of summertime fun.

Chlorine is the most widely used disinfectant. It should be used at one part per million (ppm) ideally, and must have at least 0.6 ppm of "free residual chlorine." The actual ratio is really very small, since 100 percent activity is gained by only one drop of chlorine for every 1 million drops of water.

Routine Cleaning
EASY **1–2 hours**

In addition to keeping the proper chemical balance, there are a few other things that should be done to keep your pool water clean and fresh. Some of these are listed here.

- Manually skim the pool's surface with a standard leaf skimmer, a netlike pool-cleaning tool designed especially to rid the pool's surface of leaves, bugs, debris, and other floating contaminants. Many leaf skimmers have plastic nets. Most are equipped with

KEEP YOUR LINER SAFE

Chlorine is strong stuff. It's great for keeping your water clean—but chlorine tablets and liners don't get along. If you use tablets, make sure you don't let them float freely, as some of them may sink to the bottom and burn or discolor the liner. To prevent this, use a powder or enclose the tablets in a dispenser that floats.

SAVE ON POOL CHEMICALS

It's a good idea to predict how much chlorine and shock you'll need for the swimming season and buy it all together—in bulk. This way, although you're paying up front for your supplies, you'll save money on the amount it will cost you per treatment throughout the season.

Also, it's best to buy skimmers, pipes, floats, pump and filter parts, and other accessories late in the season—this is when leftover merchandise at pool supply stores is reduced greatly in price—to make room for the next season's stock. If you're patient, you can get some good deals. Ask your pool supply dealer.

long handles to enable you to reach the pool's center while standing on the pool deck (see Fig. 13.2).

■ Brush down walls and tile. For this you'll need a stiff-bristled tile brush to clean near the waterline and a wall brush to clean the walls below.

■ Clean the skimmer's basket and the hair lint strainer. No special equipment is needed for this. Remove the skimmer basket and the hair lint strainer from the pump. Get rid of the debris that has collected there and replace them. This should be done as frequently as possible— daily is preferable—or even more often during the spring and fall when there is a heavy fallout from leaves and bushes. Failure to keep baskets clean will result in reduced circulation of the water through the pump and filter.

■ Vacuum the pool bottom. You'll need a special pool vacuum for this. There are many models and types. Some are manually operated, some are self-propelled and automatic. Consult your dealer as to the types best suited to your pool (see Fig. 13.3).

FIGURE 13.2

Daily skimming is a good way to keep your pool clean and make your filter work less.

FIGURE 13.3

Vacuum your pool regularly so swimmers can enjoy a clean pool.

■ Clean the filter. A dirty filter will result in decreased recirculation and consequently in dirty water. Consult the manufacturer of the filter (directions will be supplied when it is new) for the correct procedure for your particular filter. Most likely you should "backwash," or reverse the flow of water.

■ Hose the deck clean. A garden hose is all the equipment you'll need. This should be done during every pool cleaning.

Painting

DIFFICULT **5–7 hours**

Many pool owners leave their pools unpainted, but paint does make a pool more attractive. The trouble with painting is that you have to repaint every few years. There are two main points to note regarding pool painting. The first is to be sure to use alkali-resistant paints for concrete or Gunite (a special type of concrete) pools. Second, make sure that the surface is prepared properly.

The first step in preparation is to remove the water and repair all cracked or damaged areas to present a smooth surface throughout. If the paint is just dull or rubbed off, a thorough scrubbing is all that is necessary. If there is peeling or flaking, it may be necessary to remove the old paint completely. If so, sandblasting is the best way. You can either rent the equipment or hire a professional sandblaster to do the job.

Winterizing

DIFFICULT **5–7 hours**

In most parts of North America there are at least a few months of the year when the weather is too cold for swimming. The most important thing to remember about winterizing pools is to leave the water in. The water serves to brace the walls against pressures created by frozen or shifting earth on the outside of the walls.

Some of the other things you should do before shutting up for the winter are

1. Clean the pool thoroughly.

2. Lower the water to below the inlet suction fitting.

3. Remove lights.

4. Drain all lines at lowest points.

5. Insert rubber plugs tightly in all openings so that no water may enter.

6. Fill the pool again to within 2 inches of the bottom of the skimmer opening. Make certain that the main drain valve is closed off.

7. Add an extra-heavy dose of chlorine.

8. Spread the pool cover if you use one. Use an inflatable float in the middle to keep rain and melting snow from collecting and weighing down the cover.

9. Place all removed parts in a dry, warm place and properly oil, grease, or paint where necessary.

10. Plug all lines so that vermin or mice cannot enter the system.

11. Remove the diving board and store it on the edge of the pool.

12. Disconnect all electrical energy.

13. Stuff a semi-inflated bicycle tube into the skimmer to absorb pressures created by freezing and thawing.

14. Check the pool from time to time. If water has receded below the ice on top, refill it with a garden hose until the water meets ice. Suspended ice can cause pool damage.

Repairing Holes

EASY **1–2 hours**

A minor miracle of technology, at least to me, is that today you can repair a hole in a vinyl-lined pool, even under water. There are repair kits consisting, basically, of patches and an adhesive that "melts" the vinyl and fuses the patch to it.

To make an above-water repair, first clean the area to be patched to remove algae, soil, pool chemicals, and the like. Then cut the patch to the shape needed, apply adhesive to the back, and set it firmly in place. If the area cut is puckered, you should flatten it out first (strips of tape help) before applying the patch.

For an underwater repair, first cut the patch to the shape needed. Apply an extra-heavy coat of adhesive. Go under the water and wipe the patch clean as well as you can with a rag. Then dive again and press the patch firmly in place. That's it. Read all the instructions on the repair kits carefully, and/or ask questions of your pool supply dealer if you need help.

Correcting Water Discoloration

EASY **1–2 hours**

Discoloration of pool water can stem from a number of causes. Here are some of the causes and how to correct them.

- *Greenish and cloudy water.* Algae is usually the culprit. To restore your pool to its natural sky-blue color, treat the water with the proper amount of disinfectant and an algicide. Certain algicides may cause a very fine hazy cloudiness temporarily in some water.

- *Red-brown water.* The addition of disinfectants may oxidize the iron in water. Since oxidized iron is insoluble, rust particles give the water a reddish-brown color. To correct this, run the filter continuously for about 48 hours. At the same time, add even more of the oxidizing sanitizer. This will oxidize any remaining dissolved iron in the water. Particles not removed by the filter will settle to the pool bottom, where they should be removed with the pool vacuum as soon as they show up, to prevent staining.

- *Cloudiness.* Winds—carrying algae spores, dust, and debris— can cause the water to turn cloudy. Windblown debris may, on occasion, also change the pool water's balance—its pH or alkalinity. To correct this, adjust the sanitizer level and pH balance to remove the dirt, and clean the filter as needed.

- *pH is too high.* One form of cloudiness is caused by excessively high pH, which causes the precipitation of insoluble salts. This cloudiness may not be too apparent during the daytime, but shows up as a haziness in the water at night when underwater lights are on. This is corrected easily by restoring the water's proper pH balance (adding acid to bring the water's balance to between pH 7.2 and 7.6).

Covering and Uncovering
EASY **1–2 hours**

In the northern states, where there is a marked difference in the weather between winter and summer, homeowners close their pools down for the winter. Part of this process is covering the pool in the fall and removing it in the late spring. It simply involves getting a cover that fits your pool.

After you remove all the debris and "winterize" the pool, simply spread the cover over the top (according to the manufacturer's instructions) and secure it by setting weights on its outer surface so the wind, rain, and snow during the winter months won't damage it or send it flying. In-ground pools may have hardware and hooks embedded in the walkway around the pool to attach the cover to.

Some above-ground pools may require an inflatable device (a large balloon of some kind) to float on the top of the water. This way, when the cover is pulled over it, the cover is raised, preventing deep pockets where rainwater and snow can accumulate, and sink the cover. Secure it with a rope or elastic material (bungees, perhaps) so it can't move in strong winds.

Provided you have done a pretty good job in the fall, the cover should be pretty simple to remove in the spring. Two people working on either end of the cover usually works best. Make sure the cover has been hosed down (you may want to scrub it clean) and dried before folding it and storing it for the next year. Clean, repair, or replace any strings, ropes, bungees, or hardware used with covers.

Lastly, ladders used for entering above-ground pools should always be disconnected and removed, then stored for the winter season (see Fig. 13.4).

Pump Repair
DIFFICULT **5–7 hours**

Keeping your pool pump in working order is generally a job for a professional. Unless you are really familiar with pumps, I recommend calling in a professional to handle any problem besides routine maintenance. If you have a stationary pump for an in-ground pool, the best way to keep it running right is to start by keeping it protected from the elements. Sometimes a small enclosure such as a garden shed or pool house works best.

FIGURE 13.4

Ladders should be removed and stored for the winter.

It's a different story with portable pumps. Some simple things to remember are to keep the pump stored in a clean, secure area that is close to where it is installed every summer. Perhaps a shed is the best area to store it. When you do take it out for the season, make sure it's placed upright on a cement slab or bricks that won't shift or move in any way. You don't need it tumbling over when it's running. That's a potential headache nobody needs.

Also, be sure the electric wire, plug, and outlet are in good working order. Inspect them carefully. With water being splashed around electrical equipment, you can never be too careful about safety for swimmers and other people near the pool.

Filters

How you maintain your filter depends on what kind of filter you have. There are generally three different kinds of filters, available in stationary and portable models.

Diatomaceous Earth (DE) Filters

A DE filter requires the most maintenance of the three. Inside the filter is a cornstarch-like material, commonly referred to as DE, that acts as a filtering agent for the water that flows through it. While this has been a popular material for quite some time, the drawback comes when the pump and filter are on the backwash cycle. During this cycle the material gets sent into the pool occasionally and it gets used up. This requires that the user refill the filter with DE each time the backwash cycle occurs.

Sand Filters

Up until a few years ago, sand filers were thought to be the most reliable and maintenance-free filters available. Using sand, this type of filter efficiently filters the water and leaves the sand behind, in the filter, where it belongs. The only problem is that the sand has to be replaced every few months. You may end up having to change the sand several times during the pool season.

Cartridge Filters

Cartridge filters are the newest, most reliable, and least maintenance-intensive filters. Water passes through a cartridge that is virtually permanent. The only maintenance required is to take the filter out occasionally, run fresh water over it, and replace it. The cartridge can last for years.

Fence Maintenance   *FAIRLY EASY* **2–5 hours**

The importance of a safety fence surrounding both above-ground and in-ground pools cannot be overstated. Although safety fences around pools are required by law in nearly all areas, and privacy is another big reason to have them, the most important reason for having one is safety—especially for young children and pets.

Since it is so important, make sure your fence is in good working order and has no gaps of any kind (see Chapter 18). Children and pets can come in small sizes. They can fit into small holes. Immediately repair any hole, rip, or tear in your fence once it is noticed. It is also important to make sure the gate and locking devices are all in good working order. If a lock belongs on the gate, make sure it works.

It is also important to make sure you know the codes for your particular town regarding pool fences. If you don't, call your town office and have an inspector come out to your house to make sure your fence is up to code. The safety of neighborhood children, pets, and your peace of mind are that important.

Tools for Property Maintenance

The Right Tool

Using the right tool for the right job can turn a difficult chore into an easy task in any home landscaping maintenance project. A recent experience I had confirmed this belief.

The other day I awoke to the sound of my neighbor shoveling gravel off his driveway. He had had some loose stones delivered the day before, and the contractor left a considerable amount scattered about. Ralph was using a short-handled shovel with a pointed tip to collect the remaining rocks. I walked over to him. He was clearly frustrated. "You know Ralph, you're not using the right shovel for that," I said.

"What do you mean?" He asked.

"Why don't you try using mine?" I asked. I handed him my long-handled, square-end shovel (see Fig. 14.1). "Use this and it'll save your back and you'll be able to scoop up all the rocks quicker."

He appreciated my simple suggestion, and we've been friendly neighbors ever since. Since then I've taken pride in helping fellow homeowners tackle big and small property maintenance jobs by helping them pick the right tool to get the job done quickly, safely, and efficiently.

Caring for Your Tools

Caring for garden and landscaping tools is generally limited to consistent, relatively easy, routine maintenance and less frequent sharpening

FIGURE 14.1

A long-handled, square-ended shovel goes a long way in scooping up loose material from a hard, flat surface.

and oiling of cutting surfaces. This includes washing and drying cuttings tools each time you use them, before you store them. It also includes sharpening and oiling cutting surfaces of hatchets, axes, shovels, shears, and any other tools you use to dig or cut things.

If you're unsure how to sharpen a piece of equipment, or what device to use, consult the manufacturer of the equipment or a professional at the home center where you bought them. It's always best to err on the side of caution when dealing with tools, regardless of how simple the job may appear. Again, you can never be too safe when it comes to home landscaping tools and their maintenance.

Shovels

One tool that every homeowner needs at one time or another is the shovel. While there are many uses for a shovel, there are almost as many kinds available to choose from. The homeowner, for the most part, will usually need shovels for two purposes: digging and transporting material. Selecting the right shovel means choosing one that will hold the amount of dirt, sand, rocks, manure, peat moss, grain, or any other material that you can lift, efficiently.

For most garden and lawn digging, a long-handled, gently pointed shovel usually works best. This is because if the shaft is too short, it will cause you to bend over more, forcing you to lift away from your center of gravity.

Longer shafts reduce your leverage and seem to increase the weight of the load at the end, but they also let you decide where to grab the shovel so you feel comfortable (much like choking up on a baseball bat). A pointed tip helps you sink it into the dirt when digging (see Fig. 14.2).

Home centers and manufacturers usually sell pointed shovels for home use and commercial use. The difference between the two kinds is in the construction and the gauge of steel used.

The home-use shovel is made from a flat piece of steel. This kind of shovel must be reinforced by putting a crimp below the socket. It causes the blade to bulge in the front, which results in a hollow portion on the back. This type of shovel is usually called a "hollow-back." One disadvantage to this type is that its construction results in a slightly weaker blade and dirt tends to get trapped in the hollow. Even so, it is still fine for the homeowner.

I happen to like mine very much. I use one with a serrated and pointed front edge—it makes it easier to cut through hard soil, roots, and sod. It also has a deep dish that lets me throw a lot of soil at a time.

The heavy-duty, "commercial" shovel is rolled from a solid piece of high-carbon steel. This kind can be used for tougher jobs around the house, including transporting heavy material such as stones or gravel (see Fig. 14.3).

The blade and socket (that accepts the handle) have no seams or welds; this is commonly known as "solid-shank" construction. This kind of shovel lets you carry heavier material and can withstand more pressure when the user steps hard on the top of the blade. This allows more digging power in hard soil loaded with rocks and roots.

FIGURE 14.2

A pointed-tip shovel is easy to dig with.

FIGURE 14.3

The strength where the head attaches to the handle is important for doing heavy work.

Another variety of shovel is best suited to carrying material from one spot to another and has a flatter, square blade. This design makes it easier for the user to scoop dirt, gravel, or trash from flat surfaces and transport it with ease. The "scooping shovel" is invaluable for picking up leaves, twigs, dry grass, or other debris that has a large volume and relatively low weight. Fall cleanups are a cinch with this kind of shovel. You can find these with scoops made of lightweight aluminum or hard plastic for use moving powdery snow (see Fig. 14.4).

Spades

Another kind of shovel that is useful to the homeowner is the spade. Spades are generally strong, nearly flat, and have narrow blades that cut cleanly through soil, sod, and dirt. They are really helpful when it is time to transplant plants that are either bare-rooted or when the roots are balled and wrapped in burlap.

Other kinds of spades are narrow, rigid, and sharp. They can be used to slice rope or twine, dig, clean out trenches, pry up plants and rocks, cut roots, dig in narrow areas, cut flower beds, and perform a variety of other tasks where a standard shovel is too large.

Spades Put to Good Use

Years ago I helped a good friend who had a crazy idea: he wanted to build a miniature-sized nine-hole golf course on his property. A home golf course! He had the money, time, and the property. But it was me he turned to for the landscaping knowhow.

After two years of planning, clearing the site, grading, and seeding, we were ready for the final step: we were ready to dig the holes on the greens that would accept the cups where the golf ball falls. Out came my trusty spades! My friend questioned me as I dug the holes in the middle of each putting green. "I can't believe it!" He said with the glee of a 10-year-old. "That's all you do? Dig with that skinny shovel?" I used my skinniest spade—this blade was slightly cupped, and narrowed sharply, at the tip.

"Yep," I answered. "Why dig out more dirt than you have to? This spade has sharp edges and slices right through the dirt." As he watched, I simply dug the spade in and pulled it out, in a circular motion until I reached the first cut. Then I simply dug the spade in one last time, but at an angle, and gently pried up a circular core of dirt. He looked down in astonishment at a clean, circular hole with steep walls. He's been a fan of the spade ever since.

A good shovel or spade should last for years with proper care. Upkeep for all shovels and spades is generally the same. It is best to hose them off and dry them after use so they don't rust. After this, many homeowners find it helpful to apply a thin coat of oil on the blade. They can then be stored standing upright or hanging for safety. I know my tools I've had for years are like trusted friends to me. They feel comfortable and familiar in my hands. I do what I can to protect them.

FIGURE 14.4

These shovels are available with straight or curved handle designs. The curved handle lets you use it standing straight up—saving you back pain with heavy loads.

Spreaders

Spreaders do just what their name says: they spread loose material evenly over a desired area. They are also designed to disseminate material, in all directions, at the same rate of speed. There are two basic kinds of spreaders, and they are pretty easy to operate. They are the broadcast and the drop spreader.

A broadcast spreader spreads material over a large area and throws the material in a circular pattern, in front of the operator. Fertilizers, grass seed, peat moss, and a variety of other materials work best in broadcast units (see Fig. 14.5). A drop spreader concentrates the material in a much smaller area, focusing it in an area that is no bigger (or wider) than the spreader itself. Large wheels on the rotary spreader help it roll over the turf easily (see Fig. 14.6).

When using either kind of spreader, consult the manufacturer's recommendations about which settings you should use for which materials. Often there is also a grid printed on the bag of fertilizer and/or grass seed that explains all the correct settings. It's also important to watch the hopper as you walk behind the spreader.

It's best to fertilize and/or seed in calm, dry weather. If you want to fertilize and then seed 5 minutes later, consult the manufacturer's recommendations on the bag. This is important because fertilizers have to be specifically formulated to work in tandem with seed, and using one that isn't will likely kill the seed before it can germinate.

Trowels

The smallest of shovels, hand-held wonders called trowels, are truly the homeowner's essential gardening and landscaping tool. They are

FIGURE 14.5

It's a good idea to buy a spreader with a large hopper—you can spread a lot of material.

FIGURE 14.6

Select a spreader model that has easy adjustment controls. You can adjust the flow of fertilizer or seed as you walk.

portable, handy, and remind us of being a kid at the beach with a pail and shovel.

When selecting a trowel, look for one that is made out of one piece of steel or aluminum (see Fig. 14.7). This will ensure that it won't bend in your hand or break as you're digging with it. You'll probably want one with a nonslip surface so it won't slide out of your hand. It should be comfortable to handle and act as an extension of your hand. If you're anything like me, you may want to paint the handle of your trowel a bright color so you can spot it easily after you set it down. I'm forever forgetting where I put mine.

Rakes

Equally important as shovels to the homeowner is the rake. Again, different rakes are designed for different raking jobs. Rakes can be classified as garden, grading, lawn, and shrub rakes.

Garden rakes are usually made of steel and have rigid teeth for breaking up dirt clogs in the garden or preparing a soil to plant grass

FIGURE 14.7

Smaller hand tools should be durable and act as an extension of your hand.

FIGURE 14.8

This rake design lets you smooth out dirt easily.

seed. There are generally two kinds of metal rakes available to the homeowner. A "square-head" rake has a flat head above the teeth that attach directly to the handle, and the "bow" kind features teeth that bow back slightly a little to a rounded head. Both rakes can be used to grade or smooth out the soil, but some homeowners prefer the springlike action of the bow design (see Fig. 14.8).

Both rakes are heavy and sturdy enough to rake rocks, roots, sod, and other debris into piles. They also come attached to long, tapered, wooden handles for comfortable use.

The grading rake is used to achieve a really smooth finish for garden beds and lawns that are waiting to be seeded or accept sod. The head is usually extra wide, from 24 inches up to and including 48 inches wide, and features wooden or aluminum teeth spaced together. (This is what helps achieve a smooth finish.)

The rake's teeth ensure that the soil texture is smooth and pieces of dirt are uniform in size. The wide head helps the user prepare larger areas faster. Since it is a tool used in the final preparation of a seed bed, the remaining soil is fairly lightweight and the pieces left behind are mostly uniform in size.

The lawn rake is clearly the most popular of all rakes, and I would bet the most universally recognized. The primary function of lawn rakes is to move over and through grass without harming it. This allows the user to collect and remove grass clippings, leaves, sticks, and any other debris that may lay on the turf (another name for grass). Anything that lays on top of grass for any length of time can damage it. When grass is deprived of sunlight, water, and air flowing through it, it begins to suffer.

Although the function and basic fan design of lawn rakes has not changed dramatically, the materials from which they are made has. A desirable lawn rake should be strong and lightweight. Although bamboo is a popular material for rakes, because of its flexibility and strength, plastic is often used for the same benefits. Plastic doesn't rot, rust, or break either. A metal rake will also do the job but is prone to rusting. (See Fig. 14.9.)

Shrub rakes are given the name for their practical uses in and around shrubs, where a standard fan-shaped or iron rake may not fit. Shrub rakes are narrow rakes with long, thin, curved tines that allow the user to rake in close beneath and between shrubs to remove leaves, shavings from recently trimmed bushes, and other assorted debris.

Thatching Rakes

If you happen to be a fan of medieval torture devices, the thatch rake is a must for your garage or shed collection. With the advent of mulching mowers, there are smaller and smaller pieces of grass that fall between individual blades of grass. Over time (usually a period of years), this debris builds up and forms a barrier over the soil. When this barrier (called thatch) prevents moisture and air from penetrating the soil, the lawn is in jeopardy.

The thatch rake is the solution to a buildup of thatch. Curved, crescent-shaped metal tines form the head of this impressive tool. It is designed to work just above the surface of the soil and pull out pieces of the matted thatch to allow healthier shoots of grass to grow. Be careful, though: this tool is best used by people with strong backs and patience.

As with all rakes, safety should be a concern. Unless you store them away properly after you use them, you can risk accidentally stepping on one, asking for a broken nose or worse.

Hoes and Cultivators

Other hand-held tools for the garden, particularly small hoes and cultivators, are used primarily to fight the bane of any gardener's existence: weeds.

Hoes and cultivators allow homeowners to get close to delicate plants and remove weeds in planting beds and on the lawn.

FIGURE 14.9

Lawn rakes are designed to be lightweight and durable.

Just like people, plants need to drink, breathe, and stretch their arms (branches). They can't when they're being suffocated by weeds! A hoe can be used to furrow around and between plants, do heavy weeding, and weed between rows of plants (see Fig. 14.10).

A cultivator, a tool whose head looks like an iron rake with teeth spread farther apart, is best used in a garden with vegetables and/or flowers. It generally loosens and aerates the soil so tender roots have a chance to grow and moisture can percolate to the bottom of the plant's roots.

Picks and Mattocks

Clay picks and mattocks are at first glance crude and medieval-looking. They are actually designed for specific purposes and are highly effective.

FIGURE 14.10

Hoes are great for weeding gardens quickly and efficiently.

The clay pick has a pointed blade on one end and a wedge on the other end. Some have pointed blades on each side (see Fig. 14.11). The head slides over the narrow end of a wooden handle and stops near the top, where the handle becomes abnormally large, to prevent the head from sliding off while in use. They are very top heavy and extreme caution should be paramount when they are in use.

I can remember more than once the pain of missing my mark and landing a swing on my foot or leg. It usually happens after even slight fatigue sets in, so my advice is to rest often! The most practical uses of the clay pick are to break through tough spots in soil (hence its name—clay pick) and to break up asphalt or any other material. The wedge end is highly effective for prying up heavy objects such as tree roots, trunks, and rocks.

The mattock has a chopping blade that looks like an axe on one end and a curved horizontal blade on the other end that resembles a hoe. This heavy tool is best suited for digging out dead or overgrown bushes, chopping through surface roots, digging very narrow trenches for water or electrical conduits, and prying up heavy objects.

Safety and Fatigue

To operate these hand tools safely, goggles are a must! When chopping or digging around stones and other material, it is always wise to wear them because of the potential for flying objects. Remember, rest when you become tired! Fatigue invites tragedy. I have learned this the hard way. Last, but not least: store the heavier tools in the back of the shed after you have cleaned and dried them. This prevents accidents later.

Axes, Hatchets, and Sharpening Tools

Axes and hatchets are two mainstays of the adventurer, boy scout, and home-owner. They still hold a magical appeal for me from my memories of watching my Uncle Bernie build his own split-rail fence with nothing but his axe, hatchet, and his back. The adventurous, pioneering spirit I associate with them still has a hold on me.

Actually, they are nothing more than chopping devices that have operated on the same principal for thousands of years. Our stone-age ancestors used rocks that were strategically struck against one another, and now we use hard, tempered steel, but their uses remain the same. I like that idea. Remember earlier when I mentioned that some tools become trusted friends?

There are two primary differences between hatchets and axes. Axes have long handles and the operator uses two hands to swing it. Hatchets have short handles and the user operates it with one hand.

Axes are commonly used to chop wood, cut down trees, split tree trunks, and a host of other chores (see Fig. 14.12). Hatchets are most commonly used to chop small branches from trees, split kindling wood, drive stakes, and other small jobs.

FIGURE 14.11

Clay picks are great for digging in compacting soil and prying up large rocks.

KNOW THE TOOL

Before choosing an axe or hatchet, think about your strength and ability to control the tool. These two factors should be considered before you decide on using such a tool. When you are shopping, pick it up (don't swing it), hold it in your hands, and check its balance. Does it feel awkward or heavy? If the answer is yes, chances are that tool is not for you.

FIGURE 14.12

An axe is a very useful tool when it is used correctly. This includes wearing gloves and goggles for safety.

Safety is of paramount concern when handling axes and hatchets. These should only be operated by adults. Before using one, look around you to be sure nobody is in your swing range. Before you even begin using these tools, though, it is very important to check some things out first. When you take the tools out of storage, are the sharp edges still covered with a leather jacket or protective cover? (All are sold with protective covers for storage.) Check the very top of the handle, closest to the metal head. Is it wide enough so the head of the axe or hatchet is securely fastened to the shaft?

It may sound strange, but I've seen a few axe heads fly in my day—especially with the season's first use. Cold and hot air (and changes in moisture) weathers wood and causes it to swell and contract, thereby allowing the head of the tool to become loose. A good fix is to soak the handle in water for a few hours and make sure the head is snugly attached to the handle of the tool.

Also, if you have never been a boy scout, it's best to know that you always swing or chop with the sharp edges swinging away from you. When you are finished with a hatchet or axe, be sure and put it back in its protective jacket immediately. This practice keeps the tools from harming anybody who may accidentally step on it or pick it up.

Sharp as a Knife

Axes and hatchets should be kept sharp to be most effective. Most can be sharpened with a file and/or a sharpening stone. Both are available at home centers where hatchets and axes are sold. A good file to use when sharpening tools is one that is double-sided. The single cutting side of the file has lines that are all parallel across its surface. This is best used to sharpen axes, hatchets, and mower blades (see Chap. 1).

The other side of the file has a cross section of lines, known as a double side, for heavier work on spades, picks, and hoes.

Another sharpening device is the sharpening stone. The stone can be held in your hand and has two sides. The first side is pretty coarse and is used for the beginning of sharpening. This side gets rid of nicks and cuts. The other side is finer-textured and is used for the final finish. A good practice is to hold the stone in your hand (with gloves) and stroke the edge of the blade with a circular motion, at about a 45-degree angle. Check with your retailer or manufacturer if you have questions about the care and maintenance of these chopping tools. Remember, it's better to be safe than sorry.

Store them in a clean, dry area, away from kids, and with protective jackets that cover the sharp edges.

Bow and Pruning Saws

Bow saws have a large oblong tube of metal that curves over the blade. This allows the user to cut through pretty thick branches. They are designed for fast cutting and light pruning. They are excellent for cutting Christmas trees and other pines and soft woods. The teeth on the blade are imposing. A "skip-tooth" design features teeth that are bent slightly, making a fresh cut with each push and pull of the blade, increasing the speed of the cutting action.

Pruning saws are hand-held saws that have equally devastating teeth. The top of the blade is curved, and "raked-back" teeth dig into trees and small branches with amazing ease. A pruning saw is best used when light pruning is required but you don't have much room to place the saw. It is most useful between stacks of branches that jut out from the trunks of trees.

Dress for Success

An important part of any outdoor landscaping chore is the clothes and shoes you wear. When driving shovels and spades in the ground, particularly hard, compacted soils with rocks and roots, your feet take a beating. It's best to protect them by wearing workboots.

TREE FORT TOOLS

When my kids were little, we had a beautiful stand of pin oak trees at the back of our property. In order to install a tree fort they had to have, I needed to prune back the branches of two adjacent trees. My pruning saw came in handy. Since they were the only two trees on the property positioned well enough to support the frame of the tree fort, I was happy I had my saw.

Today, I still use the saw, and although the kids occasionally sublet the tree fort to their friends, they had hours of fun in it. Those trusty tool friends never let me down.

A bow saw blade should be replaced rather than sharpened. A pruning saw blade can be sharpened, but I suggest having it professionally sharpened. The pattern of teeth looks to me like it's hungry all the time. I know my limits.

Store saws up off the floor of a garage or shed, and hang them where you can get to them for future use.

It's important that the boots have rigid, thick soles to protect your feet. It's best to have steel toe construction and high tops. (That is, the boot material comes up over the ankle) to save them from scrapes and hits that occur when working with long-handled tools. Boots should also be waterproof, because even if it isn't raining, the home landscaper will be walking in moist material (soil, grass, etc.).

Other important dress items include cloth and heavy-duty gloves, a rugged jumpsuit or overalls, goggles, knee pads, and generally old clothes that you can afford to get dirty. Wearing gloves, even when muggy weather may make them uncomfortable, is a must when performing landscaping jobs around your property.

One reason for gloves is that they prevent splinters. Wooden handles of tools often dry, bend slightly, and change according to the air temperature over the winter. It is very easy to pick up splinters when you grab the handle of a tool to use it. Another reason is to avoid calluses. If you are not used to handling tools, you may form blisters after only a few hours.

Another reason is simply good hygiene. When you are digging in soils and handling many different tools, you could be inviting the unseen beautiful world of nature (bacteria and viruses) into the pores of your skin. Remember when Mom told you to clean underneath your fingernails?

Overalls and/or jumpsuits are practical during the cool fall months, when the ground may be wet or damp. They not only protect your clothes when you are kneeling, bending, or stretching, they provide warmth and flexibility.

Knee pads are a life saver when you must kneel for long periods (such as when working in a flower bed). If you're anything like me, I become somewhat preoccupied when I'm working around my yard and I kneel, stand, kneel, and stand without giving it much thought. I'm more concerned with the task at hand. This constant kneeling and standing taxes the knees. It's only inside the house, later, that I feel my knees. Wearing knee pads avoids a lot of wear and tear. And don't worry about what the neighbors think.

Wheelbarrows and Carts

Wheelbarrows

One of the greatest friends to the homeowner is the wheelbarrow. A good wheelbarrow can be a kid's best friend (rides on summer afternoons) and the homeowner's trusted workhorse. A good wheelbarrow can be used to carry just about anything easily, safely, and with minimum effort.

What makes a good wheelbarrow? One that has a deep, wide, hard plastic or metal body (the carrying portion), is lightweight, and is durable. Another vital feature in a good wheelbarrow is a wide, pneumatic (air-filled) tire for smooth handling over soft grass, rocky surfaces, and mud. Large legs and a wide tire also help the user keep the unit balanced while handling an awkward or shifting load. Most feature a smooth bottom surface that allows material to slide in and out easily. Even wet cement can be carried without sticking to the walls.

Although there are many styles of wheelbarrows, my advice is to stick with what the trade lingo calls the "contractor's wheelbarrow." Don't be fooled by the name. It has a wide, deep bucket, large handles for easy lifting, and a single, air- filled tire up front (see Fig. 14.13). With proper care, it can last for years and be used to carry fertilizer, dirt, mulch, grass clippings, sand, cement, blocks, wood, leaves, plants, flowers, or anything else you can imagine or dare to move around your property. This type is also easy to maintain and can be washed out after each use.

I highly suggest you also invest in this type of wheelbarrow because inferior models, with lighter-gauge steel design and hard plastic wheels, can rust or crumble under the slightest weight. A unit with a sturdy wheel and frame will last for many years.

FIGURE 14.13

Maintain large wheelbarrows like this and you'll get years of service out of them.

WHEELBARROWS

As a kid I had another use for my father's contractor's wheelbarrow. I would fill it with water and create a pond for my duck chicks. They loved swimming around in it, and as they became older, they were able to dive under the water for a moment at a time because the container was deep enough. I'm sure other homeowners would find many personal uses for their wheelbarrows, such as giving rides to small kids. Paying a little more for a quality one is certainly worth the expense. Finally, be careful.

Carts

Although I prefer using wheelbarrows for transporting materials around the yard, many people prefer using box carts, essentially wooden or hard plastic boxes on wheels, for transporting garden tools and equipment around their properties. The only drawback is that although some may be heavier than wheelbarrows, they may not have the ability to dump material easily. If that's the case, the function of the cart is limited to simply transporting equipment and supplies.

Post Hole Diggers

The post hole digger is a long-handled tool with two parallel handles made of wood that are attached to two clam-shaped metal "scoops" that face each other and work in tandem to close, thus forming one scoop for trapping and carrying out loose soil (see Figs. 14.14 and 14.15). The leading edges are sharp and cut into the ground. The handler must have a good set of arms and a strong chest.

It's a great practical tool for the construction-minded homeowner. It's a simple device that when used properly, can dig clean, round holes in dirt, sand, or a mixture of them for installing swing sets, fence posts, flag poles, deck footings, or for other devices to build a variety of things.

The benefit of the post hole digger over the shovel is important to note. When a hole is dug with a standard shovel, the earth that is removed is loose and much of the time is spent retrieving a lot of it and throwing it out of the hole. With the post hole digger, you're left with a smaller hole than a shovel can create. It's less work, less time-consuming, and creates holes with less loose dirt inside that has to be cleaned out.

Care for post hole diggers is pretty much the same as for other digging tools: Before you put them away, wash and dry them so they won't rust. It's also great practice to keep them clean and sharp as with other digging tools. Get ready, though; if your neighbors find out you have a post hole digger, they may ask you to borrow it. It really comes in handy when it's time to put up fences.

FIGURE 14.14

Post hole diggers dig deep, circular holes that are great for fence posts.

Pitch Forks

The pitch fork is an easily recognizable tool that often symbolizes farms. It's a pretty simple tool, really. It's designed for moving and transporting hay, grasses, and other long-stemmed plants that have been cut.

The obvious danger is getting stuck with the points of the tongs. It's really important that you look around and are aware of who is standing by as you work. Pitch forks are available at home centers and must be stored away (standing up in a shed or garage) for safety.

Brushes and Squeegees

There are so many varieties of brushes and squeegees that it's best to select one for the specific job you have. For example, if you need to sweep off sand from your driveway, it's best to use a stiff-bristled push broom. This is because you have to sweep a large area and remove small pieces.

If you need advice, it's best to ask a salesperson at a home center or hardware store. Describe the project you have in mind, and the salesperson can suggest the best tool for it.

FIGURE 14.15

Post hole diggers operate by "cupping" loose soil so the operator can lift it out of holes.

Pruning and Lopping Shears

Pruning and lopping shears are useful cutters for rose or "sticker bushes" that have menacing thorns. The long handle allows the user (wearing gloves) to get the cutting edge close to the branch that needs to be cut. The back-and-forth motion required for a saw would risk ripping up the arms of the user.

The "circle hook" design of these tools allows a user to exert more force with less effort on each cut (see Fig. 14.16).

Because these tools are useful while cutting plants with nasty thorns, I suggest using long-handled shears to pinch branches once they are cut and drag them away from the bush. That way the user only handles the branch once, avoiding potential injury.

Hedge Shears and Grass Shears

Hedge shears are useful for trimming flowering bushes and hedges. They are particularly helpful in cutting new growth. This is the outermost growth (tips of branches with leaves) of plants, so they are best used to shape bushes and plants.

The best way to shape a bush is to take advantage of the tool's design. The blades on hedge shears sit curved up at about 15 degrees from the handle, for cutting the tops of bushes. It's useful to turn the shears over when cutting the sides of bushes. This way, the angle of the cutting blades closely matches the angle of the sides of the bush. The difference means an evenly cut bush or shrub with little or no guesswork.

Cultivators and Weeders

Cultivators are great for scratching the top inch or so of soil in flower beds and gardens. This practice keeps weeds at bay and loosens the soil to aerate it and for continued good drainage. At the same time, you can drag rocks or other debris that may have fallen in the bed since you last tended to it.

A great weeding device is the "action hoe." This device is a double-edged, thin steel bar bent into a square. It's used to remove weeds by

FIGURE 14.16

Long handles on these shears keep your hands clear of what you are cutting.

slicing their roots and a small amount of dirt from under them. I tell people that this is the best tool to use for a large amount of weeds. It makes a lot of work easier. Pull it back and forth under weeds in a row. Also, it's best to remove cut weeds after each cut, so you know where to begin the next pass.

Other Hoes

A standard square-shaped hoe is useful in moving small amounts of dirt quickly and easily in limited areas such as flower beds, around trees, and in gardens. The tool is generally light and maneuverable.

The warren hoe is a gardener's delight. It's pointy edge is great for making furrows between plants in rows in gardens. Here's another trick: the home landscaper can use it to install plastic edging or any other edging material. Its design allows the user to quickly dig a shallow trench through good soil. Since most bedding soil is generally free from rocks, roots, and other debris, the warren hoe can be quite useful.

Edgers and Scrapers

Edgers are useful in creating clean edges between planting beds and lawns. Their rugged, thick construction, coupled with sharpened edges, make slicing sod, dirt, and roots an easy task. Do you need a great winter tip? Before taking out your snow shovel, keep the edgers and scrapers in your collection of tools handy. The fact is, a good edger is great for removing stubborn ice from walkways and driveways in the winter. Keep them sharp so you'll be able to use them when ice and snow hit. They're particularly handy when you don't have time to remove ice using ice-melt crystals.

Edgers are also helpful when cutting and shaping circular and irregular-shaped beds around trees and bushes.

Hoses

A good-quality garden hose, one that is strong and flexible but does not kink, is a convenient tool for homeowners. It's best to purchase one longer hose instead of several ones connected together. Make sure the one you get is long enough to reach all the grass and planting bed areas of your property.

Couplings (where different hoses connect) invite leaks and reduce water pressure. It's also a good idea to keep your hose neatly wrapped around a hose caddy, a device with wheels for easy transporting around your yard (see Fig. 14.17).

Knee Pads

Knee pads come in handy when working in flower beds (planting and weeding), laying sod lawns, or any other chore that requires kneeling for some time. It's usually best to use a pair with hard plastic fronts (that protect the kneecap) and soft, comfortable insides that are gentle to the knees. Hard plastic won't soak up moisture laying around and will protect your knees from gravel and hard surfaces. A wide nylon strap on the back provides comfort and allows you to stand and bend freely (see Fig. 14.18).

Push Brooms

A push broom is a must tool for nearly every home landscaping job. It's best to

FIGURE 14.17

A hose caddy keeps your hose stored neatly.

use a standard push broom (a long wooden handle attached to a hardwood block head) with synthetic bristles. These bristle last for years and can be used for course sweeping over driveways and the street.

For finer sweeping, a softer bristle, such as broomcorn or straw, is recommended. These are good for patios, decks, and walkways around the house. Keep the standard kitchen corn broom in the kitchen. Push brooms are more effective outside the home.

Aerators

An aerator is used to puncture holes in the turf to allow air and moisture to more easily penetrate it. It can be used in conjunction with a thatching rake. After removing dead grass that has formed an impervious mat (thatch), the aerator (which is designed with three, four, or any number of prongs), should be driven into the sod 3–5 inches for best results.

FIGURE 14.18

Knee pads help save your knees in the garden.

Want to know a secret? An effective aerator can be made by simply driving several nails into a block of wood. Simply set the board on the grass and step on it to press the spikes into the soil. Keep track of what area you've covered so you don't repeat areas. That should do it.

Power Equipment

The little boy in me still loves to use power equipment. There's something fun about using machines that roar to life and have them help you accomplish a job that would take much longer, and require much more effort, if you did it with your two hands. However, along with the power comes responsibility. It is important to think about and practice safe operation of these tools. Respect them. If you do, with proper care, operation, and maintenance, they will serve you well over time and behave exactly the way they were designed to.

Electric or Gas?

Outdoor power tools derive their power from electricity or gasoline. Most homeowners choose electric machines, with the exception of lawn mowers, for a few reasons. First, you don't have to store gasoline. Second, electric machines don't pollute, and they're not as noisy as gasoline ones. Finally, electric machines are generally cheaper and easier to operate than gasoline ones.

Renting versus Buying

Before deciding on which tools you need to buy and which ones to rent, ask yourself, how often am I going to use this tool? The answer for shovels, rakes, and nearly all the tools mentioned so far in this chapter will probably be often. This means it's probably best to buy these pieces of equipment. With proper care, and equipment manufacturer warranties, you'll get years and years of good use out of tools you use often.

Larger pieces of equipment, those that often run on gas-powered engines, are ones you may likely rent. You need to ask yourself the same question. How often am I going to use this piece of equipment? The answer could be not very often. (How often do you put up a fence or take out tree stumps?)

With the exception of a lawn mower, and possibly a line trimmer, there really is not a great need for homeowners to invest in purchasing a gasoline-driven piece of equipment because there really is not a consistent need for them around the home.

The advice I give to folks is to prepare for the job the best way you know how. That means having everything except the rental machine on site and ready to go. This way, when you rent a piece of power equipment for a half-day or the whole day, you spend most of your time using the piece of equipment—and getting the most for your money. This is because you're paying for the time spent using the machine—use your time (and money) wisely.

Consider the following scenario about renting versus buying. Lee Davis wants to install a fence around the perimeter of his property. He spends all morning checking the land survey of his property and begins driving stakes and attaching string along the outside perimeter of his property. Finally, when he is finished, and he can see where his property line runs, hundreds of feet into woods on both side of his house, he begins to worry that the hand-held post hole digger in his shed is going to outlast him if he tries to dig holes for fence posts every 8 feet.

Instead, he calls a local tool and machine renting shop he finds in the Yellow Pages. The conversation on the telephone goes like this:

"Hi, how are ya?" He asks.

"Good, how are you sir?" The attendant responds.

"Do you folks rent a machine that digs holes?"

"Sure! What would you like to do with it?"

"Well, I've staked out my property and I want to install a fence. My post hole digger and my back just ain't gonna make it."

The clerk at the rental store has more than likely heard the same story before. He knows what to ask.

"Do you know how many linear feet of fence you want to install?"

"It comes out to about 300 feet of fence. I've got it measured out with string."

"Well, let's see…what kind of fence are you installing?"

"Stockade."

"What size sections?"

"They measure 6 by 8 feet."

Lee hears the whir of an electronic calculator and the scribble of a pencil on paper at the other end of the phone.

"Well, let's see, if you have to cover 300 linear feet with 8-foot sections, you'll need about 37 sections of fence and 38 posts."

"Really?" Lee asks.

"Well, you'll have posts on both sides of each fence section. You'll always have one more post than sections."

"Right." Lee answers. "So that translates to 38 holes," he sighs.

"You got it." The man replies.

"Wow, how long is this going to take me?" He asks.

"What kind of soil do you have?"

"What do you mean?"

"Are there a lot of rocks and roots in the soil? Is there a lot of clay or sand?"

Lee then recalls digging in his backyard weeks before and remembers how easy it was after getting through the first 2 or 3 three inches of hard soil before hitting sand.

"Oh! It's kind of tough digging for the first few inches, but then it's sand all the way."

"Great! I'll give you the single-user model with a 3.5-horsepower engine on it."

"Will I be able to use this thing by myself?" Lee asks.

"No problem. If you come down to the store, I'll gladly show you how to use it. After digging a few holes, it'll be as easy as using a lawn mower."

Lee's confidence has grown because he feels the clerk on the other end of the phone has asked logical questions and didn't try and push any particular machine on him. The store caters to homeowners with little or no knowledge of landscaping tools and machines. But Lee does have one or two more questions.

"How big is something like this? Can I get it into the back of my Jeep?"

"No problem," the man answers. "It's no bigger than a lawn mower and when you come down, we'll help you get it into your car."

"How much will this cost me, and how long will I need it for?"

"If you get used to the machine and you have the property staked already with string, it shouldn't take more than 3 or 4 hours with small resting periods in between. We'll let you rent it for half a day and then you call us if you need it for the whole day. It's $38.00 for half a day and $56.00 for a full day.

"Yeah?"

"Sure, and we require a major credit card as a deposit. If you return the machine on time, in good condition, with a full tank of gas like when it left the yard, we'll return your credit card without even charging your account, and you pay your bill."

"That's it?" Lee asks.

"That's all there is to it."

Lee is now educated and motivated to tackle what in the recent past seemed like a daunting task. The best part is that he can accomplish this task with minimal cost and time and can save money by installing the fence himself. He will save labor, cost, time, and perhaps heartache by doing the job himself, and renting a machine to help him.

Lawn Mowers

Lawn mowers are available in many shapes and sizes. How do you know what's best for you? The answer is not as difficult as it seems. Start by asking yourself a few questions. How large is my yard? How often do I want to cut the grass? What kind of grass do I have?

The answers to these questions will help you decide which mower is best for you. Here's some more information to help you decide. One important consideration when deciding which mower to buy is one that car buyers share. Rear-wheel drive or front-wheel drive? Sometimes people ask me which is better. If they don't want the exercise of pushing the mower themselves, because their properties may be too large, or for other reasons, such as health and time issues, here's what I tell them.

If you must have a self-propelled mower, select the rear or front drive according to your needs. For instance, if anything I write can't convince you to stray from your rear-bag lawn mower you've had for years, then rear-wheel drive is the best mower for you. This is because the weight of the grass in the rear bag provides more traction for the rear wheels. It's also because that kind of mower is one you feel comfortable using.

On the other hand, a drawback is that you might have limited maneuverability with a rear-wheel drive mower. Typically, when an operator needs to turn, he pushes down on the handle, lifting the front wheels off the ground, walks the mower around, and sets the front wheels back on the ground. With rear-wheel-drive mowers, this action doesn't stop the momentum of the mower. The operator has to disengage the wheels to make turns.

A benefit of front-wheel-drive mowers is that when an operator wants to make a turn, she can push the handle of the mower down, lifting the front wheels off the ground, walk the mower around, set the front wheels down again, and off she goes. The front-wheel-drive design, using the typical turning action, naturally disengages the front wheels until the turn is completed by lifting them off the ground for a moment.

Front-wheel-drive mowers are also a little easier to handle, especially for some women and elderly people. The mower is pulled along, with the operator simply holding onto the handle. It is also easy to disengage the wheels (usually by releasing the bar under the handle) should the operator become incapacitated in any way. There's no need for a loose, unmanned lawn mower in the neighborhood.

Kinds of Lawn Mowers

Mowers are classified into three general types: reel-type push mowers (no engine—blades spin as you push it), rotary mowers (a blade that spins under its deck), and riding mowers (ones that look like small tractors). The most common are rotary mowers. These are classified even further, into push type, self-propelled, and the mulching kind. The rotary types are powered by gas engines or electricity, the reel kind relies on your muscle for its power, and the ride-on mowers are powered by gasoline engines.

Reel-Type Lawn Mowers

Reel-type lawn mowers enjoy a long history. They were around before gasoline engines arrived and are still proudly used by ecologically minded homeowners. Users enjoy obvious benefits: no gas to deal with, no pollution, few moving parts (less maintenance), and you get the benefit of exercise when you cut your grass. They are also pretty reasonably priced. You can pick up a new one for about $150. Scotts makes one that will serve you well.

The drawback to these mowers is the amount of turf they can cut. If you're cutting Yankee Stadium, I would not suggest getting this kind of mower. These are good for smaller yards and ones that have a lot of lawn ornaments and/or obstacles, but little turf.

Rotary Lawn Mowers: Self-Propelled

Self-propelled rotary lawn mowers are popular among homeowners. Although deck sizes, thickness, durability, engine sizes, and the position of the grass catcher are all different, self-propelled rotaries all operate the same way. Usually, it's the front wheels that are mechanically engaged to the engine, so it pulls itself across your lawn. You simply walk behind it and control its speed (with the use of a throttle switch) and direction.

The cut grass is discharged to the right side of the mower or is funneled to the back with a plastic or metal chute. For people with narrow spaces in their yards, it's probably best to select one with the catcher in the back. You can also remove the bag completely if you have a large area to cut and you don't mind leaving clippings on the lawn. This saves you time and effort by not having to stop and empty the catcher.

McCulloch sells a 21-inch self-propelled model for $199. This is about the cheapest price I've seen. Depending on the features, you can pay up to $399 or more for these kinds of mowers.

Rotary Lawn Mowers: Push Type

Push-type rotary lawn mowers are generally designed similar to self-propelled models, but you push them yourself. In every other way they appear (with all the bag and engine size options) like other rotary mowers. However, there are some differences that might not be immediately apparent to the untrained eye.

One is that the engine size and horsepower might be a little less for push types. This is because you don't need as much power with the push types—the engine doesn't have to turn a set of wheels in addition to turning the blades below the deck.

The other is the thickness and weight of the deck. While you need a sturdy deck on a self-propelled model because the blade turns faster and it takes more abuse, you don't necessarily need this option on a push mower. Weight is a consideration when push mowers are designed. Pushing a tank is usually not a homeowner's idea of fun. Lawn Boy sells walk-behind push mowers for as little as $199 (for a 22-inch model) and also has a 21-inch, 5-horsepower model for $429. There are other models that are in between these in price and quality.

Rotary Hi-Wheel Lawn Mowers

Another kind of lawn mower that I recommend for specific purposes is the Hi-Wheel mower. This looks like an old-fashioned mower because its rear wheels are substantially larger than its front wheels. This kind of mower is designed for uneven terrain and offers a lot of maneuverability around trees and tight corners where a standard mower wouldn't be welcome.

Some other benefits of the Hi-Wheel mower are that its design prevents it from scalping the surface of the lawn when it cuts on slopes and banks. Its rear wheel design supports the deck over uneven surfaces and offers more comfort and stability to the operator. The Hi-Wheel mower is my recommendation for people whose lawns have many trees, embankments, berms, or slopes. These are comparatively priced with rotary self-propelled mowers.

Mulchers

Mulching lawn mowers arrived a few years ago to serve a need: to conserve yard matter and stop adding it to our nation's landfills. These mowers not only cut your grass, they mulch the clippings and do something do-it-yourselfers love: They let you leave the clippings where you found them—right on your lawn, but in smaller pieces.

Mulchers look different than other rotary mowers. The deck has no discharge chute at all. If you turned the unit over, you would see the blade is not really flat. Instead, it's kind of wavy. It's designed this way so the cutting surface is increased, allowing it to cut and recut and recut each blade of grass. The volume of the cut grass is decreased tremendously, so when you're mowing, while it doesn't appear that you're cutting anything, you're really cutting it so fine, the bits of grass blades are falling between the remaining ones.

There are other benefits to mulchers as well. On a standard mower, the rear bag or side catcher fills with grass quickly and increases the weight of the machine as its pushed around the lawn. A mulching mower has no cumbersome bags and is lighter to push.

Another benefit is that every time you cut the grass you are refertilizing the lawn! When you mulch the blades of grass, you are increasing the surface area of previously fertilized blades of grass, thereby spreading out the fertilizer you may have applied and directing it to the source of growth: the roots of the grass blades and the ground surrounding it. Coupled with the decay of the bits of mulched grass blades, you're feeding the lawn twice each time you cut.

A final advantage to using a mulching mower is how clean it is. With a standard mower you have to use a bag (rear bag or side bag) and constantly keep the chute clean and free of too much grass or debris that could clog the chute. The mulching mower avoids all this extra work and cleanup. There's nothing to clean (except an occasional cleaning of the inside of the deck) and there's nothing to haul back and forth (like full grass catchers) to the trash can or plastic bag.

As more landfills close, towns have ceased taking grass clippings and yard debris such as sticks and leaves. Lawn mower manufacturers have responded to this growing recycling trend by offering lawn mowers with the latest mulching technology. If you're still emptying a grass catcher, you'll be forced to compost or spread the clippings around plants in the garden.

My recommendation is to embrace mulching technology and save yourself time and effort. Mulching mowers (22-inch models) are available for as little as $179 and go up in price from there. Check with your local home improvement retailer. There are many models to choose from.

Riding Lawn Mowers

Riding lawn mowers are commonly used by people who have a very large piece of property with a lot of lawn to cut. There's another reason they are popular: More users are growing older and have trouble walking a lot.

Ride-ons look like small tractors, and many of them now have all the amenities of cars. They have batteries, self-start features, headlights, gears for different speeds, and cushioned seats. All this equipment supports one vital part: the mowing deck. This houses the turning blades that do the work of cutting the grass.

The operator pulls levers or pushes buttons to raise or lower the deck, depending on what the grass conditions are like and how much he or she has to cut. These models usually feature grass hoppers (which hold more volume of cut grass than catchers) in the back of the operator and have 10-, 12-, 14-, or sometimes 16-horsepower engines (power enough to propel the tractor and spin the blades).

John Deere offers a 16.5-horsepower, 42-inch cut model for $600. However, because ride-ons are available with so many different amenities, prices vary. Check for warranties when you buy one. You may also want to consider buying additional service contracts with these kinds of lawn mowers. Maintenance is really more like working on a car.

DO I NEED A RIDE-ON?

While only you can really decide whether you need (or just want) a riding lawn mower, I can help you make the decision. If you have a lot of property (grass areas) to cut, and you have been using a rotary mower, ask yourself—are you exhausted after you cut the grass? Is cutting the grass becoming more of a loathed chore? Does your mower conk out a lot or spend a lot of time in the shop? If the answers to these questions are yes, you may be overworking yourself and your equipment.

It's either the ride-on (which you can have for a long time) or time to get a landscaping service.

Maintenance

Maintaining your lawn mower is the key to getting good results when you cut grass with it. If you live in an area of the country that has distinct growing seasons, you'll want to have your lawn mowers serviced by a professional just before and after every growing season. This means having the mower tuned up, lubricated, the oil changed, and parts checked for replacement (cables, engine parts, the fuel system and spark plugs, mechanical parts, etc.).

Having a professional maintain your lawn mower does a couple of things: It saves you time, aggravation, and downtime during the summer when you want to use the machine. It also allows you to worry about the important things: just keeping fresh, clean fuel in the machine and using it properly.

Always be sure to wear some kind of eye protection while mowing your grass and always stop the mower (turn off the engine) when you remove the grass catcher to empty it. Read the owner's manual and check with your dealer if you have any other questions.

Line Trimmers

Before purchasing a line trimmer, you need to decide whether to get a gas-powered or an electric-powered one. If your property is pretty small, electric is best. If it's rather large, the gas unit may be for you.

The reasons are fairly obvious. Running an electric cord around your property can be cumbersome, or you simply don't have enough extension cords to cover the whole property. Gas-powered line trimmers offer more mobility and you can get the job done quicker.

Line trimmers cut grass where a lawn mower can't—they cut it against fences, walls, around trees, flower beds, and, when turned on their side, make nice edging tools (see Figs. 14.19 and 14.20).

Electric models tend to be lighter in weight and less powerful. They are best used on small properties without longer grass. They plug in and start with a switch. Gas models are heavier, more powerful (they can be used for longer periods of time), can handle taller grass, and can run at different speeds. You control the speed of the machine's rotating head with a throttle switch.

FIGURE 14.19

Line trimmers cut grass where a lawn mower can't reach.

There are two basic model styles to choose from. One has a straight shaft and the other a curved shaft. The curved shaft is popular among homeowners because it keeps the head at a good angle for cutting grass. The straight-shaft model is usually for heavier work. On this style, users can attach different blades to it for cutting branches and heavier brush.

Operation

Most trimmers have an automatic line-feeding system that feeds new line as the old line gets used up. The operator simply taps the head of the unit against the ground. If too much line comes out, it is cut automatically by a fixed, sharp blade. This keeps the line at the right length at all times. Loading the spool when it is finished is pretty simple. Just follow the directions that come with the unit.

Remember, wear eye protection at all times when operating a trimmer. Protecting your eyes from flying debris is important.

FIGURE 14.20

The head can be twisted and the trimmer can be used as an edger. Always wear eye protection.

Blowers

In the past, the only way homeowners could get leaves, grass, and other debris off their walks, porches, driveways, and lawns was to sweep or rake it off by hand. Now, few people do this—instead, homeowners use electric- and gas-powered blowers. Blowers are much easier (on your back), faster, and do a more thorough job.

While there are many models for the homeowner to choose from, there are two categories: electric- and gas-powered. Electric blowers are generally hand-held models that weigh very little, are portable and maneuverable, and are powerful enough to blow grass clippings, dry dirt, and dry leaves from walkways, driveways, patios, decks, and porches (see Fig. 14.21).

Toro sells an electric model for as little $30 that can handle weekly chores with no problem. There are no moving parts to lubricate or any other kind of maintenance. You simply unplug it, wrap the cord up, and put it in the garage.

There are gas-powered models available for the serious homeowner. I recommend these only for people with properties that are larger than

FIGURE 14.21

Electric blowers save a lot of time and work.

average but just small enough not to require the services of a landscaper. They run on a mix of gasoline and two-cycle oil and are much more powerful than hand-held electric units.

Gas-powered blowers are worn on the back and have a throttle switch connected to an arm that can swivel. This allows the user to direct the blast of air, and backpack units can handle wet leaves and grass clippings on a lawn.

Gas-powered blowers are more expensive to buy and operate than electric units. Echo sells a gas-powered model for $300. Unless you have a huge yard and want to mix gasoline and oil, staying with an electric model is probably wisest.

Rotary Tillers

Rotary tillers are for the serious gardener. Unless you have several spacious flower and vegetable gardens you turn over every year and maintain dutifully, the typical homeowner doesn't have much of a need for a gas-powered tiller.

Rotary tillers are designed to do the backbreaking work of many people in a very short period of time. Many a farmer has turned his fields over in the spring with a shovel. If you don't want to do this, or you can't, you can rent a tiller for the one time during the year (the spring) that you'll need it.

Tillers have curved, flat pieces of metal connected to a metal rod that turns. The curved pieces of metal, the tines, dig themselves into the dirt and turn it over. For the hardy few, there are two types of tillers available. One is the front tine and the other is a rear tine. The difference between the two is simply where the tines are located on the machines—as their name says.

The front-tine style is generally for smaller work, is a little harder to operate, but is cheaper to purchase. The revolving tines pull the machine through the soil, and when they hit rocks or hard ground, the tiller bounces. The Yard Machine Company sells their least expensive model for $178.

The rear-tine model is easier to operate. The position of the tines (farther back on the machine) keeps it balanced, and it requires less physical effort to keep it straight. They can also break through harder soil, rock, and tree roots with less effort. The Yard Machine Company sells a 10-horsepower tiller for $599. Only serious gardeners should consider this investment. Read the directions carefully before operating one of these machines. Know where the kill switch is and how to operate the clutch. Check with your dealer for use and care tips.

Chain Saws

Although chain saws are real time and labor savers, they are very dangerous machines and should be used with great caution. Do not ever use a chain saw when you're tired or distracted. They can be very unforgiving if you are not completely in control of them.

Like other power tools, chain saws are available in electric and gasoline models. Nearly all homeowners will get along fine with an electric one. They are less powerful, less expensive, and certainly less costly to maintain. Unless you have trees to bring down or you have heavy tree trimming to do, you won't need a gas-operated chain saw. After all, how often do you need to take down trees?

Electric chain saws are good for trimming small tree branches (up to about 4 inches around) and cutting up tree branches that may have fallen in a storm. The only real maintenance you'll have is lubricating the chain (keeping the bar oil reservoir full) by pressing a button and keeping the bar adjusted properly. This involves loosening a nut where the bar meets the engine, prying the bar out (to tighten the chain that slides in a groove in the bar), and keeping the machine clean.

A Remington electric model with a 14-inch bar sells for as little as $43. Gasoline models, by Echo, can sell for as high as $300 to $400. Unless you live in Yosemite, however, it's unlikely you'll need one like these. Lastly, make sure you wear protective eye gear and gloves when you use a chain saw. Read all the directions before operating one. It's worth the extra time to keep safe.

Shredders/Mulchers

Shredders and mulchers are popular among homeowners because they serve a valuable purpose: They reduce a large amount of yard material to a small amount by breaking it up into pieces. In this environmental age, with landfills closing, it's smart to recycle and keep your organic yard waste (although in another form) in your yard.

Most units are designed in a similar fashion and have the same general parts. They consist of a chute that accepts straight branches and yard matter, an internal propeller (a blade or device that turns and shreds or mulches the material), an engine that powers the blade, and an exhaust chute where the material (in much smaller pieces) exits.

They are terrific for turning a lot of yard waste (leaves, twigs, branches, etc.) into fine mulch that can then be used to dress beds and act as compost. Everything is recycled in the yard and the sometimes massive volume is reduced to something manageable.

Like other power yard tools, they are available in electric and gasoline models. Electric units are generally smaller, are less powerful (can only handle branches up to a few inches in diameter), and generally can't reduce the volume of material as efficiently as gas-powered units can.

Electric units are also easier to maintain. It is simply a matter of keeping them clean and keeping debris away from the chute when they are not in use. On the other hand, while gas-powered models are more beneficial in many ways, the benefits don't come free. They require as much care as a lawn mower, some believe. There are more moving parts, gasoline, oil, and grease fittings to worry about.

The Yard Machine Company sells 5-horsepower units for $399 and 10-horsepower units for $597. Although they are expensive, if you have a large property with many trees, you might consider this investment one that will pay you back after a few years. If they are taken care of, according to manufacturers recommendations for regular maintenance, there's not any reason you shouldn't get years of use out of them.

It is important to remember that these machines can be dangerous if they are used improperly. Always wear goggles, gloves, ear protectors (they are loud), and always keep your hands clear of the chute when feeding material into the hopper. If you have any questions, see your dealer and read the manual for safe operation instructions.

FIGURE 14.22

Electric snow shovels work hard so you don't have to.

Snow Blowers

If you live in the northern part of the country, you know what kinds of winters we've had in the last few years. If you're like me, the older I get, the less I want to shovel snow. Give me a machine to take care of the problem.

Believe it or not, snow blowers are also available in electric- and gasoline-powered models. The electric ones are usually called "electric snow shovels" (see Fig. 14.22). The ones with gas engines, usually self-propelled and with crank-adjusted discharge chutes, are called snow blowers.

Personally, I don't think it pays to buy an electric snow shovel—if they call it a snow shovel, are you better off than when you did it by hand? If you're in a region of the country where you get snow, chances are you get snow for 4 to 6 months and you get a few feet at a time. If that's the case, you'll be better off with a gas-powered machine that's always ready.

These machines are pretty easy to operate. The engines are a lot like lawn mowers, but in order to work well, they should be self-propelled. You should be able to simply guide it through the snow and adjust the throw chute (where the snow is thrown). They should be maintained by having regular oil changes, fresh gasoline, a once-a-year tune-up, and regular lubrication of moving parts that call for it. Don't worry that it sits in the garage without being used for half the year—it's well worth it—and you'll appreciate having it when the time comes.

For those that must have electric snow shovels, you can pick one up for as little as $99. You can also buy an Arienns brand 11.5-horsepower model for $1299. With proper care and maintenance, there should be no reason why this shouldn't be your last snow blower purchase. Remember, ask your dealer for operation and maintenance instructions if they are unclear in the owner's manual.

Hedge Trimmers

I think of Disney World when I think of hedge trimmers. Weird, isn't it? I'm reminded of the perfectly manicured green hedges that are trimmed into letters—you can't miss them as you enter the Magic Kingdom. They've been there since I was a kid, and they were there when I took my wife Gail and my kids Andrew and Ian there two years ago. The hedges looked better than ever. Someone was using a sharpened hedge trimmer and doing a great job.

The hedge trimmer is a time-saving device for shaping and trimming hedges and bushes (usually in flower beds) against houses or ones that line driveways. Homeowners have a choice of electric- or gas-powered units. Although both seem to work equally well, unless you have a mansion with a mansion-sized property to take care of, an electric hedge trimmer is fine.

There are a few reasons for this. One is that you get plenty of power out of these for bushes and shrubs. The second is that there is little work involved in taking care of them. Lastly, most bushes and shrubs are close to houses, where there are electrical outlets. You don't have to drag around long extension cords while you are working.

The homeowner doesn't gain much by using a gas-powered machine but gas and oil spills without that much more power or cutting ability. It's important to keep the blades sharp and clean. To do this, though, take it to a repair shop. The scissor action of the blades is tricky, and maintaining the blades should be left to the pro.

Always wear goggles and gloves when operating a hedge trimmer (see Fig. 14.23). They are heavy; if you get tired, rest and turn the machine off.

FIGURE 14.23

Hedge trimmers are helpful tools, but they can be dangerous. Wear safety equipment when using them.

Read the owner's manual carefully, and if you still have questions, see your dealer before operating one.

Toro sells a 17-inch electric hedge trimmer (the length of the scissors) for about $30. You can also buy an Echo brand gas-powered 20-inch model for $249.

The Lawn

Think for a minute about the benefits of maintaining your own lawn: you are making your part of the world a greener, nicer place by providing beautiful outdoor space around your home, increasing its aesthetic and market value, reducing air pollution (healthy lawns produce oxygen and consume carbon dioxide), getting exercise, attracting wildlife, controlling erosion, and enjoying the fruits of your labor (see Fig. 15.1).

Landscaping your own property also allows you to connect with nature in a deeply personal, meaningful way. How many people can say that?

Mowing

FAIRLY EASY **2–5 hours**

As a kid I became obsessed with mowing lawns. It started when my father allowed me, for the first time, to use the power mower by myself, to cut the front yard of our home in Monterey, California. I remember wanting to do the best job possible, and wanting to leave no doubt in my father's mind that he had made the right decision in trusting me to tackle the mowing myself.

I still want to do the best job possible. Now, however, I enjoy helping other homeowners bask in a sense of accomplishment, surveying their own freshly cut, healthy, vibrant lawn. In order to achieve this, here are some guidelines to follow, and answers to some common questions.

FIGURE 15.1

Keeping your lawn maintained adds to curb appeal.

Safety First

People have asked me questions such as: Should I follow a pattern when I cut my grass? Or, what is the easiest way to cut my grass? My answers are usually the same. Before any cutting is done, safety should be the first consideration. First, always take a stroll around the grass and look for any foreign objects that may become flying projectiles if you run over them with the mower.

Years ago a friend of mine was cutting his grass and a grinding sound suddenly came from under the mower. Before he could even reach over and turn the mower off, something shot from under it and shattered his car window. Apparently, his daughter had lost her house keys when she was doing cartwheels on the grass with her friends.

To this day, he double-checks his lawn before he cuts. An efficient way to do this is to walk slowly in one direction and look straight down. This is a good way to spot small objects hidden in the grass.

Dress for the Job   *EASY* **1–2 hours**

Next, I always recommend that people dress for the job. This does not mean that you have to undergo a complete wardrobe change. Just make sure you don't have open-toed shoes or sandals on. Although sneakers are fine, I recommend workboots with a steel-tipped toe for cutting lawns. It's usually best to stick with one pair of shoes for lawn-cutting detail. Grass stains shoes, you know. It's also a good idea to wear long pants. This is really important because you never know when flying debris can injure legs or other body parts (or car windows).

Another rule to follow is to never, under any circumstances, empty the grass catcher while the engine is running. Mower manufacturers all recommend turning the engine off when emptying a grass catcher. Some have built-in cutoff switches that don't allow the bag to be removed from the unit when the engine is running. It's also a good idea to wear gloves when handling catchers and grass clippings.

Another good idea is to do an overall vision test on your mower. This simply means checking that you have clean oil in the machine, fresh gasoline, and that all the parts of the mower are in good working order. It is also important to check that the height adjustments for each wheel are the same.

Height Adjustments   *EASY*

Most mowers have height adjustments for the front and back of the deck, and some have adjustments for each wheel. If that's the case, the mower could scalp the lawn and cut unevenly, doing damage to the lawn, if only one of the wheel height adjustments is not set properly.

Look It Over   *EASY*

Regularly scheduled maintenance, recommended by the manufacturer, should cover nearly all the parts on the mower that you can inspect before operating it. After the preliminary check of the lawn and the machine are done, there is a final item to remember. That is where the mower is when you start it.

Starting the Mower

It's best to start the mower on a corner of the turf (yard). There are several reasons for this. One is that if it is started anywhere else, such as a walkway or driveway, you risk having small rocks and other debris flying out and injuring someone. Closed-toe shoes and long pants may protect the operator, but other people, pets, and objects may be close by and at risk of injury. Another important reason is to check the height of the mower deck.

By starting the mower on the grass, in an isolated area of the turf, the operator can push the mower a few feet and check to see that the deck is cutting the lawn at the proper height. If the deck height has to be adjusted, the experiment occurred on an isolated part of the lawn. Although the user has to initially estimate the proper height of the deck before staring the engine, it is best to err on the side of having the deck too high. You can always lower the deck. You can't always grow back what you cut off the lawn.

Start on the Outside

When the proper height of the deck is achieved, I recommend that operators follow the outside perimeter of the lawn that is to be cut. The chute of the mower should face the *inside* of the turf area. If you are using a mower without a chute, it's a good idea to have the inside area of the lawn to your right. Once one pass has been made around the outside perimeter, a second one can be made. When you begin the second pass, be sure that the left side of the mower deck overlaps with the previous pass by about 2 or 3 inches. This ensures that each part of the lawn is cut and you won't be left with narrow strips of uncut grass between passes.

Once that is completed, it's best to make parallel, straight passes. These should be as straight as possible, and closely hug obstacles such as trees and flower beds. This will provide uniformity to the finished lawn. Again, be sure to overlap the previous pass by 2 or 3 inches to ensure that you are not missing any part of the grass.

If you have a bag to empty, stop the engine, remove the bag, and walk the bag to a waiting trash can, plastic bag, wheelbarrow, or compost heap. It is best not to move the mower. Instead, bring the item you are putting the cut grass in to the mower. Also, by leaving the mower where it is, you remember where you left off and where you should begin cutting again.

Also, it is best to pull the mower back and remow a small portion of the previous pass after you empty the bag. This lets the mower suck up any loose grass clippings that may have fallen while you emptied the catcher.

Once the job is complete, make sure the mower's engine is off before you roll it off the grass. Empty the last catcher full of grass before the mower comes off the turf. This will prevent you from having to sweep or blow grass clipping from sidewalks and driveways.

Mix It Up

Another cutting tip is something that can be accomplished pretty easily, from week to week. Reversing the cutting pattern of your lawn every time you cut offers several benefits to your lawn and to you. A primary one is that by changing the cutting pattern each time you cut, you are training the blades of grass to grow straight up.

If you continue to cut the grass in one pattern, you are pushing the blades one way. A disadvantage to this is that, over time, they tend to grow one way, bend, and lay flatter than they should. Wheel lines will also become more prominent in the lawn. A broad, flat surface (each blade is cut to the same height) on a healthy, green lawn is much more appealing to the eye.

Another benefit is that by changing the cutting pattern, the operator picks up more debris such as old grass, sticks, and leaves. Often, when debris is imbedded in the grass, mowing over it from another angle causes it to become loose, and then it is easily sucked up off the lawn.

A final benefit is to you, the operator. Grass cutting should be fun and rewarding, coupled with a sense of accomplishment and pride. Why keep following the same pattern, week after week? Why not enjoy another pattern and get a fresh perspective of your lawn?

How Often?

An important question people ask me is how often should I cut my grass? Depending on the type of grass you have, and your watering practices (to be discussed later), once a week (with room to spare) is usually my answer. If your lawn is a tall fescue that grows relatively quickly, I suggest cutting the grass every 5–7 days, particularly if you are in an area of the country with a distinct growing season. This general rule also applies to homeowners with Kentucky blue grass blends.

On the other hand, if you have a lawn full of zoysia grass and you are in a temperate part of the country, you may only need to cut your grass every 7–10 days. Zoysia grass grows more slowly than most other grasses and doesn't require as much maintenance.

My general rule for lawn cutting is that one should never cut more than 2 inches off the lawn at any given time. This is because the top 2 inches of the blades of grass are usually the greenest and most vibrant because all plants produce new growth from only two areas: the tips of their leaves and the tips of their roots. Taking off more than 2 inches will dig too far into the body of the blade, and it will appear burned. It will eventually turn yellow or brown. Although it may recover, it will be an eyesore for some time before the lawn can recover.

Time of Day

Time of day is important when mowing your grass. The best rule of thumb is to mow in the late morning, before the hottest part of the day, or just before sunset. There are several reasons for this. You don't want to cut the grass in the early morning because of the dew that is left on the grass from the night before. This is the same as cutting wet grass. Wet grass clogs the mower deck, clumps up, and is generally a hassle to contend with.

This is even more true in areas with many trees and shade that is cast on the lawn. If this is the case, it may take longer for the dew to evaporate off the lawn. So, I recommend to people that they cut after the dew evaporates and before the hottest part of the day.

The disadvantage of cutting during the hottest part of the day is that during intense heat, the lawn could actually go into shock by cutting it. As a living, breathing thing, a plant such as grass manages its resources differently in different conditions. In extreme heat, it conserves water, and stores what little it has in its root system. The resulting blade that you see on the lawn reacts differently when it is dry than when it is full of water.

The same is true for cutting the grass just before sunset. This is because you want to cut the grass when it is cooling down: It reacts differently when it is comfortable and when the person cutting it is comfortable. Another advantage to this time of day is that dew is not getting a chance to form. This saves you time and effort with the old wet grass issue.

Enjoy Your Labor

Enjoy your lawn after you cut it. I have always enjoyed summer evenings, about an hour before sunset, when the air is cooling and the critters (which may come off the lawn when you cut) are less active. Enjoy the serenity of the cooling evening air fragrant with fresh-cut grass and flowering plants.

I wish the same for you. After all, you probably take pride in working on your property. Enjoy the fruits of your labor.

Watering

EASY 1–2 HOURS

Timing is also important when it comes to watering your lawn. The best time to water your lawn is about 8 or 9 A.M. There are a couple of reasons for this. One is that if you water during the hottest part of the day, you are battling evaporation. You may be watering and watering and it is evaporating as fast as you can apply the water. There's another, equally important reason: When a lawn is watered during this part of the day, it may burn. The fine sheen of water is heated by the sun so much that it actually burns the grass.

Conversely, if you water the lawn after 5 or 6 o'clock in the afternoon, you are inviting potential problems with fungus developing. When water sits on the lawn without benefit of the sun (which leads to some evaporation), fungus can begin to grow and breed throughout the night.

How Much Water?

My general rule is that a lawn needs about 1 inch of water a week during the spring and summer, and less during the fall. This can be achieved by natural means (rainfall) or by using a hose and sprinkler (Fig. 15.2). It's best to work with Mother Nature. She's much more powerful than we are, and will usually win if we challenge her.

To see how much water your lawn is getting, simply mark an empty coffee can at the 1-inch level, inside and out, and put the can on your lawn. As rain falls or you have your sprinkler on, occasionally check the can. Stop watering when the water reaches the one-inch mark.

If you get 1 inch of rainfall in one week, leave the hose alone. Why go through the effort that week if Mother Nature can gave you a gift? On the other hand, if you go through periods of little or no rain, you must water to have a healthy, green lawn. The general rule is that grass reacts better to fewer, very thorough soakings rather than frequent sprinklings. The reason is that you want to promote healthy, deep roots. By soaking the grass for a longer period of time, the water is able to percolate down to the roots, nourishes them, and trains them to grow straight down and deep. This will allow the grass to appear more healthy and more readily take advantage of deeper water in times of drought.

Maintaining Hoses

Leaking Rubber Hose　　*EASY* **1–2 hours**

What would a lawn be without a well-working hose? Some books have long recommended stopping a leak in rubber garden hose by wrapping tape over the hole. Actually, this is about as effective as sticking your finger in a leaking dike. The pressure of the water eventually forces it off.

The repair should be made with a thing called a *clincher mender.* This is a brass tube, in the middle of which are encircling teeth. You can get one in a hardware store for about $3. Show your dealer the hose so he'll give you the right size.

First, use a single-edge razor blade or a sharp knife to cut out the section of the hose with the hole in it. Keep your cuts straight up and down (not slanted). Slip one end of the clincher mender into one

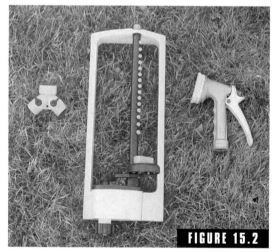

FIGURE 15.2

A sprinkler that attaches to a hose, a hand sprayer, and a diverter (for using two hoses at once) are all that are needed to keep your lawn watered.

section of the hose and hammer down the teeth so they bite into the rubber and are flat. Slip the other end of the device into the other section of hose and hammer down those teeth.

Leaking Plastic Hose
EASY **1–2 hours**

Although plastic hoses aren't that popular anymore, some readers have them and want to keep them in good repair. Tape won't stop a leak in plastic hose either. Here, as with rubber hose, use a clincher mender, but one made of sheet brass rather than pure brass. The repair is made the same way as for rubber hose. However, if you have difficulty sticking the tube into the end of the cut hose, you can soften the hose by dipping it in warm water. Cost of a clincher mender for plastic hose repair is about $3.50.

Here's a hint: If your plastic hose is still working, great. If not, it may be worth getting a rubber or vinyl hose.

Fertilizing
EASY **1–2 hours**

Fertilizing is an important part of maintaining a healthy, green lawn. For the homeowner who wants to fertilize his or her own lawn, I recommend using Scotts or another name brand that offers a four-step program. These programs include all the fertilizer you will need for each season (see Fig. 15.3). On the back of each bag are instructions on how to apply the product and when to apply it. It's as simple as can be and leaves out the guesswork and experimenting.

FERTILIZE WITH CARE

As a kid I used to help my father in the yard of our house in Virginia Beach, Virginia. One day my dad decided it was time for me to learn how to fertilize the lawn. No problem. He showed me how to operate the spreader unit and adjust the flow of fertilizer that fell below it.

I started the chore and decided that if this funny-smelling sand in the hopper (the fertilizer) made grass really green, why not use it to spell out our family's name in giant letters across the lawn? Flying over our house several weeks later in a rented plane (my dad was a pilot, and we used to rent planes), my father discovered why I always volunteered for yard detail.

When using either a broadcast or drop-style spreader (see Chap. 14), consult the manufacturer's recommendations for which settings you should use on the unit. Often there is a grid printed on the bag of fertilizer and/or

Three bags are left after applying the first bag of fertilizer in a four-step program. These applications should include the summer, fall, and late fall.

grass seed. It describes how much fertilizer to use, when (what time of year, month, and day), how to apply it, and what setting your spreader should be on when you apply it.

A good practice is to watch the hopper as you walk behind the spreader. If the material is falling faster than you think it should, it probably is. Another good practice is simply to watch the material fly out of the unit. This will tell you where you should be on another pass and prevent overlapping.

It's best to fertilize (and seed) in calm, dry weather. If you want to fertilize and seed at the same time, consult the manufacturer's recommendations on the bag. I recommend that you use gloves when working with fertilizers and store any unused material in a clean, dry spot. A tip: Granular fertilizer bags have a three-number sequence printed on them. The first number refers to the amount of nitrogen (to green the grass), the second number refers to the amount of potassium (to feed the roots), and the third number refers to the amount of potash (to sustain healthy roots and feed the whole plant).

It's best to use a fertilizer that is high in nitrogen in the spring to green the grass up quickly. Conversely, it's best to use a fertilizer with a high potassium content in the fall to feed the roots and provide enough food for them for the entire winter.

Weed Control

Weed control is also an important (and often unseen) part of lawn maintenance. Similar to fertilizer, weed killers (including broadleaf weed killers) come in granular form and provide instructions about how to apply them.

There are also preemergent weed killers available. They do just what their name says: They kill weed seeds before they emerge from the ground in the early spring. Broadleaf weed killers kill a wide variety of common weeds that you may see trying to invade your lawn.

It is important to research when weed killers can be applied. Their effectiveness depends on various factors such as time of year, possible interactions with other fertilizers, seed, and soil amendments you may have used, such as new topsoil and mulch. Read the bags you bring home carefully for instructions.

Installing Sod

Correcting a ragged, bare, or diseased lawn may require removing the old lawn entirely and installing a new one. One way to do this is to replace the existing lawn with seed or sod. Seeds will take awhile to sprout and need a good amount of tender, loving care. On the other hand, sod can be put down in one day (provided all the prep work is done) and is ready to cut shortly after. Following are the steps involved for installing sod.

Sod is grass and the dirt that it's growing in, all in one. It's grass that has been grown elsewhere for the purpose of harvesting and being planted again, on your lawn. Although installing sod is a good deal of work, it's worth the effort if you want a new, beautiful lawn—quickly. Sod has quite a rich history before you buy it at the sod farm. See the sequence in Figs. 15.4 to 15.9.

Removing Existing Turf

The first step is to remove the existing turf, including its root system, to a depth of 3 inches or so. If the area is small (say, under 100 square feet), you can do the job with a flat spade, but if it is large, you should use a sod cutter, a gas-powered device which can be rented by the half-day (which is probably all you'll need it for).

The sod cutter has a flat, horizontal steel blade that vibrates and is no more difficult to use than a walk-behind small lawn mower. The operator pushes the machine forward in a straight line and controls the vibrating speed of a slicing bar with a throttle switch on the handle. To save money, you shouldn't rent it until you are ready to use it, and you should shop rental places by telephone to get the best price.

Sod starts as newly planted seeds at a farm. This one is in Suffolk County, New York. *(Photo courtesy of Gilamiaga.)*

Sod is watered and cared for while it grows. *(Photo courtesy of Gilamiaga.)*

FIGURE 15.6

Regular maintenance at the farm includes cutting. *(Photo courtesy of Gilamiaga.)*

FIGURE 15.7

Tractors fitted with sod-cutting machines harvest the sod. *(Photo courtesy of Gilamiaga.)*

FIGURE 15.8

The sod is then folded and stacked on pallets for delivery to customers' homes. *(Photo courtesy of Gilamiaga.)*

Examine the underside of the turf you remove. Unless it is infested with grubs or other insects, it can be disposed of in a wooden area of your property or added to compost piles or used to fill in low spots in the lawn, all of which will save you having to bag it. If it is infested, however, discard it. Otherwise insects can migrate back to the new lawn and possibly damage it.

Grading the Area

VERY DIFFICULT **7–10 hours**

The exposed soil should then be *graded*—raked smooth, and all rocks, debris, and clumps of soil removed to make the surface smooth and slanted (see Fig. 15.10). The best tool is a garden rake or landscape rake (see Chap. 14). The garden rake has a heavy, rigid, metal head about 18 inches wide and has teeth that are curved. A landscape rake is usually made of strengthened aluminum and has straight teeth with a far wider head, some reaching 3 and 4 feet wide. Unless you are grading Yankee Stadium, the smaller rake should suffice.

FIGURE 15.9

Years ago, whole fields of sod were harvested with one gas-driven sod-cutting machine and then hand folded.

FIGURE 15.10

This property is ready to be graded: prepared for the installation of sod.

To save the effort of pulling rocks and clods a long way, rake the material into a number of small piles. Then use a wheelbarrow to haul it away, or use it to fill low spots on the surface. As you go, make sure the grade slants away from the house; you don't want water routed to and collecting by the foundation wall.

The best wheelbarrow to use is a contractor's type, a large, deep one which has an inflatable rubber tire (pneumatic) and can be pushed more easily than a smaller one with a metal wheel (see Chap. 14). It's better to have a wheelbarrow like this on hand even for household chores, because it lasts longer and you can handle many more tasks that require carrying a lot of weight.

Lastly, you can give the surface a final smoothing using a light rake—bamboo or plastic. Now you are ready to spread the topsoil.

Adding Topsoil

The roots of the new sod need a fresh, nutrition-rich bed of soil to anchor to, and this is the role of topsoil, which can be bought at local nurseries or at home centers in bags or loose, by "the yard"—a 3-foot by 3-foot by 3-foot cube of topsoil equals a "yard."

Bags cost much more and are more labor-intensive to use (approximately $80 per yard versus $45 for loose). They have to be individually opened and the empties disposed of. On the other hand, by-the-yard topsoil is delivered (free sometimes, or for a fee) and ready to go. What's more, if you have an average pickup truck you won't be able to haul bags that contain more than 1 to 2 yards at a time without risking damage to the truck.

Shop around for topsoil; some dealers may try and palm inferior material off on you. Ask for topsoil that has been screened, meaning that it has been filtered to remove big clumps of soil and rocks. Also, examine the topsoil. Better topsoil is a dark, chocolaty brown and has an even, spongy texture; it's not sandy, nor does it contain large clumps of clay. Sand (or "bank run," as it is known) is too porous and roots don't set well in it, and clay can prevent proper drainage of the enormous amounts of water that sod needs.

You also have to be wary of how much you buy. A greedy dealer may try to oversell you; if he does, good luck returning that small mountain of it in your driveway.

HOW MUCH WILL YOU NEED?

To determine how much you need, figure 2 inches of topsoil per 3-foot-square (1-yard) area. One yard of topsoil (or any loose material, really) will cover about 100 square feet of area at 2 inches deep. So, for example, 420 square feet of area would require 4 yards of topsoil.

Most drivers will routinely dump your topsoil at curbside, but you want it placed as close as possible to the area where it's going to be used. You can simply ask the driver or, better yet, offer him a tip. It shouldn't be difficult for him to do.

SPREADING THE TOPSOIL   *DIFFICULT* **5–7 hours**

Haul the topsoil to its final resting place with the wheelbarrow, which should be filled, but not overfilled so much you find it hard to push. To save steps, push the wheelbarrow to the farthest point where the topsoil is needed. Immediately dump and rake it even.

Load the wheelbarrow again and repeat the procedure. Continue like this, working your way back to the pile. You may be surprised at how quickly what seems like an enormous pile of soil can be used up. Any remaining soil can be disposed of like turf. It's best to hold back on cleanup until the entire job is done.

Fertilizing the Topsoil   *EASY* **1–2 hours**

Enriching the soil by adding fertilizer with a high phosphorus content and medium nitrogen content is a good idea (see the "Fertilizing" section of this chapter for more information). Phosphorous will help stimulate healthy root structure, and nitrogen will help keep the sod green. A good starter fertilizer, such as Scotts Starter Fertilizer, is fine. Follow the instructions on the bag for spreading it (the spreader settings will be printed).

Choosing the Sod

Sod comes in two basic sizes, giant rolls (if you're Godzilla) or bite-size sheets measuring 5 feet long and 18 inches wide, each covering 4.5 square feet. Unless you have a contract to do the outfield of Yankee Stadium, the latter is what you want. The sheets are delivered to the site on pallets (wood frameworks), each containing 600 square feet of material.

As with topsoil, sod quality can vary, so shop around. To get tips on where to go, try to think of someone you know who may have installed sod, or check at a garden nursery you trust and ask them who sells good sod. Prices will vary around the country, but in my home base (Long Island), it costs approximately 25 cents a square foot, delivered. Also, while sod suppliers may or may not charge you a delivery fee, nearly all of them will charge you a refundable deposit on the pallets to ensure that you're motivated to return them when your job is finished.

As with topsoil, have the sod delivered as close as possible to its final location, and check its quality. The blades of grass should be very green—not discolored or pale—and the root side should be free of insects.

To handle sod better, it's good to think of it as what it is; a living, breathing thing that needs your help to survive—immediately. After all, why wouldn't it? When you order it, it's cut from a field, folded over, loaded on a truck, and trucked to your home. By the time you get it, it is usually dry, thirsty, hungry, and tired.

Laying the Sod

DIFFICULT **5–7 hours**

Start installing the sod next to the house. Just lay the sheets on the ground and pull each by the edge to its approximate final position, then push and pull the joints together with your hands.

When the first line is installed, install the next, placing the next sheets so the joints are staggered—not aligned with those of the first sheets and so the ends of the new sheets fall about halfway along the sheets above. When this is done, lay the next sheets the same way, and so on until you are finished. Staggering like this hides the seams better and helps the sod interlock better—there's less movement.

At some point (or points) as you go, the sod will have to be cut to fit, such as at the ends of lines or perhaps to get around an obstacle such as a tree, bush, or flower bed. This is done with an easily bought tool called—appropriately enough—a sod cutter. It looks like a cobbler's knife. Use it as you would any knife to trim the sod.

Rolling the Sod

EASY **1–2 hours**

Once it is in place, roll the sod, that is, tamp it in place. For this you use a manual sod roller, which is really a hand-operated steam roller. Its metal barrel is filled with water (for weight), and you just roll it over the sod in a straight line, from one end to the other; at the longest part you turn around and come back the other way.

Overlap each pass by a few inches to make sure all the sod has been rolled evenly. Rolling sod is very important, because it levels any high spots. It helps to ensure that the whole sheet makes contact with the topsoil (in fact, embeds the roots into the soil) so as to promote root growth.

After the area is cleaned up, the new lawn should be watered. Sod, as mentioned, will be thirsty and should receive at least 1 to $1^1/_2$ inches of water twice a week. You can do the job with a hose, but a portable sprinkler works well and, of course, a sprinkler system may be installed. It's best to water during the cooler part of the day, such as in the morning, so evaporation is minimized. You should not water at night. Water can stay on the turf all night, an open invitation for fungi to form.

Cutting the Sod   *DIFFICULT* **5–7 hours**

Your new lawn should be cut after you have about $1/2$ inch of growth. It's very important not to take off more than $1/2$ inch during the first cut, and never more than 2 inches off the grass blade height. The lawn mower blades should be sharp, not dull, which can shock the grass, causing the tips to turn yellow and brown.

Planting a Seed Lawn   *VERY DIFFICULT* **7–10 hours**

Planting a seed lawn is very similar to laying sod in the preparation stages. The top dressing (the topsoil that the seeds will germinate in) must be high-quality. It must be dark in color, consistent in shape, and spongy to the touch. If it's good enough for sod, it's good enough for seed.

Not only should the soil be good, it's probably a good idea to add a step to planting seed. This is what's called amending the soil.

Amending the Soil   *DIFFICULT* **5–7 hours**

Unless the area you are planting is shaded most of the time, adding peat moss and/or lime to the soil is helpful because it will help it hold moisture when it is not being watered. Simply pour the contents into the new soil (according to the directions on the package) and work it in with a shovel. If you have a large area to do, you can use a gas-powered tiller to mix the soils together (see Chap. 14).

It's best to have seeds germinate in moist soil (not pools of water or dry soil), because the healthier it is when it germinates, the healthier it will be when fully grown.

In order to fully prepare the soil for seed, you must remove stones, roots, and any other debris. When the ground is level and you are ready to plant seeds, the final step of fertilizing the soil is important. It's important to get the right kind of fertilizer because there are not many available that allow you to plant and fertilize at the same time. Scotts makes such a product. Read the back of the bag and measure the area you plan on planting. This is the best way to judge how much seed you will need.

Selecting the Seed   *EASY* **1–2 hours**

It is important to consider a few things before you select a seed. Assuming you have good soil, and I am because you have just amended it, you should consider how much traffic you will have on your new lawn, how much sun and shade it will receive during the day, and how much care you are willing to give it after it is installed.

For instance, a cool fescue is pretty hardy for high-traffic areas, and a Kentucky blue grass is darker green and hardy, but not as tough. A rye grass is quick to come up, but it's an annual grass. It will look pretty good in a short time, but it won't be back next year.

For a homeowner the best seed is usually a mixture of some rye, fescue, and mostly blue grass. This way it comes up a little more slowly but establishes itself firmly. As it does, it also provides the durability needed for kids, dogs, and people. For the best advice, though, ask your neighborhood garden center employees. They'll surely walk you through selecting a seed that's right for you and your property. In fact, they can help you choose between seed or sod.

Spreading the Seed
EASY **1–2 hours**

The seed should be loaded into a spreader and spread the same way fertilizer or lime is spread. Again, make sure you make straight passes one way, turn around, and on the next pass, overlap with the previous pass to ensure proper, even coverage.

Consult the manufacturer of the spreader and the package of seed for the correct spreader settings. The handle should be pulled to release the material; when the pass is over, release the handle until the turn is finished. A smaller, portable, hand-cranked spreader is available for smaller lawns that don't require a lot of seed. Your local home center has these for less than $10.

Pest Control
EASY **1–2 hours**

Spreaders can also be used to spread insecticides and other granular material for getting rid of grubs and other pests. How do you know you have grubs or other pests in and on your lawn? Look at the grass. If you have brown, bare spots, it's best to dig some soil in that area and bring it to a home garden center, a nursery, or a cooperative extension office near you that specializes in agricultural issues. Most states have them, and they provide free information to homeowners looking for answers to common lawn problems.

Look for other parts of your lawn that don't have a bright, green color with grass blades that look upright, vibrant, and healthy. Chances are, when you bring the soil and grass sample of areas that have been compromised in some way to a respectable gardener or nursery person, he or she will be able to help you solve your problem.

Grubs, especially in the beginning of the growing season, after the ground thaws, are hungry after being dormant all winter. They love to eat the tender grass roots that begin to grow. This kills the grass and it turns brown. Grubs are just one of the pests that can invade your lawn and soil, and do it secretly. There are granular products available for controlling grubs (see Fig. 15.11). Ask the experts, they won't steer you wrong.

FIGURE 15.11

Grub-control products are applied the same as fertilizers are applied.

Thatching

DIFFICULT **5–7 hours**

Thatching is the process of removing old and matted-down grass from your lawn. Over time, when grass is not picked up, water gets on it and enough builds up to form a sometimes impenetrable layer on the dirt. This suffocate the grass. It doesn't allow air and moisture to travel to its roots.

You can use a thatching rake to take care of this. The job involves setting the head of the rake on the ground and pulling the head toward you, in short strokes, over and over. You'll see the old layer of grass come up. Discard it when you're finished.

You can also rent a thatching machine for this purpose. Again, unless you are planning on dethatching Giants Stadium, it won't be necessary. You'll see a big difference in your lawn's color and texture within a few weeks during the growing season. Your lawn will thank you for allowing it to breathe and drink again.

Edging

FAIRLY EASY **2–5 hours**

Edging is simply the process of making a nice cut along a grass border so it's clearly distinguishable from other areas, such as flower beds, walkways, curbs, or driveways. In the olden days, this was done with an edger, a long-handled garden tool with a rectangular, flat head that was used to chop at the edge of the grass to produce a clean edge.

Now, line trimmers can be used by holding the machine at a 90-degree angle and letting the revolving trimmer wire slice a clean edge. They work really well and produce a sharp, clean-looking edge that gives your lawn a clean, manicured look. Be careful, though, because debris can fly up at you. Whether you use an edger or a line trimmer, always wear goggles and protective safety gear. You'll want to be able to see your work when you're done.

Fall Cleanup

DIFFICULT **5–7 hours**

Professional landscapers call leaf cleanups spring and fall cleanups. Seasonal cleanups really involve a lot more than simply removing leaves and debris from your lawn and garden. The homeowner may not be as thorough on his own property, but if he wishes to be, there is a lot to do. In the fall, when trees lose their leaves, it's an exciting time of year. And a busy time.

Not only do leaves need to be picked up, branches and other debris should also be taken off the lawn. Also, after the debris is removed, the turf should be raked clean and given a final cut. The next thing to be done is a final fertilizing for the winter ahead.

Doing this gives the grass a final feeding and some food for the roots—they get nourishment to last through the dark winter months. Moisture shouldn't be a problem. If you live in an area of the country where deciduous trees are (they lose their leaves and regrow them every year), chances are you'll get some rain, freezing rain, and snow during the winter months. Either way, the grass will have plenty to drink.

If you have a chipper/shredder, it's a good idea to use it on your yard so you don't have to take leaves and debris off the property. Instead, as you shred and mulch the material, you reduce it in volume by a lot. The processed material you took off the lawn also is consistent in size and texture, making it much easier to work with.

In fact, it's probably a good idea to wheelbarrow the material to your flower beds and deposit it there. It will protect young plants and give the bed a manicured appearance throughout the winter.

Composting

EASY **1–2 hours**

There is another option: Compost the material or simply deposit it into a wooded area on your property. Anything organic can go into wooded areas. In fact, in addition to having an alternative to bagging it and bringing it to the curb, you're amending the soil in the woods. Adding to the organic mix helps all your plants.

Although the work has to be done, homeowners have a choice here. Because trees lose their leaves over several weeks or months, you could choose to remove them as they come down, or simply wait until they're all down and do it all at once. I've always preferred to do two cleanups or so. This way, you're not stuck with all of them in late fall (wet leaves are no fun), and you don't have to do them all at once.

Composting is a good idea because as you mulch and shred the material, the volume decreases dramatically, but the surface area of each leaf also increases. You're essentially speeding up the rotting process by doing this. With good composting techniques—which means occasionally turning the material in on itself—you can produce high-quality organic fertilizing material for the following spring. You can use it when planting new plants and feeding existing ones in your flower beds.

Spring Cleanup

DIFFICULT **5–7 hours**

Spring is a beautiful time of year. It's a great feeling to be outside, and the fragrances in the air are sweet with forsythia and other early-budding flowers and bushes. Your first order of business in the spring is to start at the top of your house and clean off the roof and gutters of the inevitable leaves and twigs and debris that fall. Get everything on the ground.

Next, starting at the foundation of your house, rake or blow the leaves and material away from the house and toward the yard. Work this way until you have all the material, including dead grass in the turf, in piles to be picked up later, or to the curb for collection.

Work this way, from start to finish, on each side of your house. Within a few hours, or a day, you'll have cleaned the turf and beds and be ready to fertilize for the season.

Next, depending on whether you have a lot of trees and shade or you have sunlight all day long, you can apply fertilizer and/or seed. Before doing this, make sure the likelihood of frost during the night is next to nothing. Frost is a way to kill seed and have fertilizer not be effective at all.

Finally, use a blower to blow the tiniest debris (bits of leaves, twigs, and dirt) off all walkways, patios, and driveways. Also, you can deposit the debris you remove from the property the same way you did in the fall. Either dump it in a wooded area on your property or shred and mulch it for the compost pile. You'll use it soon enough.

SAVE ON YARD PRODUCTS

A good way to save on fertilizer, seed, and mulch is to buy these items from a home improvement center at the end of the spring. Because these items are seasonal, the store needs to clear them out to make room for new merchandise. To do this, the prices are reduced. If you have a dry, somewhat cool place to store this material, you can take advantage of the discounts.

Flower Beds

Years ago (25 or more), homeowners often let plants in their flower beds grow up and out to obscure their windows (see Fig. 16.1). Even if the bushes and shrubs were occasionally trimmed, bigger was better, and it stayed that way until the home improvement wave (and subsequent home improvement centers) caught on in the mid-1980s.

Then and now, a lower profile of plants (smaller ones) is in vogue, and flower beds are designed with a few other things in mind. Two of the most important are allowing the house to be seen (the flower bed complements the house as a total plan instead of the other way around) and the other is to allow light and air through windows.

Bed Makeovers: From the Ground Up

One sure-fire way to give your house and property a whole new look is to redesign the flower beds, particularly in front of the house and near the entrance. I've done it a few times on different houses I've owned, and it's always a lot of work, fun, and very satisfying when you look at the finished product.

Before starting, it's important to consider the size and scope of the project. If

TALK ABOUT A FLOWER BED!

During the last days of World War II, the Netherlands befriended Canada for their support. To show their gratitude, the Netherlands bequeathed 1 million tulips upon Canada. Today, the tulips bloom every spring in Canada's Capital Region— a colorful thank you that has repeated itself every year since 1945.

FIGURE 16.1

Plants that obscure windows should be removed.

you feel it's too much work for you, it probably is, and a landscape contractor should be consulted. If not, doing it yourself could still require a visit to your local nursery and/or garden center for advice.

Start by looking at what kinds of plants you have in the bed. If there are any that you may want to keep to plant elsewhere on your property, mark them somehow (tie a string around them), and when you dig out the old plants, set them aside. Be sure and plan where you are going to put them so they don't lay around too long. This could mean predigging the new holes or simply putting a tarp on the lawn where you can put the plants for the time being and keep the root balls (the roots with the dirt attached to them) moist with a garden hose.

Digging Out the Old Plants   *DIFFICULT* **5–7 hours**

Before doing any digging, check the site plan of your house and make sure that where you dig is free of buried electrical lines, gas lines, or any other objects that you could hit.

Next, using a pointed shovel and perhaps a garden pick, dig around the roots of the plants you want to remove. If you see that you are cutting through roots, dig a little farther out from the base of plants. When you can wiggle the plant enough to lift it out of the ground, before you lift it out, be sure you're taking enough dirt with the roots (to form a root ball).

Doing this will ensure that the roots stay healthy and intact. Discard the plants or set them aside as you take them out. This will keep your work site clear. Believe it or not, this simple act can prevent needless spills.

Grading the Bed   *FAIRLY EASY* **2–5 hours**

Grading is not about school; it's about moving dirt around. More dirt should be added against the foundation to create a gentle slope away from it. The rest of the bed should be flat, or berms (small raised areas) can be made where you would like them. If the ground in your flower bed is uneven and slopes down more than a few feet, you may want to consider planting ivy, cotoneaster, or some other ground cover plant that will provide protection from soil erosion. Use an iron rake to finish the rough grading. This involves getting the ground level (where it is supposed to be) and smooth. A smaller, plastic fan-shaped rake can be used for the final grading. This means removing stones or dirt clogs.

Planning the New Flower Bed   *DIFFICULT* **5–7 hours**

During this step it is important to take your time, consider a few key things, and start correctly. First, consider which way the land faces. Exposure to the sun and winds are important criteria for deciding which plants to install in the bed. (Your plant suppliers will answer your questions about which plants will do best in sun or shade, and their water requirements.)

Next, consider the slope of the land. It's vitally important to make sure the soil in the flower bed against the house slopes away from the foundation. This way, moisture seeps away from the house, saving you potentially big problems in the future.

Next, it's probably a good idea to make a drawing of the plant layout. Using graph paper will make this task easier. This will give you a design to work from and give you a peek ahead of what it will look like when finished. It may seem strange to do this, but it's a lot easier to erase a pencil mark than to dig a new hole or pull out plants. Start by getting a copy of your property survey. This includes your whole property (and its dimensions) and the position of the house on it.

Begin by transposing the location of the house and boundary lines onto the graph paper. To keep things simple, let each of the squares equal 1 foot. Draw the outline of the house and include porches, steps, driveways, and walkways that are connected to the house. Next, lay a sheet of thin tracing paper over the graph paper and draw the rough shapes of the plants and where you want them. It's also a good idea to include any rocks or other objects you might want to put in the bed.

After taking into consideration the amount of light and moisture each of your plants require, the best general rule of thumb is to plant larger plants in the back, closest to the foundation, medium-size ones in the center of the bed, and the shortest ones closest to the edge of the bed. This way all the plants are seen from the curb and provides texture, depth, and an aesthetic, pleasing look that complements the house (see Fig. 16.2).

It's important to measure the total space you have in the bed and then get the approximate measurements of your plants when they are fully mature. (Nursery employees can tell you how large your plants will grow.) Finally, when you get the plants on site, you'll want to place them on the ground in their relative positions (where they'll be planted). A hint: it's OK if the plants appear too small for the size of the bed. They need the room to grow. Before planting, though, there's one more thing to do.

Amending the Soil

DIFFICULT **5–7 hours**

A home flower bed, and every plant and bush in it, are only as good as its soil. After all, every plant in it will spend its life in it. Soil has two

FIGURE 16.2

Plants of different sizes and shapes often make up flower beds.

layers: topsoil and subsoil. The subsoil is directly beneath the topsoil and has been there for hundreds of years. Depending on where you live, it can very in depth from a few inches to almost 2 feet deep.

Most important, however, is the composition of the soil. It can be sandy or claylike. If it is too sandy, water will drain right through it, leaving plants thirsty. If it is too claylike, water will stay around, drowning plants. Depending on what your soil is like, you may have to amend it to get your plants off on the right track.

Adding peat moss or other organic matter to the soil is wise. It helps nourish the soil for the plants in the flower bed and it makes it the right consistency. Another benefit is that amending the soil allows a healthy amount of moisture to be held in it to nourish the plants growing there.

You can simply empty a bag of peat moss and/or lime onto the ground and work it into the existing soil with a shovel. If you prefer, and you have a large area to do, use a tiller (see Chap. 14) to mix it in. You can rent these for a few hours at a time.

If, after amending the soil, you still need some advice, take a sample of the new soil and have it tested at a nursery or home garden center. Most often, a trained professional can predict the quality of soil by looking at it and feeling it. Once you have quality soil, you're ready to plant—almost.

Borders and Landscape Fabric
EASY **1–2 hours**

Before planting, it is important to make sure the borders of the bed are securely in place so no dirt will fall out, and that the bed is self-contained. This means that whether the borders are plastic, brick, metal, or concrete, there should be no gaps or spaces in them.

Weed control in flower beds is important. Without it, beds can look unkempt and shabby. Most homeowners don't like the idea of weeding the beds every few days. There's a solution to this problem: landscape fabric. This is a roll of fine meshlike fabric that gets spread out on the dirt. It allows water and air to pass through it and at the same time stops weeds from emerging. It's pretty easy to install.

Buy enough to cover the whole bed and simply cut holes in it where you install the plants. Make sure the hole in the fabric is a little larger than the plant root ball.

Planting
DIFFICULT **5–7 hours**

Set all the plants on the ground in their respective positions. Let the containers they are in make an impression in the dirt. This will be your mark where you should start digging. Using a pointed shovel, dig a hole nearly twice the size of the root ball of your plant and slightly deeper than the height of the container it's in. Make sure the soil inside the hole is loose and not compacted. This will allow the roots to embed themselves inside the walls and the bottom of the hole.

If a plant is in a container, slide it out and make certain the roots are not compacted (wrapped around each other). If they are, gently untangle them with your fingers and let them swing free. If a plant is wrapped in burlap, make sure the plant is next to the hole and then untie the rope that holds the burlap together.

Loosen the burlap that may be knotted or twisted around the caliper (base) of the bush. Set the plant into the hole, twist it if you have to, and straighten it to its final position. Backfill the hole around it with the soil you took out of the hole. When you are finished with all the plants, gently walk around and, with the sole of your shoe, tamp in the dirt around the plants.

A Quick Regrading

EASY **1–2 hours**

Since you did the initial grading, you've tramped around in the bed. You've dragged bushes and equipment in and out of it. After the plants are all in, it's time to do a final regrading with your iron rake. Make sure the hills and valleys are where you want them and that the flat parts are smooth.

Start closest to the house and work your way out. Next, if there's no rain in the immediate forecast, take a garden hose and sprinkle water on the whole flower bed. Make sure you wet the leaves and branches of bushes and the ground around them, especially at the base. The water should drain pretty quickly because the soil has been amended and aerated. It's best to avoid creating pools, but give the plants enough to drink and settle into their new environment. Let the soil dry.

BUY IN BULK TO SAVE MONEY

If you'd like to save money on soil, mulch, or any other loose material, it's usually cheapest to buy it in bulk, from a nursery, and have it delivered to your home. You won't have to transport it, and you won't have to lug bags of material in and out of your car. Instead, you'll save money and time—you'll only have to move the material once—to its final location in your flower bed.

Mulch—The Ultimate Top Dressing

EASY **1–2 hours**

Any material that is spread between and around plants is a mulch. It's best to apply between 2 and 4 inches of material.

Applying mulch to the bed does several things. First, it is pleasing to look at. It adds a lot of aesthetic beauty and provides a clean, well-manicured look to the house and property. Second, it provides moisture control. It doesn't allow the water to evaporate, so you have to water less. Third, it covers the weed-barrier fabric and provides a natural or rustic setting. Lastly, mulch is an organic material, prone to decaying over time, which contributes to improving the quality of the soil.

Your choices are many when it comes to top dressings. You may be surprised by what you can use as mulch. You can use sawdust (alone or mixed with peat moss), hay (or straw), or simply grass clippings. You can also choose pine bark nuggets or shredded mulch, cedar chips or shredded bark, redwood mulch, pine chips, nuggets or mulch, and a host of other materials.

Your local home center probably has at least three to five different kinds of top dressings. Again, if you have a generally small area, it's best to buy this material in bags. If you're covering the "back 40," get it trucked in (loose form) and dumped close to where you will use it.

Trimming Bushes and Shrubs   *DIFFICULT* **5–7 hours**

Pruning is part of regular maintenance and serves several purposes. The most obvious is that it shapes plants and maintains a manicured, pleasing look. Another is to remove damaged or dead branches and parts. Still another is to allow circulation of light and air. Finally, with proper care, pruning directs the growth of plants and, over time, increases the amount of flowers (if that's your intention).

Pruning   *EASY* **1–2 hours**

General hacking is no good for the plant or you. It's important to remember that you can't put back what you take off. It's best to make cuts above flower buds or small side branches. It's best to avoid leaving small stubs, because over time they will wither and that's an open invitation for insects.

Instead, cut branches in the general direction you would like them to take. For example, if you want the flower bed to maintain a low profile, you'll want to cut the top branches of bushes. Likewise, if you'd like to form a vertical look, keep the lower branches pruned, but only after a season or two in the ground. Lower branches help feed newly planted bushes.

What Tool Is Best?

Hand-held pruners work best for small branches and larger ones closer to the middle of the bush. Hand-held pruning shears (they look like giant scissors) are best for the outer tips of bushes. It's important to keep the edges of these tools sharp; cutting with them should be relatively easy going. Electric trimming shears are also recommended, but only when you have a whole row of bushes to trim or a large flower bed full of rows of bushes. Rake up the clippings with a plastic or bamboo rake and dispose of them.

On a Slippery Slope?   *DIFFICULT* **5–7 hours**

Planting ground cover (plants that grow in a spreading fashion) is important on steep embankments and slopes. They provide much-needed erosion control and beauty. It's important to have the plants establish themselves rather quickly, before rain runoff and wind can take soil away.

Popular ground cover plants include pachysandra, ivy, cotoneaster, and spreading junipers. The soil conditions should be the same as described in the planting section of this chapter. Asking plant suppliers about ground cover planting should yield some pretty good results.

Ground cover plants generally come in "cell" containers that resemble the bottoms of egg cartons and have long, stringy roots embedded in a clump of potting soil. When planting, these roots need to be spread out in the hole. Make sure the hole you dig is as deep as the clump of potting soil and about twice as wide.

Plant them about 4 to 6 inches apart in a grid pattern. This means straight rows—width and lengthwise. This is because they grow by forming networks of roots under the ground. When they do, new buds (which will become the leaves or flowers) emerge above ground later.

After planting and cleaning up the containers, rope off the area (to prevent it being walked on) and water lightly. Water enough to keep the plants and surrounding dirt moist, but don't create puddles.

Bushes and Shrubs

Shrubs are the mainstay of any home yard, and they are everywhere. In fact, they are so plentiful, most of us don't see them because they blend in with our houses and properties. I hope this chapter will help solve this problem and help do-it-yourselfers not only maintain their bushes and shrubs, but learn the ins and outs of designing and planting them.

The trick is selecting bushes that will establish themselves nicely in the soil and the general environment (sun and shade) that you have on your property. Giving them a strong, healthy start means less maintenance for you down the road. Another important consideration is their size when you buy them.

You need to know how large they will grow, so you can plan for this in your design. It's not easy to plant two small bushes 10 feet apart in a garden or along a walkway. This is because initially it will look bare, and you have to have faith that they will grow and fill out.

It takes patience and hope that the bushes will grow together and eventually form a hedge, or the look you want to achieve. The garden may have to look spotty for a while. In the meantime, before planting, ask yourself a few questions as you consider what bushes should be planted. How the bush grows is also important. Does it naturally grow tall? Spread out? Both? How fast does it grow? Ask at your local nursery or home center if you need some answers.

THE LARGEST HEDGE

Think you have a lot of bushes and hedges to maintain? Think again. The longest hedge (made into a maze) is the Dole Pineapple Garden Maze in Honolulu, Hawaii. It measures 1.7 miles long and has an area of 100,000 square feet. That's a lot of trimming to do!

Buying Bushes
EASY **1–2 hours**

Bushes are sold primarily in two forms. They are available with their roots and the dirt clinging to them (a root ball) in containers, or balled and burlapped. This means the root ball is wrapped in burlap and tied together with rope. Either way you buy them, the most important indicator of health and quality is a hardy color, strong leaves or needles, and a moist root ball.

If the root ball is dry, or the leaves seem discolored, faded, or drooped, it's probably a good idea to stay away from it. It's also a good idea to bring a sample of the soil from where you want to plant to your local garden center. Experts can inspect the soil, and with some information from you (about how much shade, sun, and water the garden will receive), help you select the right bushes for your property.

Logistics are important when buying bushes. You may want to have the holes for the plants already dug when you go shopping. That way, when you get them home, you can plant them right away. On the other hand, if you cannot plant them right away, keep the roots moist by spraying balled and burlapped root balls with water until you can plant them.

Planting Bushes and Shrubs
DIFFICULT **5–7 hours**

Before you plant, consider that evergreen bushes and hedges are best planted in the fall and deciduous ones (shrubs that shed and regrow leaves from year to year) in the spring.

SAVE MONEY ON BUSHES AND SHRUBS

A good way to save money on bushes and shrubs (particularly balled and burlapped ones) is to buy them directly from the grower. Believe it or not, you can buy plants from growers just as home improvement centers do. And you can get them cheaper than the stores sell them. Look in the Yellow Pages under "growers" or "nurseries." If you don't find them there, look up your local agricultural extension office. They can give you the names of local growers. I've even heard of some growers who let you dig them out of their fields yourself. Talk about saving!

The good part about planting to form hedges, to line walkways, or as a backdrop for a garden, is that you don't have to dig separate holes. Instead, a furrow or trench will suffice, because individual bushes should be placed close to each other.

Although you may be removing more dirt, it's easier because you don't have to shape the steep walls of the holes. Next, stretch a string along the length of the trench and use that as your guide for where the line of bushes will sit.

The general rule is that large evergreen shrubs or deciduous ones should be planted between 24 to 36 inches apart, depending on their individual size (generally, the smaller the shrub, the farther apart they should be planted, to allow for size at maturity). Smaller plants popularly used to form hedges, such as privet, should be planted about 12 inches apart.

Remove the root balls from the containers and untie the ropes from around the base of plants (which hold the burlap on); leave the burlap on the root balls. Place the plants in the trench and twist them to the position you want.

Backfill the trench with the dirt you removed. The dirt should come up to about 2 inches above the top of the root ball. If it doesn't, take the plant out, add or remove dirt, and try setting the plants in the trench again. Water the plants and the surrounding soil immediately. Do it lightly. Keep the soil surrounding the plants moist, but don't create puddles.

Planting with a Purpose

Planting hedges to screen objects that should remain unseen is a natural way to solve the problem. Objects such as electrical boxes, filters and pumps around pools, and garbage cans can easily be hidden behind a tall hedge.

Another reason for planting hedges is for privacy. Often, if houses are situated on busy roads or very close to neighbors, hedges that screen doorways, particularly front entrances, are helpful for providing security and privacy without giving the house the look of a fortress.

In fact, hedges for these purposes can be planted and shaped in a variety of ways to make the house look like it was built inside a natural setting, a cluster of trees and bushes (see Fig. 17.1). The same rules of planting shrubs apply here. Soil conditions, sun, shade, moisture, and circulating air should be considered.

Feeding Time
EASY **1–2 hours**

Unless you want to trim your hedges more than a few times a year, don't fertilize them. Giving them a shot of fertilizer can cause growth

FIGURE 17.1

Bushes and shrubs next to a house make it appear like a natural part of the landscape.

spurts and slow-releasing fertilizer can promote long-term growth, requiring lots of time and maintenance with the hedge clippers. Using a natural mulch in the bed and around the base of bushes will be enough to keep them fed.

A Cool Drink

EASY **1–2 hours**

Evergreen hedges usually don't require a lot of water after they have become established. When they are first planted, it's important to keep them moist so the roots sprout new growth and embed themselves in the surrounding soil in their new homes. However, after a time, unless you experience a prolonged period of dryness (a drought), rain will usually do the trick.

Ground Cover

Natural ground cover such as mulch material or ground cover plants can be planted among hedges. Not only do they add to the beauty and the texture of the bed (adding depth and distance), they also help control erosion and maintain moisture for the plants (see Fig. 17.2).

Color Design

Part of the reason evergreens are used to form hedges is because there is more to an evergreen than meets the eye. However, it's the eye that

FIGURE 17.2

Ground cover plants add an important look and texture to bushes in a flower bed.

counts in this case. Evergreens are relatively hardy, easy to maintain, and inexpensive to buy. The other obvious benefit is their color. Green says natural. Grass and most of the trees and bushes in nature and natural settings (unless you're in the tropics) are green. Having a background of green hedges works with any other plants in the same flower bed or landscape. It appears natural, and the colors complement each other (see Fig. 17.3 here).

Trimming Your Hedges

EASY **1–2 hours**

Selection of the best shrubs for an area begins long before they are planted. The right shrubs will eventually be the desired width, height, and appearance, and will need little pruning and care. Some are better suited to form hedges than others.

Still, in the real world, all shrubs need some care. Unless you have a half-mile-long hedge to trim, it's best to use hand shears that look like giant scissors. This way, you can work without being encumbered by trailing the long extension cord required for electric trimmers.

After waiting until the bushes have developed new growth, while the new shoots appear tender and lighter in color than the rest of the branches, trim them carefully to the desired shape. Be careful not to dig into the woody part of branches. If you do so, they will look bare and brown.

FIGURE 17.3

Evergreen shrubs, ready to be planted, will add a soft, green touch to this house.

Start by trimming hedges wider at the base than at the top. This will allow much needed light and air to circulate among the lower branches. When the bush fills out, you can begin to make the top and the bottom the same width.

If the bushes line a walkway, trim the sides of the bushes to match the contour of the walkway. Also, if the walkway is on an incline, try and trim the top to match the incline.

In other words, before trimming the top, measure the height of the top of the bush to the walkway on one end of the hedge. Do the same at the other end of the hedge. Just to be sure, do the same in the middle of the hedge. Wherever you have differences, make adjustments. Remember, you can always take off more, but you can't put back what you take off!

Fences

Fencing your property is important, because fences provide boundaries between your paradise and the rest of the world. They also provide privacy and security (see Fig. 18.1). However, in these times, fences provide a lot more. Homeowners now have so many design and material choices, fences can be a statement of your personal tastes and likes.

If fences are included in a landscape architect's plans, they can become an integral part of the whole house and property plan. For example, some houses look best with a rustic wood fence, contemporary homes often look best with PVC (hard, durable plastic) fences, and traditional homes very often have stockade or chain link fences surrounding their property (see Fig. 18.2).

Finally, because good building sites are becoming harder to find as populations increase, fences are also becoming useful as protection from the weather (to diffuse strong winds or filter strong sunlight), or to help in reducing noise such as from traffic.

Maintaining your fence is as important as ever because of its relationship with the house and the rest of the property. All fences need occasional maintenance to ensure that they operate the way they were designed to.

Stockade Fences

Stockade fences are usually made of spruce, redwood, cedar, or pine. They have parallel, vertical pickets about 3 inches wide that taper at the

FIGURE 18.1

Stockade fences are used primarily for privacy and security.

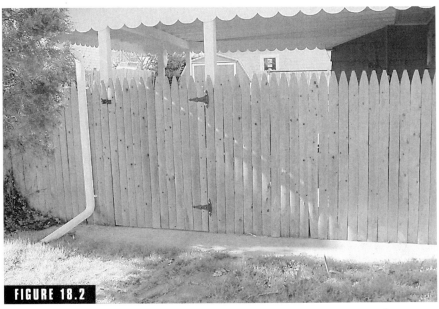

FIGURE 18.2

Stockade fences are also available in smaller sizes, and gates are easy to make.

top. They are attached to three horizontal slats behind them. Sections are sold at home centers and lumber yards in sizes of 4×8, 5×8, and 6×8 feet. Other stockade designs include solid panels, louvers, horizontal slats, or any other configuration the imagination can conjure up.

Fences made of cedar need the least amount of maintenance. Cedar is a naturally soft, oily wood that takes a long time to discolor from the elements. Still, after a few seasons of rain, wind, and sun, even these, like other wooden fences, should be cleaned and sealed with a waterproof sealer or paint.

Cleaning with a Powerwasher
DIFFICULT **5–7 hours**

The best way to clean a wooden stockade fence is to use a powerwasher or a pressurized hand pump sprayer (see Fig. 18.3). Try and do the job on a warm, still day, without much wind. This will prevent a lot of the liquid material you use from becoming airborne.

When using a powerwasher, you will be limited as to what solutions you can use. This is because bleach and other harmful cleaners will ruin the seals in a power washer. Instead, there are fence and deck solutions that are labeled for their particular use, and they will not harm your powerwasher.

Read the directions on how to operate the powerwasher (most are pretty simple to use—it involves connecting to a water source, filling the solution chamber, and turning on the machine). Before you begin spraying, experiment with the trigger settings (that release the pressurized water) on a small section of the fence. This allows you to adjust the trigger settings to clean the fence in a uniform fashion. It is important to know that powerwashing uses pressurized water to remove a layer of wood and expose the good wood underneath. Adjustments to the nozzle should then take on a new meaning.

SAVE MONEY ON STOCKADE FENCES

A good way to save money on stockade fences is to buy ones that may be slightly damaged. Lumber yards and home improvement stores don't bother repairing them—often they will sell them for a fraction of the original cost. They also sell individual pickets—you can buy these individually and make the necessary repairs at home. It will save you a lot of money, if you're willing to do the repair work.

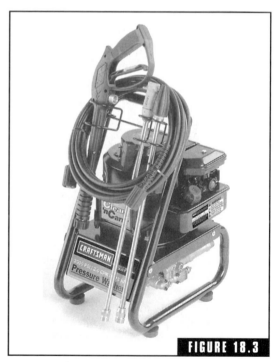

FIGURE 18.3

A powerwasher saves time and effort, especially with a long fence.

Start at the top of the fence and make uniform, vertical passes with the jet of water. Do a picket at a time and make sure the jet follows the downward flow of water off the picket. This will allow you to keep track of how much you have done. Powerwash solutions are usually available in 1-gallon containers and sell for about $5 or $6 a gallon. Each gallon of cleaning solution can cover approximately 400 square feet of fence. This may differ slightly, depending on the porosity of the wood.

Cleaning with a Pump Sprayer   *EASY* **1–2 hours**

Cleaning a wooden fence with a pump sprayer (see Fig. 18.4) will generally yield the same results as powerwashing, if the pump sprayer is used properly. The nice thing about a pump sprayer is that it allows you to use a water-and-bleach mixture. Bleach will clean almost anything, and its effects on wooden fences are almost immediate: you can watch the dirt roll off the fence. Although it seems more time-consuming than using a powerwasher, the bleach-and-water solution lets you work as fast as you can apply the solution.

The process is the same as powerwashing. Work a picket at a time, starting at the top and letting gravity do its work. If you choose to buy a cleaning concentrate, it may come out to a cheaper price per gallon. You will also have to dilute it with water. A gallon of concentrate can

FIGURE 18.4

Pump sprayers are pretty simple to operate and highly mobile.

cost between $18 and $20 a gallon and is enough to make 5 to 8 gallons of cleaning solution. The same rate of coverage applies: you can cover about 400 square feet of fence, give or take a few feet, depending on the porosity of the wood.

Let the fence dry, and then later you can use the same tank (after it has been washed and thoroughly rinsed) to apply a sealer (stain) or paint to it. Other ways to apply these products are with a paint sprayer, a roller, or a brush.

Applying Stain   *DIFFICULT* **5–7 hours**

Generally speaking, stain is the best material to apply to fences to seal them from the elements. The best, most durable, and most often used stain is a solid color stain. It looks like paint (you can get it in a variety of custom colors) and it is durable enough not to flake, peel, or run. It goes on smoothly and hides the grain of the wood.

Semitransparent stain goes on just as smoothly but allows the grain of the wood to show through. This is available in a few different shades and can be applied just like any other stain.

A transparent stain can also be used to seal fences. The transparent stain allows the natural beauty of the wood to come through. This includes the grain and any other imperfections that add to its rugged beauty. It makes the fence appear brand new, and helps it stay that way over time.

Stain can be applied using a pump sprayer. Just fill the tank to the appropriate level and pump the handle to the correct amount of pressure (according to the manufacturer's recommendations). The nozzle should be set to let a wide spray be released (to save time by covering a wide area), and you should start at the bottom. Work vertically and move slowly up each picket until the entire area is coated. Be careful not to put on too much, or it will run or smudge.

Stain can also be applied using a roller. A deep-nap roller is suggested to get into the cracks and the spaces where one side of a picket meets another. A paint pan is suggested because it is easier to move as you progress down the fence line and because the roller fits nicely into it when you apply stain to it.

Another way to apply stain is with a brush. Make sure it is big enough to cover knots, cracks, and imperfections. Brushing is not recommended when you have a large area to seal. Although there might be some slight differences depending on what method you choose to apply stain, and the porosity of the wood, the general rule is still about 400 square feet of coverage for every gallon of sealer.

There are many brands of stains and sealers available. Some are Thompson's Clear Wood Finish (CWF) and Behr's Wood Sealer. Depending on the quality and the kind of stain (solid, semitransparent, or transparent), they can cost anywhere from about $9 to $25 a gallon, and they are available at home centers and paint stores.

Applying Paint   *DIFFICULT* **5–7 hours**

Make sure the fence is dry and free of dirt or any other moisture. A good primer should be applied using a spray paint machine, roller, or a brush. It should be applied in the same fashion as described in the stain application procedure as stated before. When the primer dries (it can be the color of the final coat of paint), the paint can be applied.

The paint should be applied in the same fashion as stain is applied. Use only exterior paint that is durable, and you can have your choice of colors. Although stain and paint can be used to seal a fence, paint will eventually blister, crack, and peel, and may require more maintenance than stain in the long run.

Expect to pay between $17 and $23 a gallon for exterior paint. It is also available in 5-gallon buckets. Buying the paint in bulk like this may help you save a dollar or two per gallon. The rate of coverage is also about 400 square feet per gallon, depending on the method of application and the porosity of the wood.

Chain Link Fences   *DIFFICULT* **5–7 hours**

Cleaning a chain link fence is simply a matter of spraying it with a garden hose. Although most chain link fences are made with plastic-coated chain link or galvanized metal, rust and corrosion do occur. In fact, rust is probably the major enemy of chain link fences.

When you spot rust or corrosion, take a wire brush to it (wear a pair of sturdy gloves so as not to injure your hands) and scrub off any excess metal or rust particles. The idea is to expose as much clean metal as possible. Next, wipe it down with a regular cloth or terrycloth fabric. Apply a metal primer, then one or two coats of exterior enamel. It may save you time to apply it with a roller with a very long nap.

Another way to paint chain link is with a spray paint. Rustoleum brand works well. This paint is designed to seal and protect metal from the elements. This should stop the rust from spreading by coating the existing bare spots with good, waterproof paint.

A long nap of 1$^{1}/_{2}$ inches or more is also good for painting a chain link fence. Sopping wet, those fibers wrap themselves around the links and you can virtually paint both sides of the fence from one side.

For wrought-iron fencing and other detail work, a painter's mitt may work well. You wear it like a glove, dipping it in paint and, in effect, paint with your fingers.

PVC Fences

The newest fences on the market are PVC (hard plastic) fences (see Figs. 18.5 and 18.6). They are marketed as virtually maintenance-free. Because they are made of thick, durable plastic, they won't warp, rot, crack, or peel like other fences. Although this is generally true, they do require a little bit of maintenance. This includes spraying the fence with a garden hose to remove dirt, smog, or debris from trees. Tougher stains may require a mild detergent-and-water mixture (warm). You can simply wipe the fence down with a towel or rag and rinse it off with a hose and let it air-dry. That's it.

Repairing/Replacing Broken or Missing Parts

Repairing and maintaining a stockade or any other kind of wooden fence is pretty straightforward. Start with a visual inspection of the fence. If there are holes, cracked and broken boards, or missing pieces, it's pretty obvious they need to be replaced. For instance, if you see a picket that is broken at the top but fine all the way down, you may decide to leave it alone because the aesthetic value of the fence is not as important as its usefulness for privacy and security.

However, if a piece of the picket is missing at the bottom, more likely or not you'll wind up replacing the whole picket. Single pickets are available at lumberyards and/or home centers and go for less than a dollar each. If you're not sure what to look for, bring a piece of the broken picket with you and the salesperson will match it up for you.

FIGURE 18.5

No need for gates here, just pick up where you left off.

FIGURE 18.6

These fences are attractive and very easy to maintain.

It's also a good idea to bring in a nail that attaches the picket to the cross brace in the back, so you can match that also.

Loose Parts

EASY **1–2 hours**

Another common repair is tightening loose pickets or other parts. Nails that wiggle themselves out and pieces that become loose due to winds, critters that crawl on them, and driving rains, all need to be tightened and secured. It's best generally to walk the length of the fence a few times a year with a handful of galvanized nails (the same size that are used in the fence) and drive them in where they are missing or loose.

It's also important to make sure each section is still properly attached to each post. With most fences, three horizontal crossbeams in the back should be secured to the post. If these nails are missing, it's best to replace them. If whole sections are bent or twisted, it might be best to replace them altogether. Before deciding, however, check the condition of those that might not seem to fit snugly against another one, especially where two fence sections share a post.

Wobbly Posts

FAIRLY EASY **2–5 hours**

The last part of maintaining a fence is the posts themselves. If they have shifted in the ground (or if the posts are wood that can rot—and are not preserved with chemicals that resist rotting), it may mean that the fence is leaning one way or another or ready to come down altogether with the next big wind. A visual inspection will do the trick, but you may also want to grab the top of a post (usually 4 inches × 4 inches × 8 foot CCA treated to prevent it from rotting when it contacts earth) and see if you can wiggle it. If you can move it more than an inch or two, you may want to brace it.

Bracing involves getting a long metal tamping bar. It looks like a giant nail except that the pointy edge sometimes has a sharp edge. The top part has a flat head that can be used to tamp the earth down hard around the edges of the post. More dirt (from elsewhere) should be added as you press down the remaining dirt. If this doesn't work, somewhat flat pieces of bricks or rocks can be shoved between the post and the surrounding earth.

Tamping these rocks and debris down beneath the dirt's surface nearly always stabilizes the post, and thus stabilizes the fence. Hardware such as hinges, straps, and latches should be replaced if they are rusty and should also be lubricated occasionally with a medium-weight household oil so they work properly.

Rotting Posts
EASY **1–2 hours**

If some posts are too far gone (more than a large part is rotting or splitting), replace the posts with ones that have been treated (waterproofed) with chemicals to resist rot. Your local lumber yard can direct you in this area.

If you don't have to replace the posts, dig out as much of the soft wood as you can. Next, seal the hole and the top of the post with tar or wood putty (if the carved-out space is not too large). Next, you may want to attach a slanting piece of painted (sealed from the elements) wood or aluminum flashing at the top.

Wobbly Chain Link Fence Posts
EASY **1–2 hours**

If posts wobble because the concrete they are set in is crumbling, chip out the pieces with a shovel and blow out the remaining smaller chips. Pack in quick-setting cement and round it off at the top so water has a chance to drain away from the posts. That should secure them and stop them from wobbling.

Other Chain Link Fence Repairs
DIFFICULT **5–7 hours**

Chain link fences are also not entirely maintenance-free. As previously mentioned, rust and corrosion and painting needs to be taken care of, but other jobs remain. Although

TALK ABOUT A FENCE!

The Great Wall of China is probably the largest "fence" in the world. It winds up and down through deserts, valleys, and mountains, stretching 4163 miles. The builders did a magnificent job: after 2000 years, nearly all of it is still standing!

galvanized posts for chain link fences are usually set in concrete, occasionally they do need to be replaced if they get bent or broken off by a car or something else. This is a big job, and I suggest hiring a contractor with professional equipment (say, a jackhammer and sledge hammers) to do the job. Everything else can be done by the homeowner.

For instance, the hardware that connects the chain link to the posts and horizontal top bars should be checked. Sometimes they become loose and end up missing over time. They include shorter and longer pieces of solder-type metal that is soft and can be easily bent. They are twisted around the poles and the chain link, thus attaching both together. If you end up with a hole in the chain link, you may have to fasten the same material (or chicken wire—a similar material) to the mesh and attach it with pliable strips of metal. This is because chain link comes in long rolls and there are no seams that can be taken apart.

Another repair might be replacing broken slats that are woven in between the chain link mesh for privacy and sound protection. It's much easier to replace these slats than to try to repair them. Hardware such as hinges, straps, and latches should be replaced if they are rusty and should also be oiled occasionally with a medium-weight household oil so they work properly.

Most homes have a lot of metal around—decorative fencing, light fixtures, and the like—and it often gets a little rusty or chipped. To paint these items, first use a wire brush or rust remover liquid to remove all traces of rust, then apply a prime coat and a finish paint designed to combat rust.

Repairing PVC Fences
EASY **1–2 hours**

Maintaining PVC fences involves keeping them clean, occasionally lubricating moving parts such as hinges and latches, and replacing whole parts when they break. This is because although the fences are virtually maintenance-free, accidents still happen. If a part breaks, perhaps because a car or even a high-speed baseball from the neighborhood kids hits it, parts must be replaced.

Installing Sections
DIFFICULT **5–7 hours**

Installing sections of fences is a pretty straightforward process. However, there are some pitfalls that I've had to learn about the hard way. Hopefully, my mistakes will prevent you from doing the same.

When I was a kid on my first fence installation job, I was installing ten 4-foot × 8-foot sections of stockade fence along a customer's yard that was pretty flat and free of a lot of obstacles such as trees or other fences. Pretty straightforward job, right?

I strung my line (for a straight line) and had two posts in the ground holding it up. I took my trusty post hole digger, dug my first hole, and sank the post. I measured to be sure it was not going to stand taller than the fence section. Then I grabbed my level and worked it into position, and backfilled the hole. No big deal, right? Wrong.

The next step is one nearly every beginner gets wrong. I looked at the first section and measured how wide it was. Then I took that measurement and transferred it to the space between the first post and approximately where the second post would be. The wrong word here was "approximately."

I dug the second hole before I put up the fence section. I sank the second post. I leveled it and sank it to the right depth. When I readied the section (to be nailed to the two posts), it was off! Why? I had miscalculated when I transferred the measurement to the space between the posts. I dug in the wrong spot. I dug just a few inches off, and it made all the difference. If I had continued in that fashion, I would have had to redig each and every hole and move the posts as I proceeded. It would have meant lots of extra time and work.

How do you solve the problem? Always hang the section and secure it completely (on all three horizontal slats) before guessing where the next post should go. Then position the section and the attached post exactly where you want it and then move it just slightly to dig the new hole for the next post. This way, when you are ready to attach the section to the second post, it will fit precisely. After all, you're only going to use one half of the post at first. The other half is reserved for the next section.

By following this rule, and installing post, section, post, and then section, you can keep track of the top of the fence and install the whole run as if it were one. It will end up simple, straight, and true.

The same can be said for other fences. Whenever you have a fence that's made up of sections, the same installation technique should be used.

Trees for Natural Privacy and Wind Screening

Many people—before, during, and after the green environmental movement—prefer natural barriers around their properties rather than man-made fences or walls. There are benefits to having trees and other plants border your property. If they are placed properly, they can screen out a great deal of noise (say, from a nearby well-traveled road). They can also block the view of the same road or any other undesirable sight that is close to your property. Trees and plants can continue to grow, and you can plan on this: After planting them, you may have to endure an undesirable sight or noises for only so long, until your trees grow tall enough to ensure your privacy and relative quiet. Plus, of course, you will get to look at nature (see Figs. 19.1. and 19.2).

Planting the Right Plants

DIFFICULT **5–7 hours**

Part of maintaining your property is strategically selecting kinds of trees and plants as borders for your property. While almost any tree can be used to screen out a view and cut down on noise pollution, evergreens often seem to be the best choices. One reason is because they are not deciduous. Instead, they maintain their needles, often in dense clusters (for good coverage), throughout the year, and they are generally hardy (easy to care for once they are established in the ground).

FIGURE 19.1

Trees and shrubs add beauty and privacy to your property.

FIGURE 19.2

Trees soften the corners of your home, provide shade, and soften stiff winds.

Trees with dense foliage are able to reduce more noise than sparsely leaved trees. Evergreens also serve as good wind breaks because they are dense. Wind cannot easily pass through all their branches.

What Plants Are Best to Plant?

Some of the best trees are white pines, cedars, Douglas firs, hemlocks, and spruces. Depending on what area of the country you live in, not all of these trees may be available from local nurseries.

Another good plant to use is arborvitaes. They remain a favorite because, with little maintenance, they hold their regal (and highly recognizable) narrow, tall shape. Planting them close together to form a continuous, dense barrier is best, although some room is needed between them, for growth.

For effective noise control, when planting, the plant belt should be as wide as possible. This simply means that, depending on how much property you have, several rows of plants (one behind another) should be planted and maintained. It's usually best to plant the tallest trees in the back and shorter ones in the front. This serves two very important purposes. It stops the noise with the tallest trees first. Second, it is aesthetically pleasing to the eye for the homeowner. It gives the property barrier some depth and texture.

SAVE ON TREES

A good time to shop for trees is in the fall. This is when nurseries and home improvement stores reduce their prices. If they don't sell them, the trees become worthless to the stores—they are perishable (they only have a certain lifespan if they don't get planted). Also, the stores want the trees gone because they need the space for different, seasonal merchandise. From the homeowner's point of view, fall is a good time to plant trees in any case.

Pruning

DIFFICULT **5–7 hours**

Homeowners should maintain their trees and bushes much the same way growers do in nurseries (see Fig. 19.3). Depending on the age of your trees when you plant them, they can be pruned for several purposes. One is to train the tree to grow a certain way. When you trim a branch, you're asking other, untrimmed branches to grow. Another reason (in some more mature trees) is to maintain a desired shape. The extremities of branches (around the trees and from top to bottom) should be trimmed. By doing this, the tree is trained to keep its desired shape and you are helping maintain the health of its lower branches. If this is not done, the natural tendency of trees takes over: They grow straight up and start to lose their bottom branches.

Pruning tall trees and bushes as part of regular maintenance is important because doing it the right way determines how full and robust they will grow. If they are left to grow naturally, the bottoms will

FIGURE 19.3

Pruning can create quite a mess, but it's worth it in the long run.

most likely lose their branches, leaving gaping holes and defeating your original purpose of planting them to provide privacy and noise control.

Start by looking at the tree. You'll be able to tell new growth because the shoots will be a different color (usually a paler version of green) and will be tender. You can use a hand tool and shape them the way you want. Start by taking off dead or withered shoots. Then, carefully select smaller branches and shoots that are not in the general shape of the tree. If the tree is young, you may want to wait another season—and let it grow—to determine the shape the tree will take.

Be careful not to take off too much. Remember, you can always take off some more, but you can't put back what you cut off. Also, it's a good idea to look up your tree in a good landscaping book. From the picture, you'll see what your tree should look like when it is fully mature.

When to Prune

Usually, the best time to prune is during the late fall and winter (see Fig. 19.4). Conifers may be pruned at any time of year, but pruning during the dormant season may minimize sap and resin flow from cut branches.

My advice for hardwood trees and shrubs without flowers is to prune in the dormant season, because then you can easily visualize the structure of the tree, the wound can close and heal during the growing season after you prune, and to reduce the chance of spreading diseases.

A good time to prune is in the fall, when trees are losing or have already dropped their leaves.

If you have questions, contact your local tree specialist to find out when it's best to prune the various tree species in your area of the country. Your local horticulture cooperative extension can help you here.

Flowering trees and shrubs should also be pruned during the dormant season for the same reasons as stated above; however, to protect the flowers, you should prune according to the following schedule:

■ Trees and shrubs that flower in early spring (redbud, dogwood, etc.) should be pruned right after flowering (flower buds usually appear a year before they actually bloom, and will form on the new growth).

■ Trees and shrubs that flower in the summer or fall should be pruned during the dormant season (flower buds will form on new twigs during the next growing season, and the flowers will bloom normally).

■ Dead branches can be removed any time of the year.

Pruning Tools

Using the right tools is important when you prune. The choice of which one to use depends on the size of branches to be pruned and the amount of pruning to be done. If possible, use the tool before you buy it, to ensure it suits your specific needs. As with most things, a higher quality of tool equates to higher cost.

Generally speaking, the smaller a branch is when pruned, the sooner the wound you created will seal. Hand pruners are used to prune small branches (under an inch or so in diameter), and many different kinds are available. They can be grouped into bypass or anvil styles, based on the way the blades are designed.

Anvil-style pruners have a straight blade that cuts the branch against a small anvil or block as the handles are squeezed. Bypass pruners use a curved cutting blade that slides past a broader lower blade. These work like scissors. To prevent unnecessary tearing or crushing of branches, it is better to use a bypass-style pruner. Left- or right-handed versions can be purchased.

Slightly larger branches that can't be cut with a hand pruner can be cut with a small pruning saw or lopping shears. These have larger cutting surfaces and greater leverage. Lopping shears are also available in bypass and anvil styles.

Even larger branches can be cut with lopping shears or a pruning saw. Pruning saws vary greatly in handle styles, the length and shape of the blade, and the design of their teeth. Most have tempered metal blades that keep their sharpness for many pruning cuts. Remember, unlike most other saws, pruning saws are often designed to cut on the "pull" stroke.

Chain saws are the recommended tool for cutting the largest branches. Chain saws should be used only by qualified people. Sometimes it is best to avoid cutting larger branches altogether, by pruning them when they are small. You can use a pole pruner to cut branches beyond your reach.

Because of the danger of electrocution, pole pruners should not be used near utility lines except by professionals. They have the proper equipment and know-how.

To ensure that satisfactory cuts are made and to reduce fatigue, keep your pruning tools sharp and in good working condition. Hand pruners, lopping shears, and pole pruners should be periodically sharpened with a sharpening stone. Replacement blades are available for many styles. Pruning saws should be professionally sharpened or periodically replaced. To reduce cost, many styles also have replaceable blades.

Treating Wounds
FAIRLY EASY **2–5 hours**

Sap, the gooey stuff that sometimes leaks from trees, is natural. It's the trees' way of staying healthy. Sap flowing from pruning wounds is not generally harmful; however, excessive "bleeding" can weaken trees. When oaks or elms are pruned or wounded during a critical time of year (usually spring for oaks, or throughout the growing season for elms), either from storms, pruning wounds, or from necessary branch removals, some kind of dressing should be applied to the wound. It's probably a good idea to contact a tree specialist for this kind of maintenance. Look under "trees" in your Yellow Pages or contact your local horticulturist extension service for advice.

THE BEAUTY OF BONSAI TREES

The Japanese bonsai tree, a small, beautiful plant that has become popular in recent years, has a rich history. It arrived here from Japan via China during the Kamakura period (1185–1333) by means of Zen Buddhism. The Japanese people, along with others who own them and care for them, feel inspired by them. They have good reason to: bonsai represent a fusion of strong, ancient beliefs with the Eastern philosophies of the harmony among man, the soul, and nature.

Water and Sunlight

Another important part of maintenance is making sure your trees and bushes have enough water and sunlight. If two trees are planted too closely together, chances are that one tree will lose as they both compete for light and growing rights. When you visit your local nursery, you should be ready to ask a few questions so they can help you select the right trees and bushes for your property. They will ask you some questions: What kind of soil do you have? (Bring a small sample of soil with you.) How much sun and shade mix do you have throughout the day? How much water is available? Do you have automatic sprinklers?

Answers to these questions will help them advise you on what trees you should select for your property.

Staking Young Trees   *EASY* **1–2 hours**

Before young trees can establish themselves securely, it's a good idea to help them along. Staking means tying them to stakes driven into the ground on either side for support.

After planting a young tree, drive two stakes (usually locust posts designed and sold for staking purposes—available at nurseries and home centers) on either side of it. They should be driven into the ground at angles, with the tops pointed away from the tree. Use ropes to tie the trunk of the tree to the posts. To avoid the rope digging into the bark, you can fashion "sleeves" made from old hose sections that slide over the rope.

You can get these supplies at nurseries or home improvement centers.

Feeding Trees

There are a variety of fertilizer products available for trees. Some are called "food spikes," and they are driven into the ground at the base of the tree. They release fertilizer slowly, and it leaches into the ground to feed the roots. The instructions are pretty simple and describe the kinds of trees they feed. Check with nursery personnel about other products you can use.

Deep Root versus Shallow Root

Feeding, watering, and staking trees are based on another quality of the tree—whether they have shallow or deep roots. Oaks and some other hardwood trees usually have deep roots and a taproot—a centrally located root that grows deep into the soil—for finding water sources (see Fig. 19.5).

Weeping willows, on the other hand, have shallow root systems. Knowing what kinds of root systems your trees have will help you decide how to feed them, water them, and support them when they are young.

FIGURE 19.5

These trees have deep roots—they are mature and don't need any maintenance.

Climate and Geographic Considerations

Where you call home goes a long way to determine what plants and materials are available to maintain your house and property. For instance, if you live in the Southwest, potential problems with moisture are not going to be considered the way they would for a homeowner in the Northeast.

In fact, while a homeowner in upstate New York may have a sump pump working to prevent water from seeping into his basement, a homeowner in Arizona may have a rock garden for a front lawn instead of grass because of restrictions on water usage.

Different climates in different areas of the country may affect your decisions about a huge variety of things, from what kind of driveway sealer to use to what kinds of windows you'll have to get, to what kind of siding you'll need on your house—and anything in between, inside or out.

How do you know what's best for your house and property? In your area of the country? In your particular climate? In addition to consulting with people from your local nursery and/or home improvement center (and letting your fingers do the walking through your Yellow Pages), what follows are important contacts—and sources of information—for different areas of the country.

National Climatic Data Center
Climate Services Branch
Room 468
151 Patton Avenue
Asheville, North Carolina 28801-5001
Phone: 828-271-4800
Fax: 828-271-4876
E-mail: ncdc.info@noaa.gov

There are also six regional climate centers:

High Plains Regional Climate Center
School of Natural Resources
University of Nebraska—Lincoln
236 L.W. Chase Hall
Lincoln, NE 68583-0728
Phone: 402-472-6706
Fax: 402-472-6614

Midwestern Regional Climate Center
2204 Griffith Drive
Champaign, IL 61820
Phone: 217-244-8226
E-mail: mcc@sws.uiuc.edu

Northeast Regional Climate Center
1123 Bradfield Hall
Cornell University
Ithaca, NY 14853
Phone: 607-255-1751
Fax: 607-255-2106
E-mail: nrcc@cornell.edu

Southern Climate Control Center
E-328 Howe Russell Building
Louisiana State University
Baton Rouge, Louisiana 70803
Phone: 225-578-5021
Fax: 225-578-2912

Southeast Regional Climate Center
2221 Devine St., Suite 222
Columbia, SC 29205
Toll-free phone: 1-866-845-1553
Phone: 803-734-9560
Fax: 803-734-9559
E-mail: sercc@dnr.state.sc.us

Western Regional Climate Center
2215 Raggio Parkway
Reno, Nevada 89512
Phone: 775-674-7010
Fax: 775-674-7016
E-mail: wrcc@dri.edu

Special Problems

Radon

Radon is a very toxic, colorless gas that can possibly seep into your home. It comes from the earth, rocks, and/or well water beneath your house. There are ways you can test for it.

The National Safety Council offers low-cost short- and long-term radon test kits through its National Radon Hotline to people who want to test their homes. The kits should be used according to the directions on the package and then sealed and returned to the lab for analysis. Results are provided within a few weeks, along with information on how to reduce radon risks in your home. Kits can be ordered directly from the National Safety Council Helpline at 800-557-2366. They can also answer any questions you have about radon. If you'd like, you can write them at:

National Safety Council
Radon Test Kit Offer
P.O. Box 65721
Washington, DC 20035

In addition, here's another resource:

1-800-SOS-RADON
[1-800-767-7236]

If you have tested your home:

The Radon FIX-IT Program at:
1-800-644-6999
www.radonfixit.org

Asbestos

Asbestos is a toxic mineral fiber that can be identified only with a special type of microscope. In the past, asbestos was added to a variety of products to strengthen them and to provide heat insulation and fire resistance. There are ways to test for it. If you think this might be a problem in your home, here are some resources you can use.

For more information, contact your local American Lung Association for copies of

Indoor Air Pollution Fact Sheet—Asbestos

Air Pollution in Your Home?

Other publications on indoor pollution

For more information on asbestos in other consumer products, call the CPSC Hotline or write to the U.S. Consumer Product Safety Commission, Washington, DC 20207. The CPSC Hotline has information on certain appliances and products, such as the brands and models of hair dryers that contain asbestos. Call CPSC at 1-800-638-CPSC. A teletypewriter (TTY) for the hearing impaired is available at 1-800-638-8270. The Maryland TTY number is 1-800-492-8104.

To find out whether your state has a training and certification program for asbestos removal contractors, and for information on the Environmental Protection Agency's asbestos programs, call the EPA at 202-554-1404.

For more information on asbestos identification and control activities, contact the Asbestos Coordinator in the EPA Regional Office for your region, or your state or local health department.

Floods

Knowing how to protect your home against flooding is important. For information on how to protect your home and what to do if it happens, here are some resources you can contact for answers to your questions.

The Federal Emergency Management Agency (FEMA)
500 C Street
Washington, DC 20472
Phone: 202-566-1600
Web site: http://www.fema.gov

The American Red Cross
National Headquarters
2025 E Street NW
Washington, DC 20006
Phone: 202-303-4498
Web site: www.redcross.org

Here's another helpful source of information for your home and property—how to order publications from EPA:

IAQ INFO
P.O. Box 37133
Washington, DC 20013-7133
Phone: 1-800-438-4318/703-356-4020
Fax: 703-356-5386
E-mail: iaqinfo@aol.com

You can order these publications directly via the EPA's National Service Center for Environmental Publications (NSCEP) (http://www.epa.gov/ncepihom). Your publication requests can also be mailed, called, or faxed directly to

U.S. Environmental Protection Agency
National Center for Environmental Publications (NSCEP)
P.O. Box 42419
Cincinnati, OH 42419
Phone: 1-800-490-9198
Fax: 513-489-8695

INDEX

ABOUT THE AUTHOR

Joe Beck has been a contractor for 15 years and has owned a landscaping company. A veteran author as well, he co-wrote *The 100 Greatest Inventions of All Time* (Citadel Press, 2003), and numerous articles for such publications as *The Long Islander*, *Schools in the Middle*, and *The Hispanic Outlook in Education* magazine. He lives in Bethpage, New York.